PAST PERFORMANCE HANDBOOK

PAST PERFORMANCE HANDBOOK

Peter S. Cole
Joseph W. Beausoleil

MANAGEMENTCONCEPTS

Vienna, Virginia

ꟿ
MANAGEMENTCONCEPTS

8230 Leesburg Pike, Suite 800
Vienna, Virginia 22182
Phone: (703) 790-9595
Fax: (703) 790-1371
Web: www.managementconcepts.com

Copyright © 2002 by Management Concepts, Inc.

All rights reserved. No part of this book may be reproduced or utilized in any form
or by any means, electronic or mechanical, including photocopying, recording, or by
an information storage and retrieval system, without permission in writing from the
publisher, except for brief quotations in review articles.

Printed in the United States of America

Library of Congress Cataloging-in-Publication Data

Cole, Peter S.
  Past performance handbook/Peter S. Cole, Joseph W. Beausoleil.
    p. ; cm.
  Includes bibliographical references and index.
  ISBN 1-56726-103-5 (hb)
    1. Public contracts—United States. 2. Letting of contracts—United States—
Decision making. 3. Performance standards. 4. Contracting out—United States.
I. Beausoleil, Joseph W. II. Title.

HD3861.U6 C655 2002
352.4'39'0973—dc21

2002018838

About the Authors

Peter S. Cole has more than 35 years of experience in acquisition and contracts management. During his military service, he was a contracting officer in the Navy's laboratory system, he taught basic and advanced procurement at ALMC, Fort Lee, and he worked at the headquarters staff level on procurement policy matters. He is currently an independent consultant based in Bowie, Maryland. He provides consulting and training services in government contracting for government and commercial clients.

Since his retirement from the Navy, Mr. Cole has researched and developed textbooks and presented training programs in incentive contracting, cost-plus-award-fee contracting, competitive negotiation, implementation of OMB Circular A-76, FAR implementation, contract management for technical personnel (COTR training), technical evaluation, and how to write a statement of work. He is the author of *How to Write a Statement of Work* and *How to Evaluate and Negotiate Government Contracts,* both published by Management Concepts.

Joseph W. Beausoleil served as an advisor to the U.S. Agency for International Development in implementing procurement reform as a result of the Federal Acquisition Streamlining Act of 1994. He was assigned responsibility for implementing the past performance initiative. He developed the agency's policy and procedures for evaluating past performance information and for evaluating contractor performance. He has had extensive experience in training contracting and technical officers in their responsibilities with regard to past performance. He also served as the agency's liaison with the Office of Federal Procurement Policy (OFPP). He participated in OFPP's interagency working groups in developing the sample form for evaluating contractor performance and in rewriting the best practices guide for past performance.

Mr. Beausoleil is the author of "Contractor Performance Reports: An Effective Tool of Contract Administration" and "Past Performance Is Not Working," articles published in *Contract Management*. He has a PhD in Management from the University of California for Advanced Studies, an MA in Economics from UCLA, and a BA in Philosophy from Maryknoll College.

Authors of Chapter 13, Legal Issues in Past Performance:

Thomas L. McGovern III is a partner with Hogan & Hartson LLP. A member of the firm's government contracts group, his practice emphasizes administrative and judicial appeals, including bid protests, disputes, claims, and defense of allegations of defective pricing, procurement fraud, and misconduct. He represents a broad range of clients, including start-up, small, and minority companies, major defense contractors, and universities.

Mr. McGovern is a member of the ABA Public Contract Law Section and the D.C. Government Contracts and Litigation Section. He is the author of numerous articles and is a member of the Bars of the District of Columbia, California, the U.S. Court of Federal Claims, and other federal courts. He received a JD from Stanford Law School, an MBA from Babson College, and a BS from the United States Air Force Academy.

Timothy D. Palmer has worked in the field of federal government procurement for more than 10 years, first as a contract negotiator with the Department of the Navy, then as an attorney in private practice, and currently as in-house counsel with a major government contractor. He has counseled a variety of clients on proposal preparation, contract formation, and contract administration matters, and has been active in bid protest and contract claims litigation.

Mr. Palmer practiced government contract law with the law firms of Hogan & Hartson LLP and Piper Marbury Rudnick & Wolfe LLP in Washington, D.C. He currently serves as Assistant General Counsel, Lockheed Martin Systems Integration—Owego. He received his JD from the Georgetown University Law Center.

Table of Contents

Preface xiii

Chapter 1—Evaluating Past Performance 1
by Peter S. Cole and Joseph W. Beausoleil
Related but Different Evaluations 1
  Source Selection Evaluations 1
  Contractor Performance Evaluations 2
Measurable Performance Standards 3
Establishing the Basis for Evaluation in the Solicitation
  and Contract 4
  Evaluation Basis for Source Selection 4
  Evaluation Basis for Contractor Performance Evaluations 4

Chapter 2—Pre-award: Using Past Performance As an
  Evaluation Factor 7
by Peter S. Cole
Determining Which Evaluation Factors to Use 7
  Cost or Price 8
  Technical Excellence 8
  Management Capability 8
  Prior Experience 9
  Personnel Qualifications 10
  Compliance with Solicitation Requirements 11
  Past Performance 12
Selecting Evaluation Factors 12
  Tailor the Evaluation Factors to the Procurement 12
  Ensure That the Evaluation Factors Discriminate
    among Offerors 13
  Limit the Number of Evaluation Factors 13
  Always Include Cost or Price and Quality 13
Determining Whether to Use Past Performance As an
  Evaluation Factor 14

viii PAST PERFORMANCE HANDBOOK

Determining the Relative Importance of Past Performance
  As an Evaluation Factor 16
  Determining the Relative Importance of Evaluation Factors 16
  Determining the Relative Importance of Past Performance 17
  Distinguishing Between Past Performance and
      Prior Experience 18
  Combining Past Performance and Prior Experience 19
  Distinguishing between Past Performance As a Responsibility
      Factor and As an Evaluation Factor 20
Determining What Will Be Evaluated As Past Performance.............. 22
  OFPP-Suggested Past Performance Subfactors....................... 22
  Using the OFPP Subfactors 24
  Areas of Specific Concern....................................... 27
Determining How the RFP Will Address Past Performance 29
  Define Past Performance 29
  Indicate How Past Performance Will Be Evaluated 30
  Indicate the Documentation Required 31
Determining How Past Performance Will Be Rated or Scored
  in the Evaluation 32
  Numerical Scoring Systems 32
  Color Coding Scoring Systems 33
  Performance Risk Assessments 34

**Chapter 3—Pre-award: Obtaining Past Performance
Information** 37
  by Peter S. Cole
For the Government 37
  Sources of Past Performance Information 37
  Conducting a Reference Check 40
  Asking the Right Questions 41
  Getting Answers 43
  Making Offerors Responsible for Reference Checks 44
  Using Contractor Performance Reports 45
For the Contractor 46
  General 46
  Describing Past Performance in a Proposal........................ 49
  Planning for Contract Performance 59

**Chapter 4—Pre-award: Factors that Affect the Evaluation
of Past Performance** 63
  by Peter S. Cole
FAR Factors... 63
  Currency and Relevance of the Past Performance
      Information.. 63
  Source of the Past Performance Information....................... 64

Context of the Data 64
General Trend of Past Performance 65
Other Factors 65
Impact on Prospective Performance 66
Extent of Government's Responsibility 71
Relevance of Past Performance Information 72
New Firms/Firms with No Past Performance History 74
Performance of Other Companies, Key Personnel,
    or Subcontractors 78

Chapter 5—Pre-award: Evaluating Past Performance **85**
by Peter S. Cole
Checking References 86
Using Information Close at Hand 89
Using Personal Knowledge 91
Allowing Offerors to Rebut Adverse Past Performance
    Information 94
What the Government Should Do 94
What the Offeror Should Do 98
Applying Rating Systems 99
Numerical Systems 101
Color Coding Systems 103
Performance Risk Assessments 105
Documenting the Evaluation Findings 106
Avoiding Problems 107

Chapter 6—Pre-award: Past Performance and Source
    Selection **111**
by Peter S. Cole
Past Performance Tradeoffs and Source Selection Decisions 113
Determining Best Value 113
Making Past Performance/Price Tradeoffs 115
Documenting Tradeoff Determinations and Source Selection
    Decisions 118
Evaluating Past Performance Is Not Easy 121

Chapter 7—Post-award: Contractor Performance
    Evaluations **125**
by Joseph W. Beausoleil
Low Compliance 125
Purpose of the Evaluations 126
Contractor Performance Evaluations 127
Not a Complex Procedure 127
Performance Evaluations Are Based on Current
    Information 127

Report Cards for Contractors 128
Evaluating versus Accepting/Rejecting Performance 128
Shared Responsibility 129
Timing/Frequency 129
Content 130
Distinguishing Features of Contractor Performance
Evaluations 131
Different Approach, Added Value 132

**Chapter 8—Post-award: Designing a Contractor
Performance Evaluation System** **135**
by Joseph W. Beausoleil
Content 135
Basic Assessment Areas 136
Additional Assessment Areas 136
Tailoring Content to Contractual Requirements 137
Areas Not Assessed 137
Rating Principles 138
Narrative Supporting Ratings 139
Format 139
Using a Form 141
Design of a Form 141
Standard Forms for Evaluating Contractor Performance 141
Sample Form in OFPP Guide 142
Proposed Sample Form 143
Automation 144
Signatures 146

**Chapter 9—Post-award: The Initial Evaluation of
Contractor Performance** **147**
by Joseph W. Beausoleil
Contracting Officer's Responsibility 147
Format, Not Form 147
Use a Form to Record Information, Not to Collect It 148
The Initial Performance Assessment 149
Basis for Appraising the Assessment Areas 150
Rating Performance 151
Satisfactory Is a Good Rating 152
Objectivity 152
Incomplete Information 153
Comments 153
Guidance for Rating the Four Assessment Areas 154
Quality of Product or Service 154
Timeliness 155
Cost Control 155
Business Relations 156
Time Needed to Perform the Evaluation 156

Table of Contents **xi**

Chapter 10—Post-award: Contractor Review and Response **159**
by Joseph W. Beausoleil
Contractor's Input 159
   Alerting the Contractor 159
   Contractor Should Understand the Process. 160
   Guidance for Contractors 160
   Contacting the Contractor 161
Contractor's Review 161
   Review Process. 162
   How to Respond to the Agency. 162
   How Not to Respond 163
   Special Problems 164

Chapter 11—Post-award: Resolving Disagreements **165**
by Joseph W. Beausoleil
Definitions of Terms 165
How to Avoid Agency Reviews. 166
Requesting a Review 167
Responsibility of the Reviewer 169
Decision Is Final 169
Advising Contractor of Decision. 169

Chapter 12—Post-award: Maintaining and Making
Accessible Past Performance Information **171**
by Joseph W. Beausoleil
Maintaining Past Performance Information 171
   Treat As Source Selection Information 171
   Past Performance Information System 172
Sharing Past Performance Information 172
Experiences in Maintaining Past Performance Information 173
   Evaluation Reports on Construction Contracts. 173
   Evaluation Reports on Architect-Engineer Contracts 174
   Lessons Learned. 174
   Applying the Experience 174
   Problems with Multiple Past Performance Information Systems 175
   Integration of Agency Past Performance Information Systems 176
   Virtually Shared Information Network 176
Provisional Solution 176
   Submitting Evaluation Reports with the Proposal 177
   Emphasis on Evaluating, Not on Collecting, Past
      Performance Information 177

Chapter 13—Legal Issues in Past Performance **181**
by Thomas L. McGovern III and Timothy D. Palmer
How Contractors Can Use Past Performance Information to
   Their Competitive Advantage 182
   Submit Comments on Performance Evaluations 182

xii PAST PERFORMANCE HANDBOOK

Obtain Review at a Level above the Contracting Officer 183
Prepare Proposals to Present Past Performance in the
    Best Light Possible. 184
Use Discussions to Enhance Your Position 184
Challenging Agency Past Performance Evaluations 185
Scope of the PPI Review—Relevancy and Currency 185
Challenging the Accuracy of PPI. 188
Exchanges Regarding Past Performance 190
Evaluation Consistent with the Solicitation Factors. 192
Reasonableness of Evaluation Methodology. 194
Offeror's History of Claims/Disputes 196
Offeror's Status As Incumbent 197
Use of PPI of Subcontractors, Affiliates, and Key Personnel 198
Conclusion 201

**Appendix A—Best Practices for Collecting and
Using Current and Past Performance Information** 203

**Appendix B—A Guide to Collection and Use of
Past Performance Information** 251

Index 309

Preface

Evaluating past performance in competitively negotiated contracts is not a new concept, but how past performance is evaluated has changed. Even the changes are not new—the first regulatory requirements were promulgated in the Federal Acquisition Regulation (FAR) in 1995—but general implementation of the changes has been slow because the changes were much easier said than done.

The basic premise was that it would be a good idea to evaluate an offeror's past performance as part of the proposal evaluation process. The concept made sense: Past performance can be an excellent indicator of future performance, so why not use it as an evaluation factor to select the proposal that offers the best value to the government? The realization of this premise, however, would depend on the availability of past performance information.

In 1995, few agencies had procedures for collecting past performance information. Initially, past performance information was obtained mainly through questionnaires administered to references identified by offerors. This process, however, proved to be difficult and time-consuming. Another problem was assuming that the past performance evaluation factor could be evaluated and scored just like any other evaluation factor. This too proved to be more problematic than envisioned.

Over the past few years, these problems have been addressed and resolved. Most agencies have developed systems for collecting, maintaining, and making accessible past performance information on their contractors. Revisions have been made in the FAR to clarify past performance regulations. The Department of Defense published past performance guidance in 1999. The Office of Federal Procurement Policy rewrote its best practices guide in 2000. However, while many of the problems related to the evaluation of past performance have been addressed and resolved, the potential for past performance to be an effective factor in source selection still depends on the ability of government agencies to collect and to share past performance information on their contractors.

The *Past Performance Handbook* is a comprehensive source of information about the evaluation of past performance prior to contract award as well as at the end of contract performance. It expands on the guidance already available from the various sources and suggests how this multifaceted, complex process can be simplified. The *Handbook* follows the procurement cycle, beginning with the solicitation and continuing through contract award and the evaluation of a contractor's performance upon completion of the contract effort. It concludes with a discussion of the legal aspects of using past performance.

The *Past Performance Handbook* was written for both the government personnel who participate in the procurement process and the contractors who provide the goods and services. Government personnel need this information to avoid the pitfalls of a process that is more complicated than it looks. Contractor personnel need this information to improve their competitive position because the evaluation of past performance is becoming a key factor in the award of competitive contracts.

We hope that the *Past Performance Handbook* will give you one more tool in your arsenal for successfully accomplishing your goals in the federal procurement process.

Peter S. Cole
Joseph W. Beausoleil

Chapter 1

Evaluating Past Performance

by Peter S. Cole and Joseph W. Beausoleil

The evaluation of past performance is not a new concept. It has been a long-established requirement that an offeror's past performance be examined as part of the responsibility determination made just prior to contract award.[1] Relatively new, however, are the requirements to evaluate an offeror's past performance as an evaluation factor for source selection[2] and to evaluate a contractor's performance upon completion of contract performance.[3] In addition, agencies are required to retain the contractor performance evaluations and make them available to other agencies when needed in making source selection decisions.[4]

RELATED BUT DIFFERENT EVALUATIONS

Although the evaluation of an offeror's past performance information for source selection and the evaluation of a contractor's performance executing a contract are related, they are very different kinds of evaluations. They have different purposes, are done at different times, use different evaluation criteria, and rely on different information sources. These two evaluations are linked, however, because the results of the contractor performance evaluation upon contract completion become a primary information source for the evaluation of past performance for future source selections.

Source Selection Evaluations

Purpose—The purpose of past performance evaluations during source selection is to determine the quality of an offeror's performance on comparable past contracts and then match it to the past performance of competing offerors. An offeror's past performance on other contracts is a good indicator of how well it might perform on future contracts and can be a significant factor in the determination of the competitive range or in the source selection decision if award is made without discussions. The evaluation results also may be a significant factor in tradeoff decisions and the final source selection.

2 PAST PERFORMANCE HANDBOOK

Timing—Evaluating past performance information for source selection is a solicitation activity primarily performed before establishing the competitive range or making an award without discussions; however, an offeror's past performance also may be considered when making the source selection decision.

Evaluation Criteria—During the initial evaluation, each offeror's past performance on other similar contracts must be evaluated based on the specific evaluation criteria set forth in the request for proposals (RFP). The evaluation criteria may be generalized, as in the Office of Federal Procurement Policy (OFPP) criteria (performance quality, schedule performance, cost control, and business relations), or stated specifically (see Chapter 2). The evaluated proposal—there usually are other evaluation factors in addition to past performance—is then comparatively assessed against each competing proposal to determine the proposal's relative ranking in the competition.

Information Sources—The sources of information about an offeror's performance on past contracts are contract references provided by the offeror, contractor performance evaluations conducted by the contracting agency or other agencies, and information gleaned from agency records or from third-party sources.

Contractor Performance Evaluations

Purpose—The purpose of contractor performance evaluations is to provide past performance information for use in source selection. The evaluations also serve to motivate contractors to optimum performance because the results of the evaluation—past performance information—may be used in future award decisions.

Timing—Contractor performance evaluations must be conducted upon completion of contract activities (not contract closeout) and may be conducted on an interim basis if the contract period exceeds one year.

Evaluation Criteria—The criteria that are used to evaluate a contractor's performance are the performance standards for the critical actions required of the contractor in furnishing the supplies or services. The performance requirements are set forth in the contract schedule and clauses.

Information Sources—Contractor performance evaluations are based on input from the acquisition team, which always includes representatives from the contracting and technical offices and, when appropriate, end users. The acquisition team also includes the financial, legal, audit, and other personnel involved with the contract as well as the contractor who is furnishing the supplies or services.

MEASURABLE PERFORMANCE STANDARDS

The requirement to evaluate a contractor's performance changed the way that performance standards are written. In the past, performance standards were sufficient if they served as the basis for a judgment regarding the acceptance or rejection of the contractor's performance in furnishing a service or supply. Now the performance standards must enable making a judgment regarding how well the contractor performed all aspects of contract performance, not just the end results. This places an added responsibility on the government to establish measurable performance standards that will enable an evaluation, and not merely the acceptance or rejection, of a contractor's performance.

The purpose of contractor performance evaluations is to provide past performance information for source selection. The more accurate and objective the past performance information, the more useful the information will be in source selection. The information will be accurate and objective to the extent that the evaluation was based on measurable performance standards.

Generally, it is not difficult to establish measurable performance standards for acquisitions that are expressed in terms of physical characteristics, i.e., construction and supply contracts. The physical characteristics—the description or specifications—contain measurable standards against which a contractor's performance can be evaluated accurately and objectively.

This is not the same for acquisitions that are expressed in terms of functions to be performed or performance required. The performance standards must be tailored to the instant acquisition, and their measurability varies depending on the nature of the acquisition. Using performance-based contracting methods,[5] however, ensures that the performance standards are expressed to the highest degree of measurability for the instant acquisition. These methods include: (1) expressing the requirements in terms of the results required; and (2) establishing, to the extent practicable, measurable performance standards with respect to quality, timeliness, and quantity.

In summary, if the requirements are expressed in terms of physical characteristics, the performance standards are measurable and the contractor performance evaluation can result in an accurate and objective assessment of the contractor's performance. If the requirements are expressed in terms of functions to be performed or performance required, the accuracy and objectivity of the evaluation of contractor performance depends on the extent to which the government can establish measurable performance standards. Thus, the usefulness, i.e., the accuracy and objectivity, of past performance information in the source selection depends on the measurability of the performance standards used in the contract.

ESTABLISHING THE BASIS FOR EVALUATION IN THE SOLICITATION AND CONTRACT

The basis for past performance evaluations for source selection is established in the solicitation. The basis for contractor performance evaluations is established in the contract.

Evaluation Basis for Source Selection

When using the uniform contract format,[6] the past performance evaluation criteria used for source selection are set forth in the RFP's Section L, *Instructions, Conditions, and Notices to Offerors or Respondents* and Section M, *Evaluation Factors For Award*, and apply only to the evaluation of proposals. The specific evaluation criteria and the evaluation procedures are set forth in Section M, and the information the offeror must provide in its proposal are set forth in Section L.

Note that when acquiring commercial items, a different contract format applies.[7] Instructions to offerors on submitting past performance information are found in solicitation provision FAR 52.212-1, and the past performance evaluation criteria are incorporated into solicitation provision FAR 52.212-2.

Evaluation Basis for Contractor Performance Evaluations

Irrespective of whether past performance is used in source selection, all contracts will be evaluated upon completion. Performance standards are found in various parts of the contract. For example, when using the uniform contract format, performance standards are found in Section C, *Description/Specifications/Statement of Work*; Section E, *Inspection and Acceptance*; Section F, *Deliveries or Performance*; and Section I, *Contract Clauses*. If the acquisition is for a commercial item, the performance standards are contained in the schedule of supplies/services (block 20 of the SF 1449) and in the contract clauses 52.212-4 and 52.212-5.

Note that performance standards may be explicit, i.e., specifically stated in the contract, or implicit, i.e., generally accepted professional or business practices regarding relations with the government. The contractor performance evaluation is an overall evaluation of how well the contractor met its contractual commitment and is not restricted to specifically identified evaluation criteria, as is the case with the evaluation for source selection.

The results of contractor performance evaluations are the primary source of past performance information for use in source selection. The accuracy and objectivity of the past performance information depend on the measurability of the performance standards used in evaluating the contractor. The more measurable the performance standards, the more accurate and objective the past performance information. The more accurate and objective the past performance information, the more useful it will be in future award decisions.

The evaluation of past performance information in source selection and the evaluation of a contractor's performance on current or completed contracts are two very different kinds of evaluations. Each has its own policies and procedures. This book treats each evaluation separately. Source selection evaluations are a pre-award activity and will be treated first in Chapters 2 through 6. Contractor performance evaluations, a post-award activity, will be addressed in Chapters 7 through 12. The final chapter will address the legal aspects regarding the collection and use of past performance information.

NOTES

[1] FAR 9.104-3(b).

[2] FAR 15.304(3). Past performance must be used as an evaluation factor in all source selections for negotiated competitive acquisitions expected to exceed $100,000 unless the contracting officer documents the reason past performance is not an appropriate evaluation factor for the acquisition.

[3] FAR 42.1502. "Agencies shall prepare an evaluation of contractor performance for each contract in excess of $100,000 at the time the work under the contract is completed. In addition, interim evaluations should be prepared as specified by agencies to provide current information for source selection purposes for contracts with a period of performance, including options, exceeding one year."

[4] FAR 42.1503(c). "Departments and agencies shall share past performance information with other departments and agencies when requested to support future award decisions."

[5] FAR 37.102.

[6] FAR 15.204.

[7] FAR 12.303.

Chapter 2

Pre-Award: Using Past Performance As an Evaluation Factor

by Peter S. Cole

This chapter addresses pre-award past performance issues that must be considered before issuing the RFP. While primarily directed at government personnel, this information also should be of interest to contractor personnel because it addresses those things that government personnel should do when preparing to evaluate past performance in a competitive acquisition, thus providing insights that should help contractors prepare their proposals better.

The evaluation of past performance is not a simple process. The government should consider a number of areas when planning to use past performance as an evaluation factor, including:

- Which evaluation factors to use

- Whether to use past performance as an evaluation factor

- The relative importance of past performance as an evaluation factor

- What will be evaluated as past performance

- How past performance will be addressed in the RFP

- How past performance will be rated or scored in the evaluation.

The following section will address these points, suggest how they might be handled, discuss some of the problems that might be encountered, and suggest possible solutions.

DETERMINING WHICH EVALUATION FACTORS TO USE

Before deciding if and how to use past performance as an evaluation factor, you should consider what other factors might be important in the evaluation. After all, past performance is only one of a number of evaluation factors that

8 PAST PERFORMANCE HANDBOOK

may be used to evaluate proposals in a competitively negotiated procurement. The FAR[1] identifies seven areas that could be evaluated to determine the quality of an offeror's proposal. In addition to cost or price, there are six non-cost evaluation areas: technical excellence, management capability, prior experience, personnel qualifications, compliance with solicitation requirements, and past performance.

Cost or Price

Cost or price is a mandatory evaluation factor in all procurements. While cost or price need not be the most important factor, no award is valid unless cost or price has been considered in some fashion during the source selection process.

Technical Excellence

Technical excellence has to do with evaluating the quality of an offeror's technical proposal in terms of meeting the contractual requirements. The technical proposal is evaluated considering such things as technical understanding, as demonstrated by the offeror's analysis of the requirement; technical approach, as demonstrated by the techniques or methodology to be employed; and technical planning, as demonstrated by the scheduling and sequencing of the planned effort. Overall, the technical evaluation must consider the feasibility of the technical proposal, the probability (risk) of technical success, and the offeror's ability to do what is proposed and meet the contractual time frames.

Technical excellence is a commonly used evaluation factor. Its use is most appropriate when the requirement is unique or complex and the government needs to see how the competing offerors propose to meet the technical requirements of the RFP. Its use is also appropriate when there are a number of different ways to meet the technical requirements and the government wants to select best technical approach.

Generally, technical excellence is used as an evaluation factor if the government feels that: (1) it must evaluate how the offerors propose to meet the contract requirements, (2) the differences in the technical proposals will be a discriminating factor in the evaluation, and (3) there is likely to be a need to discuss aspects of the technical proposals with the offerors in the competitive range.

Management Capability

Management capability involves the evaluation of how well an offeror's proposal demonstrates that the offeror can effectively manage all aspects of contract performance. The management proposal is evaluated considering such things as: (1) how well the management plan demonstrates that the work effort will be managed effectively and establishes well-defined lines of authority, responsibility, and communication; (2) the establishment of management techniques that will facilitate the early identification and resolution of problems and the prompt response to changes; (3) the extent to which the staffing represents an appropriate level and labor mix and reflects the technical input and ability for successful and timely contract performance; and, as appropriate, (4) the offeror's ability to react to workload fluctuations.

Management capability is a commonly used evaluation factor. Using management as an evaluation factor is most appropriate for large, complex requirements when how the work is staffed and managed could be a major factor in the success or failure of the contract effort, such as in systems acquisition, research and development, technical support services, bundled contracts, and other complex acquisitions. Evaluating management issues is less important in standard, noncomplex acquisitions, such as acquiring commercial items and standard supplies or services. Management capability also may be used as a subfactor to the technical evaluation factor.

Management capability is probably an overused evaluation factor. Often it is automatically coupled with the technical evaluation factor. Except for the large, complex efforts noted above, how an offeror proposes to manage its contractual effort is not necessarily a discriminating factor in an evaluation. However, even when other management aspects are not particularly important, how an offeror proposes to staff the work effort could be a discriminating factor.

Basically, staffing is evaluated to determine if the offeror is proposing adequate staffing; the evaluation should also consider, however, how the offeror proposes to manage its staffing, considering such things as staffing distribution, staffing for standard and peak workload conditions, cross-utilization, personnel turnover, and retention plans. Staffing might be used as a primary evaluation factor rather than management when acquiring complex technical support services or in other acquisitions in which how an offeror proposes to manage its staffing effort could be a discriminating factor. It also should be noted that proposed staffing is inherent to assessing the offeror's understanding of the requirement, and staffing could be used as a subfactor to the technical evaluation factor.

Prior Experience

Prior experience (often referred to as corporate experience) involves the evaluation of an offeror's expertise, as demonstrated by its work on past and current contracts of the same or similar nature, and is related to whether the offeror has done such work before, not to how well it performed the work. Prior experience is evaluated based on information provided by the offeror (and verified as necessary) that identifies specific past or current contracts demonstrating the offeror's expertise with work relevant to the current procurement.

Generally, prior experience is evaluated in terms of the number of years of general or specialized experience or the number of comparable or relevant contracts. Prior experience also can be evaluated in terms of the experience of an offeror's senior technical or management personnel, subcontractors, or other members of a joint venture.

Prior experience is a commonly used evaluation factor and is important because the government needs some assurance that the offeror knows how to perform the required work. The degree of importance depends on the size and complexity of the required work effort. Prior experience is valuable for evaluating an offeror's ability to complete a complex effort that involves many personnel and multiple work units and requires interfacing both inside and outside the corporate structure. In large efforts, the existence of prior experience often provides some assurance that corporate memory will be retained.

Prior experience may be less important on smaller efforts that involve only a few personnel because the retention of corporate experience is less ensured if only a few personnel were involved in the contract. Prior experience is, after all, little more than the corporate memory of the individuals currently working for the offeror. The fact that an offeror previously performed the same or similar work is not necessarily a qualifying factor if the key experienced personnel who performed the work are no longer employed by the offeror.

Evaluating prior experience can be a problem when new firms or established firms seeking new markets for their products or services enter the competition. Such firms will not have a track record in performing the same or similar services but nevertheless might have the requisite expertise, if permitted to demonstrate how their prior experience qualifies them to compete.

When prior experience is used as an evaluation factor, the RFP should permit offerors to show how the innovative use of their products or services or of subcontractors or joint venture partners will enable the offeror to meet the contractual requirements.

Personnel Qualifications

Personnel qualifications (often called key personnel) involve evaluating the availability, competency, pertinent education, and related experience of an offeror's proposed key technical, management, and administrative personnel, as appropriate, with respect to their potential contribution to successful contract performance. Personnel qualifications are evaluated based on information provided by the offeror regarding each individual's qualifications and commitment to work on the proposed contract.

Personnel qualifications often are used in evaluating proposals for research and development, information technology services, technical and other complex support services, and other requirements in which the qualifications of proposed key personnel are vital to the success of contract performance and would be a discriminating factor in the evaluation. Personnel qualifications may be used as a primary evaluation factor or as a subfactor under technical, management, or staffing.

The use of personnel qualifications as an evaluation factor has been the subject of numerous protests. Generally, protests in this area can be minimized if the RFP: (1) identifies the key positions so that the offeror can provide specific names and résumés, (2) identifies the minimum qualifications required of the personnel proposed to fill these positions so that the offeror can provide the appropriate qualification information, (3) identifies the documentation required (such as résumés and letters of commitment) to support the offeror's identification of such personnel, and (4) warns that it is the offeror's responsibility to ensure that the proposed key personnel are available and committed to perform under the contract throughout the acquisition process and to propose new personnel should the originally proposed personnel become unavailable.

Compliance with Solicitation Requirements

Compliance with solicitation requirements is used as an evaluation factor in place of technical excellence when a technical presentation is not needed but the offeror must demonstrate that the proposed product or service meets the requirements of the solicitation. Generally, compliance with solicitation requirements is used in fixed-price acquisitions in which the requirements are not complex and the technical and management aspects are not likely to be discriminating factors among the potential offerors.

Compliance with solicitation requirements is appropriate to use when the prime consideration, besides price, is that the offeror's proposal demonstrates that all of the mandatory solicitation requirements will be met, as might be the case with fixed-price construction contracts or contracts for the manufacture or provision of standard supplies, equipment, or services. It is also appropriate in solicitations in which award will be made to the lowest-priced, technically acceptable proposal. In such cases, technical excellence is not a factor; the only requirement is that the proposal demonstrates that it meets the minimum standard for compliance with the solicitation requirements. All proposals that meet

12 PAST PERFORMANCE HANDBOOK

the minimum standards, i.e., are technically acceptable, are then competed based on the proposed prices.

This evaluation factor usually is the only non-cost evaluation factor used; past performance, however, also may be used to demonstrate how well the offeror met compliance requirements in other contracts.

Past Performance

Past performance is used to evaluate the quality of an offeror's prior performance and is evaluated on the basis of how well the offeror performed the same or similar effort on past or current contracts and how that past performance is likely to affect the current effort. The evaluation should consider the currency and relevance of an offeror's past performance, the source and validity of the past performance information received, the context of the data, and the general trend of the offeror's past performance.

The use of past performance as an evaluation factor is required by the FAR[2] for all procurements in excess of $100,000, except[3] when the contracting officer documents the contract file to indicate why using past performance as an evaluation factor is not appropriate for the acquisition. Generally, past performance is an appropriate evaluation factor in most procurements.

SELECTING EVALUATION FACTORS

When selecting the evaluation factors to use in a competitively negotiated procurement, certain key criteria must be met. You must: (1) tailor the evaluation factors and their descriptions to the needs of the specific procurement, (2) use only those evaluation factors that are likely to show the differences among the proposals, (3) limit the number of evaluation factors, and (4) always include cost or price and quality as evaluation factors.

Tailor the Evaluation Factors to the Procurement

Evaluation factors must be tailored to the requirement being procured. The relationship between the evaluation factors and the statement of work and other contractual requirements should be clear. The evaluation scheme should include *only* those evaluation factors and significant subfactors that represent the *key areas of importance and emphasis* to be considered in the source selection decision and that can be applied *equitably* to all offerors. In a competitive acquisition, the evaluation factors (as with the statement of work—SOW—requirements) cannot be designed so that only one offeror can meet the requirements.

It should be noted that with the exception of cost or price (which is always required) and past performance (which is required when appropriate), the evaluation areas cited in the FAR are not required for all procurements and are not the only criteria that can be used. Any factors appropriate to the evaluation may be used.

Ensure That the Evaluation Factors Discriminate among Offerors

Evaluation factors and significant subfactors must support meaningful comparison and discrimination among the competing proposals. They must reflect that which is most important in determining which offeror can perform the contract successfully and which, when considering cost or price, offers the best value. Using evaluation factors that are likely to result in similar evaluation results is not effective. Select those factors and subfactors that are most likely to point out the differences rather than the similarities between the proposals. Keep in mind that the purpose of the evaluation is first to identify the most highly rated proposals (for the competitive range determination) and then to determine which of these proposals offers the best value (for source selection). This cannot be done effectively unless the evaluation criteria provide the basis for identifying the differences, and the respective value of those differences, among the competing proposals.

Limit the Number of Evaluation Factors

Keep the number of different evaluation factors and subfactors to a minimum. Do not try to evaluate every facet of an offeror's proposal. Limit the factors and subfactors to only those *most* important to the success of the procurement. Proposal scoring often becomes diluted if there are a large number of evaluation factors and subfactors. The overall scores tend to level off and become roughly equal, making it difficult to distinguish between and rank the relative worth of the competing proposals and to select the proposal offering the best value. Generally, using more than three or four primary factors and a similar number of subfactors will have a leveling effect.

Always Include Cost or Price and Quality

All procurements must include cost or price as an evaluation factor, although neither need be the most important factor. Cost or price does not even need to be weighted or scored, but it *must* be considered in the source selection because an evaluation scheme in which cost or price is not considered in some fashion can be successfully protested.

14 PAST PERFORMANCE HANDBOOK

Quality also must be addressed in some fashion. As noted earlier, quality may be expressed in terms of such non-cost evaluation factors as technical, management, prior experience, personnel qualifications, compliance with solicitation requirements, past performance, or any other non-cost factor appropriate to the procurement. Past performance must be used in acquisitions exceeding $100,000, unless the contracting officer documents a decision that the use of past performance is not appropriate. Other non-cost factors are used when appropriate to the particular procurement.

Before addressing the decision to use past performance as an evaluation factor, a few words about the other non-cost evaluation factors are in order. Prior to the current emphasis on the use of past performance in the evaluation, the standard primary evaluation factors were technical, management, and prior experience. Often these were used automatically, with personnel qualifications as a subfactor to either technical or management when appropriate. Compliance with solicitation requirements was used when the acquisition did not require the evaluation of technical and management. Past performance was used as an evaluation factor, but its use was not common.

Now, with the FAR requiring the use of past performance, we are seeing some variances in evaluation schemes, particularly with fixed-price contracts. Agencies are now looking more critically at using non-cost evaluation factors. Some agencies are soliciting on the basis of price and past performance as the only evaluation factors when acquiring standard supplies or services. Other agencies, when appropriate, are substituting past performance for the technical and management evaluation factors, where how an offeror has performed in the past is determined to be a better indicator of how it will perform in the future than the promises set forth in technical and management proposals. In other instances, agencies are combining past performance and prior experience into a single evaluation factor and diminishing the importance of technical and management, if not eliminating one or both altogether. A critical analysis of exactly which evaluation factors are appropriate for each procurement is a good thing.

DETERMINING WHETHER TO USE PAST PERFORMANCE AS AN EVALUATION FACTOR

Despite the emphasis on using past performance in competitive evaluations, keep in mind that the final decision is up to the contracting officer. The contracting officer must determine if using past performance as an evaluation factor is appropriate and how it should be used. If past performance is not used in the evaluation, however, the contracting officer must document the reason why in the contract file.

Using past performance as an evaluation factor should depend on the significance of past performance as a discriminator in the current procurement. Do not automatically assume that past performance is an important factor without first considering whether you need it to discriminate among offerors. For example, if all potential offerors are good performers, the evaluation of past performance may not enhance the evaluation process. If the acquisition is a once-in-a-generation acquisition, there will not likely be any significant past performance to evaluate (assuming that there is no sufficiently similar effort). The effective use of past performance also may be diminished if a number of new firms with no performance history are competing or when the acquisition is for a new item or service that has no germane performance history. The rationale for not using past performance as an evaluation factor should indicate the circumstances of the procurement that preclude using past performance as a discriminating factor and state that because past performance will not be a significant discriminator, it should not be used in the evaluation.

Generally, past performance can be used effectively in most procurements, either as a primary evaluation factor or as a significant subfactor. For example, if previous contracts for the same or similar items or services have a history of performance problems, then past performance, as an indicator of performance risk, is a very important criterion and should be used as a primary evaluation factor. Past performance is also an effective evaluation factor in the repetitive acquisition of standard supplies or services when there are many competing offerors and a significant performance history.

Past performance also is significant if strict conformance with the specifications and delivery times is critical to the program the procurement supports. For example, the acquisition of military clothing requires strict conformance to the specifications and delivery schedule. This field is very competitive, and the evaluation of past performance helps limit the competition to proven suppliers. Past performance also is important in the acquisition of supplies and equipment when the required items are sensitive and complex devices and the proven ability to produce the items successfully in conformance to specifications and to make timely delivery are critical to selecting the successful offeror.

The evaluation of past performance is also applicable to services, such as technical support services, when the proven ability to respond successfully to complex technical requirements is critical to source selection, or even standard services, such as janitorial services, where successful past performance is an important indicator of an offeror's likely future performance.

Past performance also can be evaluated separately from the standard non-cost evaluation factors as a performance risk factor, in which the risk of successful performance is evaluated through assessing risk and determining the likelihood that instances of poor past performance (or superior past performance) will be repeated in the prospective contract. Do not confuse performance risk with proposal risk. Proposal risk is an assessment of the likelihood that the proposed technical and management approach will be successful, based solely on the contents of an offeror's technical and management proposals. Performance risk evaluation is based on outside information, i.e., the verification of past performance information provided by the offeror and information about past contracts obtained from third parties, rather than being restricted to information contained in the proposal.

DETERMINING THE RELATIVE IMPORTANCE OF PAST PERFORMANCE AS AN EVALUATION FACTOR

To submit accurate and realistic proposals, offerors must understand the criteria against which their proposals will be evaluated. Therefore, the evaluation factors and significant subfactors and their relative importance must be set forth in the RFP in a manner that clearly expresses their value and interrelationships.

Determining the Relative Importance of Evaluation Factors

Once the evaluation factors and subfactors to be used have been identified, the relative importance of each should be determined based on an assessment of the value of each factor to the overall evaluation. Generally this is done by first determining the relative importance of each primary evaluation factor and then the relative importance of each subfactor to its associated primary factor.

To determine relative importance, you must first review the solicitation requirements to decide what it is that you need to know from each offeror to determine the worth of the offeror's proposal. Those things you need to know are represented by the evaluation factors (e.g., technical, management, prior experience, past performance), and the relative importance of each factor depends on how important each is to the identification of those offerors to be included in the competitive range and the eventual source selection.

Evaluation factors are listed in the RFP in a descending order of importance, and their relative importance is set forth either in a narrative (if the relationships are simple, easy to understand, and there are not very many factors) or by publishing the specific evaluation weights in the RFP. Keep in mind that the primary purposes of describing the relative importance of the evaluation factors and subfactors are: (1) to ensure that offerors address the issues represented by the evaluation factors with the appropriate emphasis, and (2) to ensure that offerors understand how their proposals will be evaluated.

Determining the Relative Importance of Past Performance

The Office of Federal Procurement Policy's (OFPP) May 2000 publication, *Best Practices for Collecting and Using Current and Past Performance Information*, recommends that past performance be used as a primary evaluation factor weighted at 25 percent or more, or at least equal in significance to the other non-cost evaluation factors, to ensure that significant consideration is given to past performance. It goes on to say that a very low weighting may reduce the overall perception of how important good contract performance is as an element of the source selection process.

Note, however, that the importance of past performance as an evaluation factor must be based on its importance in determining which proposal offers the best value, which in turn depends on a number of varying factors, all relating to the current acquisition and not to a policy statement or general guidance. The overall requirement must be assessed carefully, first to determine which evaluation factors to use and then to determine the relative importance of each. Automatically assigning past performance some predetermined evaluation weight would be a poor practice.

When used, past performance usually is one of the primary evaluation factors, but not necessarily one of the most important. The technical and management factors provide insight into how the offeror proposes to perform the current requirement, and the prior experience factor indicates the offeror's expertise. If this is important—such as when the requirement is large and complex, specific technical expertise is required, or there are a number of different ways to accomplish the requirement—how an offeror proposes to do the work and its technical and management expertise could be critical discriminators in the evaluation. In such instances, past performance might be of lesser importance in the evaluation scheme.

There are times, however, when the technical or management factors might not be significant to the source selection. For example, in the procurement of continuing services (particularly when using performance-based service contracting), how a contractor plans to perform or manage the contract might not be as significant as its track record in performing the same or similar services. When the performance of services is standardized, as in commercial or commercial-like services, the competitors generally will be alike in their technical and management approaches. If their technical and management proposals were to be evaluated, it is likely that they would be rated as roughly equal, in effect rendering technical and management capabilities ineffective as evaluation factors. In such instances, substituting past performance for the technical or management evaluation factors rather than adding past performance as another evaluation factor would make the evaluation more effective. A number of agencies, when acquiring standard supplies or services on a fixed-price basis, have

18 PAST PERFORMANCE HANDBOOK

found that using past performance and price as the only evaluation factors is an effective and efficient approach.

Distinguishing between Past Performance and Prior Experience

Past performance must be distinguished from prior experience. The evaluation of past performance and prior experience uses the same database—previous contracts for the same or similar effort—but each is evaluated differently. Prior experience is used to evaluate an offeror's technical expertise and is related to whether the offeror has performed such work in the past, not how well it performed. Past performance is used to evaluate how well the offeror has performed the same or similar past or current contracts and is not concerned with the offeror's expertise, except as demonstrated by how well the offeror met its contractual requirements.

Another way to look at the difference between the two factors is to consider prior experience to be personnel-oriented (i.e., it demonstrates the corporate memory of the personnel involved). Past performance is results-oriented (i.e., it demonstrates how well the offeror performed).

When both past performance and prior experience are used as evaluation factors, each should be specifically defined in the RFP. Define prior experience as an indicator of the offeror's expertise, as demonstrated by its work on past and current contracts of the same or similar nature. Define past performance as an indicator of how well the offeror is likely to perform on the current contract, as demonstrated by how well it performed on comparable prior contracts.

Please note, however, that using both prior experience and past performance can dilute the importance of past performance, as shown in Example 2.1.

Example 2.1—The relative importance of past performance can be diluted by adding prior experience.[4]

In a fixed-price solicitation for refuse collection and disposal services, proposals were to be evaluated based on: (1) past performance/experience and (2) price/cost, which were to be approximately equal in weight. Past performance and experience were also to be approximately equal in weight. Award was to be made on a best value basis. Past performance was to be assessed to determine offerors' relative capability and trustworthiness, and thus their relative reliability to perform the contract requirements, and prior experience was to be evaluated to assess offerors' experience in performing work on similar refuse collection and disposal services contracts.

The award decision was successfully protested (see Example 6.4) because the reasonableness of the tradeoff decision was not adequately documented. Of interest here, however, is the perhaps unintended consequences of the evaluation scheme as noted by the Comptroller General in footnote 2 to its decision.

Since past performance/experience and price/cost were to be given approximately equal weight, each was worth approximately 50 percent of the overall rating; since, within past performance/experience, each of the two component[s] was approximately equal, past performance was worth approximately 25 percent of the overall rating.

It is unlikely that the agency meant to have the relative importance of past performance rated at 25 percent, given that the award was to be based on past performance and price as approximately equal. By adding prior experience as equal in importance to past performance, the relative importance of past performance was diminished, which would make a tradeoff favoring superior past performance difficult to support. Evaluation schemes should be objectively assessed prior to the issuance of the RFP to ascertain the possibility of such unintended consequences.

Combining Past Performance and Prior Experience

The problem noted in Example 2.1 could have been avoided if past performance and prior experience had been combined as a single past performance evaluation factor. This can be done by defining past performance as the evaluation of the quality of an offeror's performance on relevant past or current contracts and further defining "relevant" as contracts of the same or similar nature and scope as the requirements of the current solicitation (i.e., prior experience). This combination is particularly important if past performance and price are to be the only evaluation factors, but it also can be applied to minimize the number of primary evaluation factors when using other non-cost evaluation factors is appropriate.

If past performance is to be a significant evaluation factor, it might be best not to use prior experience as a discrete subfactor but to use instead the combination noted above. After all, an evaluation of past performance should be made using relevant past effort. How else can you relate an offeror's past performance to its likely performance on the prospective contract? Example 2.2 demonstrates the need for relevancy.

Example 2.2—Relevancy is important in evaluating past performance.[5]

In a UNICOR solicitation for a best value award of a fixed-price, indefinite-quantity contract for leather to be used in manufacturing work gloves, the solicitation cited three evaluation factors in a descending order of importance—past performance, compliance with technical specifications, and price. With respect to past performance, vendors were (among other things) required to submit from three to five references for previous similar contracts performed within the past three years.

PCI listed four past performance references—two for leather contracts and two for communications components contracts. After concluding that the communications components contracts were not similar to the current leather requirement, the contracting officer checked UNICOR's database and found that PCI had a current contract to supply leather to UNICOR. Because she viewed this contract as similar to the solicited requirement, she used it as the third reference instead of the communications components contracts. Based on the ratings for these three contracts—one excellent, two good—the contracting officer evaluated PCI as overall good for past performance.

After another firm received the award, PCI protested, asserting, among other issues, that the contracting officer improperly failed to consider the two communications components contract references. PCI claimed that had these contracts been considered, PCI would have received all excellent ratings and would have been in line for award.

The Comptroller General denied the protest.

In evaluating past performance, an agency has discretion to determine the scope of the vendors' performance history to be considered, provided that it evaluates all submissions on the same basis and consistent with the solicitation.[6] An agency may base its evaluation on contracts it believes are most relevant to the solicitation,[7] it has discretion to consider information other than that provided by the vendors,[8] and need not consider all references a vendor submits.[9]

UNICOR's actions fall within the above standard. The contracting officer sought to identify the most relevant contracts for purposes of assessing PCI's past performance and, in doing so, considered a relevant contract not listed in PCI's quotation and disregarded two listed contracts which were not similar to the current requirement. This was reasonable, and well within the agency's discretion. Moreover, although we think the logic of evaluating similar contracts to assess past performance is obvious, the RFQ requirement that firms provide references for "similar" contracts put PCI and the other vendors on notice that the agency wanted to evaluate similar contracts; thus, the agency's reliance on PCI's ongoing leather contract was fully consistent with the evaluation scheme.

Thus, while past performance and prior experience may be defined as different evaluation factors, they also may be defined as a single evaluation factor when appropriate. Prior (or corporate) experience has been a commonly used evaluation factor. However, unless there is a specific reason to use it as a discrete evaluation factor along with past performance, it might be best to combine it with past performance, as noted above. Such a combination will ensure that past performance is accorded an appropriate relative importance.

Distinguishing between Past Performance As a Responsibility Factor and As an Evaluation Factor

Using past performance as a *responsibility* factor must be distinguished from using it as an *evaluation* factor to ensure that both are handled properly.

FAR 15.304(c) requires that past performance be used as an evaluation factor in all competitively negotiated procurements in excess of $100,000 *unless* the contracting officer documents the reason why it is not an appropriate evaluation factor for the instant procurement.

FAR Subpart 9.1 requires that all contracts be awarded to responsible contractors and establishes the responsibility standards that must be met. Past performance is one of the responsibility standards. FAR 9.104-3(b) requires the use of past performance in making determinations of responsibility, stating that, "A prospective contractor that is or recently has been seriously deficient in contract performance shall be presumed to be nonresponsible, unless the contracting officer determines that the circumstances were properly beyond the contractor's control, or that the contractor has taken appropriate corrective action. Past failure to apply sufficient tenacity and perseverance to perform acceptably is strong evidence of nonresponsibility. Failure to meet the quality requirements of the contract is a significant factor to consider in determining satisfactory performance."

Distinguishing between past performance as a responsibility factor and as an evaluation factor is necessary because determining responsibility and evaluating proposals are two distinct and separate functions, performed for different purposes at different times by different people during the procurement process.

As an evaluation factor, past performance is evaluated for purposes of source selection in competitively negotiated acquisitions. All *evaluation* factors are evaluated by the application of specific criteria set forth in the RFP, through a *comparative assessment* that establishes the relative value of each proposal and the relative ranking of each offeror. Past performance is evaluated during the initial evaluation for the establishment of the competitive range and later during the final evaluation to establish which proposal represents the best value to the government. It should be noted that in a comparative assessment, a failure to meet the minimum requirements of an evaluation factor does not in itself require automatic rejection of a proposal. It simply results in a lower assessment or score. A technical evaluation team performs this evaluation.

Responsibility factors are assessed in all acquisitions to determine if a proposed contractor is a responsible business able to perform the contract. Past performance is one of a number of responsibility factors that are assessed by the application of specific responsibility standards established in the FAR. This assessment is made on a pass/fail basis, and a failure to meet the minimum requirements of any responsibility standard requires rejection of the proposal. A contractor is either responsible or not responsible; there is no middle ground. The contracting officer performs this assessment after completion of the final evaluation and immediately before award.

The need to distinguish between past performance as a responsibility factor and past performance as an evaluation factor lies in how failures are handled if a small business is involved. If a small business firm fails to meet the responsibility standards and is determined to be not responsible, the matter must be referred to the Small Business Administration (SBA), which may issue a Certifi-

22   PAST PERFORMANCE HANDBOOK

cate of Competency (COC) declaring that the firm is a responsible business concern. If the SBA does not issue a COC, the firm's proposal *must* be rejected.

However, if a small business firm's proposal is downgraded under past performance during a comparative assessment (evaluation) of all proposals, the matter is not reviewable by the SBA because, as noted earlier, a failure to meet the minimum requirements of an evaluation factor does not require automatic rejection of a proposal but simply results in a lower assessment or score. The SBA's authority extends only to matters of non-responsibility and does not encompass matters involving comparative assessments.

Using past performance as an evaluation factor is not a substitute for assessing past performance in the responsibility determination. Past performance is an established responsibility factor and *must* be considered in a determination of responsibility. Therefore, if past performance is used as an evaluation factor, it could be evaluated twice—first, as part of the assessment of the value of an offeror's proposal in comparison to the proposals of other offerors, and second, to determine if the offeror's past performance meets the minimum standards of responsibility.

Generally, however, if past performance is an evaluation factor, an offeror whose past performance is such that it would be considered non-responsible would not remain in the competition long enough for a responsibility determination. Only the most highly rated offerors are included in the competitive range, and an offeror's significantly deficient performance record will, in most cases, lower the offeror's score enough to result in proposal rejection during the initial proposal evaluation. However, there are always exceptions to the rules, and knowing the difference between an evaluation factor and a responsibility factor before issuing the RFP will help avoid mistakes that can be protested successfully.

DETERMINING WHAT WILL BE EVALUATED AS PAST PERFORMANCE

A number of areas can be evaluated under past performance, depending on the needs of your particular procurement. While past performance is generally evaluated in terms of problems encountered, noting any significant successes in each area evaluated is equally important. Past problems are usually determinative in the initial evaluation for the establishment of the competitive range, but past successes can be determinative in the final evaluation for source selection.

OFPP-Suggested Past Performance Subfactors

OFPP suggests the following past performance subfactors,[10] which provide broad evaluation areas.

Performance Quality—This area includes the evaluation of the quality of the products or services delivered under past or other current contracts and the extent to which the interim and end products or services conformed to the contractual requirements. This evaluation involves more than the quality of deliverable items or services; it also involves technical excellence (including quality awards and certificates), the accuracy of reports, rejections and reworks, and any other successes or failures with respect to the contractor's conformance to contract requirements.

Quality problems should be examined to determine the reason for them, the extent to which government actions may have contributed to them, and if the problems were corrected. Determine if contractual modifications were made to accommodate the contractor's inability to meet the stated requirements and why these accommodations were made. A contract modification that lowers the quality standards may be an indication that problems were not corrected.

Schedule Performance—This area has to do with how well the contractor adhered to delivery and administrative schedules under past and other current contracts. This involves a contractor's record of adhering to delivery schedules for interim and end products and services as well as meeting technical milestones and the schedules for administrative deliverables, such as progress reports. It also includes intangible deliveries, such as the timeliness of the contractor's response to technical direction and the contractor's ability to meet interim and final milestone schedules on a timely basis.

Examine any schedule failures to determine why the schedule was not met and the extent to which government actions may have contributed to the schedule problems. Determine if contractual modifications were made to accommodate schedule failures and the circumstances under which they were made. A contract modification that accepts schedule failures may be an indication that problems causing the schedule failures were not corrected.

Cost Control—This area is applicable only to cost reimbursement, time and materials, and labor-hour contracts, which are used when the government requirements are not defined sufficiently to use a fixed price. This lack of definition often creates cost or hour problems as the contractor reacts to performance realities. As the contract progresses and the work requirements become better defined, the cost or hour requirements may well increase. Examine such increases to determine if contractor inefficiency or matters beyond the contractor's control caused them. The extent to which government actions may have contributed to the problems also should be determined.

This area also includes an assessment of the accuracy of contractor estimates, the relationship of negotiated costs to actual costs, the use of cost-efficient techniques, and any other problems related to cost, including the timely submission of current, accurate, and complete billings.

Business Relations—This area involves the evaluation of a contractor's history of reasonable and cooperative behavior and commitment to customer satisfaction. This evaluation deals with the working relationship between the contractor and the government during contract performance, including how well the contractor responded to government requests for information and reports, how well the contractor responded to contract changes, and how well the contractor met contract requirements other than quality, schedule, and cost, such as subcontract management, meeting of socioeconomic goals, user satisfaction, and integrating and coordinating contract activities.

A contractor concerned with customer satisfaction will respond quickly and cooperatively to problems and changes and demonstrate an interest in delivering a quality product. Be alert, however, to situations in which a contractor's reported problems represent an assertion of the contractor's rights under the contract as opposed to situations in which the contractor has simply failed to respond properly. For example, the fact that a contractor has submitted a number of contract claims in the past cannot be used to downgrade the contractor's past performance on the basis of a lack of reasonable and cooperative behavior (see Example 4.5).

A contractor has the right to submit contract claims even if doing so irks the government. A contractor also has the right to challenge the government over such things as the interpretation of contract specifications or contract clauses, as long as such challenges are not frivolous.

Using the OFPP Subfactors

The OFPP-suggested past performance subfactors are by no means mandatory. If other subfactors or areas of interest are deemed more appropriate, they should be used instead. Tailor the areas to be evaluated under past performance and their definitions to your current requirement.

You may choose to define past performance as consisting of the OFPP subfactors listed above in a narrative (e.g., past performance will be evaluated in terms of the quality and timelines of the offeror's performance, its ability to control costs, and its business relations), rather than listing them as discrete subfactors. This would provide some evaluation flexibility, particularly when describing the relative importance of the past performance evaluation factor, because you would not have to establish the relative importance of each of the subfactors. Keep in mind, however, that if an issue arises, the Comptroller General probably would rule that each element of the definition bears an equal weight in the evaluation.

Quality and Schedule Performance—Quality and schedule performance are critical in evaluating an offeror's past performance; their use is inherent in the evaluation of past performance. These are objective criteria and are not difficult to evaluate because the offeror either did or did not meet the contractual quality and schedule requirements. There may, however, be mitigating circumstances in which the problems were beyond the control of the offeror and not due to its negligence, such as acts of God or actions by the government that directly or indirectly contributed to the problem. Any other performance failures would have to be explained in terms of the corrective action taken. If the offeror cannot show effective corrective action, the failure should adversely affect the past performance evaluation. When the preponderance of past performance reports about an offeror are good, a single negative report should be examined closely to determine the cause of the problem and whether there were mitigating circumstances.

The number of contract changes is another area to consider. Contract changes often adversely affect timely delivery and adherence to the requirements, especially when the changes are significant. The impact of such changes is difficult to assess unless these issues were documented at the time the contract was changed. Nevertheless, the effect of numerous contract changes should be considered, to the extent possible, when evaluating an offeror's past performance.

Cost Control—Cost control applies only to contracts other than fixed-price (e.g., cost reimbursement, time and materials, labor hour); these contracts are used only when it is not possible to use a fixed-price contract and are performed on a best-efforts basis because of performance uncertainties. Despite OFPP's suggestion that cost control be considered as a past performance subfactor, the use of cost control in evaluating an offeror's past performance should not be automatic because a contractor's ability to control costs depends on what happens during contract performance and may be beyond the contractor's control.

Overruns, for example, can be caused by the fact that the required effort—not fully defined at the time of contracting—proved to require greater effort than either the government or the contractor anticipated. Because the contractor is committed only to applying its best efforts, it may not be fair to rule an overrun as poor performance—unless the overrun can clearly be attributed to contractor inefficiency. Delivery times often slip in such contracts as the requirement is redefined during contract performance.

These redefinitions may or may not be supported by official contract modification of the delivery dates. Adherence to contract requirements in such contracts is often difficult to determine because in many instances, the requirements are not fully defined at the time of contracting and no definitive baseline can be applied. Because of the initial uncertainties, contract changes are often necessary, and their effect on the offeror's ability to control costs also may be difficult to assess accurately.

Does assessing how well the offeror controlled costs in one contractual situation in which costs (or hours) could only be estimated really serve as a valid indicator of how well the offeror might control costs in a different contractual situation? The simple fact that there was an overrun of costs (or hours) is not automatically poor performance. There are many valid reasons why the work might cost more or take additional hours to complete, not the least of which is that the costs or hours were estimates at best.

Before using cost control as an explicit past performance subfactor, consider your ability to evaluate effectively an offeror's past cost control and its value to your evaluation of past performance. Note that the evaluation of an offeror's cost control could be included indirectly by including management in the definition of past performance, i.e., *past performance will be evaluated in terms of the quality and timeliness of the offeror's performance and its effective management of current and past contracts.* Cost control is an inherent part of the management of contracts other than fixed-price and could be evaluated without listing cost control as an explicit subfactor.

Business Relations—A contractor's cooperative behavior depends on what happens during contract performance, and an assessment here is necessarily subjective because there are no objective standards that apply. From a practical standpoint, how important are good business relations? If a contractor meets the quality and schedule requirements, does it matter how well the contractor got along with the government?

Generally, an offeror with a history of meeting its quality and schedule requirements would also have a good history of business relations—but what if it didn't? Would you *not* contract with an offeror with a history of meeting all of its contractual quality and schedule requirements but who is hard to get along with? What added value do business relations bring to the past performance evaluation? Are business relations likely to be a discriminating factor in most past performance evaluations?

A contractor with poor business relations also is likely to have quality and schedule problems. Why, then, use it as an evaluation factor? These questions should be addressed before using business relations as a discrete past performance subfactor.

If the RFP states that certain elements will be evaluated, they must be evaluated. If you do not have a good idea how you will evaluate the more difficult areas of past performance such as cost control and business relations, it might be best to exclude them from the evaluation. Save these areas for those times when they are really important to contract performance, such as when the solicitation is for a cost-plus-award fee contract or other instances where the nature of the contract will call for extensive interaction between the contractor and the government.

On the other hand, both cost control and business relations are inherent management functions, and management (encompassing both cost control and business relations) could be listed as a past performance subfactor or simply included as part of the definition of past performance.

Evaluating every aspect of past performance is not necessary. The area of adherence to delivery and administrative schedules encompasses the most common problem with a contractor's cooperative behavior—the ability to get the contractor to deliver administrative requirements on time. Keep in mind that the more factors you include in the evaluation, the more complicated the evaluation will become and the greater the potential for controversy.

Using cost control and business relations in evaluating past performance is a policy matter—to encourage contractors to pay closer attention to these areas if they want future government contracts. But what is good policy for the government as a whole may not be in your best interests in terms of an instant acquisition.

Areas of Specific Concern

In addition to, or instead of, the past performance subfactors suggested by OFPP, there may be specific areas of concern particular to your requirement, such as staffing, quality control, or subcontracts (particularly if subcontractors will be doing a significant portion of the work), that you may want to emphasize in evaluating past performance. When evaluating at the subcontractor level, be sure that you explain exactly what will be evaluated and what documentation is required because the offeror must pass this information down to its proposed subcontractors. The following are two examples of how past peformance was defined in actual RFPs.

- One agency cited "quality and timeliness of offeror's work; reasonableness of pricing, costs, and claims; reasonableness of its business behavior; concern for the interests of its customers; and its integrity" as the factors to be evaluated under past performance. It should be noted that "reasonableness of claims" is not a proper evaluation criterion (see Example 4.5), and the term "integrity" is dubious because integrity is primarily a responsibility factor—a contractor either has integrity or not, so a comparative assessment of integrity does not make sense. The rest of the subfactors, however, were sufficient for a valid evaluation.

- Another agency cited "offeror demonstrated performance record in effective contract and subcontract management, responsive scheduling, timeliness, workload fluctuations, customer satisfaction, quality, government interface, effective use of resources, environmental and safety compliance, and major subcontractors" as past performance evaluation factors. While this may have covered the agency's concerns, it included too many different evaluation areas. Using many evaluation criteria not only makes the evaluation more complicated, but it also has a leveling effect on the evaluation results. The agency would have been better off using fewer and more generalized evaluation subfactors.

These examples demonstrate that agencies are evaluating past performance in many different ways. Some agencies have simply listed past performance and price as the only evaluation factors and, under past performance, have required offerors to provide details of its past contracts, including sufficient information to demonstrate the relevance of the referenced contracts to the proposed effort. This approach has proved beneficial in the award of fixed-price contracts, particularly those involving the repetitive acquisition of standard supplies or services (see Example 4.6).

Other agencies have listed past performance and prior experience as two of the subfactors under a technical evaluation factor, with price as the only other evaluation factor. In essence, under "technical," these agencies have said that they will evaluate an offeror's past performance on other contracts to see how well they performed and their prior experience to see if they have performed contracts of the same or similar nature as the current requirement. Prior experience must be assessed to determine if the offeror's experience is relevant. It should be noted, however, that when used this way, or whenever past performance and prior experience are used as separate subfactors, the relative importance of actual past performance may be diminished because both subfactors would share the overall weighting of the primary evaluation factor (see Example 6.5).

Use of the broad evaluation areas suggested by OFPP covers virtually all aspects of past performance, and other specifically identified subfactors may not be needed. Problems falling in these general areas are inherently part of the past performance evaluation factor. Use other specific subfactors or evaluation areas only where you have a specific evaluation purpose in mind, such as when subcontracting will be a major part of the prospective contract and how well the offeror managed its subcontractors and how well a specifically identified subcontractor performed in the past is important to the award decision.

It is not necessary to use the OFPP wording or to define explicitly each past performance evaluation area, but how you describe what you will evaluate must be sufficient to put offerors on notice of the areas to be considered. When defining past performance as an evaluation factor, specificity is not in your best interests. You must evaluate proposals to the factors stated in the RFP, and you cannot evaluate unstated factors without first amending the solicitation to include them. Thus, if you are too specific in describing the past performance evaluation factor, you may preclude the evaluation of unanticipated problems.

You may use unstated evaluation subfactors, however, if they are deemed "inherent" to the primary evaluation factor, i.e., commonly accepted as part of what would be evaluated under the primary factor. For example, performance risk may be considered in evaluating past performance, even when it is not specifically listed as an evaluation factor.[11] The OFPP-suggested evaluation areas are general enough to cover most problems that you might encounter. If you want to use other wording, be sure to include the following key words: "quality," "timeliness," and, when appropriate, "cost control" and "business relations."

The evaluation of past performance is used as an indicator of how an offeror will perform under the current requirement. Note that good past performance is a positive indicator, but not a guarantee, that an offeror will perform well. Poor past performance, however, unless adequately explained, is a good indicator that an offeror *will not* perform well. Tailor the description of past performance as necessary to ensure that you get only the information you need (i.e., do not use any of the evaluation areas noted above if they will not be important in discriminating among offerors). Ensure that the information to be obtained is relevant, meaningful, and related to the key performance criteria in the SOW.

DETERMINING HOW THE RFP WILL ADDRESS PAST PERFORMANCE

Assessing past performance is no easy matter; contractors are sensitive to allegations that they do not perform well. It is important, therefore, that the RFP clearly explain how past performance will be evaluated. Ensure that Sections L and M of the RFP appropriately address what the term "past performance" means and how it will be evaluated.

Define Past Performance

Define past performance in Section M of the RFP in terms of the kinds of information that will be evaluated. As noted earlier, past performance may be defined by listing the specific subfactors (i.e., quality, schedule, cost, business relations, and areas of specific concern), or it can be defined in a narrative in terms of the offeror's performance in the areas of interest (i.e., "past performance will be evaluated in terms of the quality and timeliness of the offeror's performance, its ability to control costs, and its business relations under current or past contracts"). The difference lies in the amount of information that must be provided. If the areas of interest are listed as subfactors, each must be defined and their relative importance indicated. If a narrative approach is used, only the relative importance of the primary past performance factor need be identified.

The definition of past performance and the specific subfactors (or areas of interest in a narrative) should be tailored to your requirement. While the definitions need not get into specific detail, the definitions should be such that offerors will understand which areas of past performance will be evaluated. The definitions should not include anything that will not be evaluated.

Indicate How Past Performance Will Be Evaluated

In addition to identifying the past performance areas to be evaluated, RFP Section M should state that an offeror's past performance will be evaluated to assess its relative merit with respect to the current requirement and then as compared to that of competing offerors. Indicate that the evaluation will be based on current and past performance information furnished by the offeror as well as information from other available sources, such as other government agencies, suppliers, subcontractors, or customers of the offeror. Section M also should state that offerors without a record of relevant past performance or those for whom information on past performance is not available will not be evaluated favorably or unfavorably on past performance but will be given a neutral rating.

If past performance will be evaluated separately from the other technical evaluation factors, as a performance risk factor, this should be specifically noted with an explanation of the evaluation criteria to be used.

As noted earlier, the evaluation must be conducted as set forth in the RFP. If the RFP indicates that certain areas will be evaluated and certain methods will be used, the evaluators cannot deviate from this unless the RFP is first amended to show the changes and offerors are given an opportunity to revise their proposals accordingly. A failure to evaluate in accordance with the RFP can result in a successful protest.

When establishing the factors to be used to evaluate past performance, therefore, keep in mind that the more subfactors you use, the more complicated the evaluation will be, and you are committed to evaluating each subfactor listed in the RFP. Therefore, you should keep the number of past performance evaluation subfactors to a minimum, using only those that would be significant to the performance of the proposed contract. Or, as noted earlier, define past performance as containing those areas you might otherwise use as subfactors, and do not list any specific past performance subfactors when identifying the RFP's evaluation factors and subfactors and their relative importance.

Indicate the Documentation Required

In the proposal preparation instructions (RFP Section L), identify the information that the offeror should submit as past performance information. Require offerors to identify current and past contracts (these may be federal, state, local government, or private contracts) for the same or similar work, including the contract number, dollar value, dates, name of the contracting agency, a contact telephone number, and a description of the work effort. State that it is important that the offeror clearly show how the work under each referenced contract is relevant to the proposed effort. Inform the offerors that some, but not necessarily all, of the references will be checked to verify the quality of the past performance.

Indicate that offerors may describe the quality of their performance on the referenced contracts and may (or must, as appropriate) also provide information on predecessor companies, key personnel who have relevant experience, or subcontractors that will perform major or critical aspects of the requirement, when such information is relevant to the instant acquisition.

It is important to require offerors to identify any performance difficulties in the referenced contracts and to discuss the corrective action taken. The offeror must provide evidence that it was able to identify the cause of the problems and demonstrate that the problems were resolved. Tell the offerors that if past problems are not fully addressed, it will be assumed that they still exist, and the proposal will be evaluated accordingly. If deemed appropriate, you should identify specific areas of concern, such as late deliveries, cost overruns, or product deficiencies, but do not limit the information to just those areas. Indicate that copies of agency-developed contractor performance reports on past or current contracts should be submitted as part of their past performance information, if available.

You also should indicate that offerors should provide information on awards or commendations that they may have received regarding work on referenced contracts. These are positive indicators of an offeror's past performance and could significantly affect the past performance evaluation.

DETERMINING HOW PAST PERFORMANCE WILL BE RATED OR SCORED IN THE EVALUATION

Before issuing the RFP, you must consider how offerors' past performance will be rated or scored. In the initial evaluation, each offeror's proposal is evaluated based on the evaluation factors stated in the RFP. This evaluation facilitates developing an initial rating and ranking the proposals for the contracting officer's use in establishing the competitive range. While some comparative assessment may be done when establishing the competitive range, the primary emphasis is on assessing how well the offeror met the past performance evaluation criteria.

In the final evaluation for source selection, an offeror's past performance is primarily assessed on a comparative basis with the competing offerors to determine which proposal offers the best value. Tradeoffs between past performance and other non-cost evaluation factors, or between past performance and price, are often determinative in the source selection decision.

Where award will be made without discussions, an offeror's past performance is first evaluated based on the RFP's evaluation criteria and then comparatively assessed (with tradeoffs as necessary) with the competing offerors to provide a basis for the award decision.

Past performance, however, is not necessarily scored or rated in the same manner as the other evaluation factors. Generally, there are two ways to rate past performance: (1) in the same manner as the other non-cost evaluation factors (i.e., numerically, by color code, or some other method); or (2) with respect to the degree of performance risk in the same manner that proposal risk is evaluated (i.e., by a broad scoring range such as "low risk," "moderate risk," and "high risk").

Numerical Scoring Systems

Numerical rating systems usually use six adjectival ratings: Excellent, Very Good, Good, Fair, and Poor, with a numerical scoring range and a definition assigned to each of the ratings; and Neutral, for offerors with no past performance history. In effect, the range of scores within each rating allows you to measure how good is good and how bad is bad. This rating system is applied to each subfactor of each evaluation factor.

To evaluate past performance effectively using this scoring system, contract references must be obtained from each offeror, information related to each subfactor must be obtained or verified by the references, or similar information must be obtained from third-party sources. This can be a significant undertaking and may be more information than you really need to evaluate past performance.

The effective use of a numerical system, or any system with a lot of ratings, depends to a large degree on the information base being used. The other non-cost evaluation factors are evaluated based solely on information provided in the offeror's proposal, using the offeror's own words, thus providing a singular information base. While prior experience is evaluated based on information provided by the offeror, the reference checking is restricted to verifying the offeror's description of the work requirements.

The evaluation of past performance, however, requires a larger information base. In addition to the references and information provided by the offeror, the past performance information base includes information gleaned from checking the references (i.e., verifying the information provided by the offeror), information obtained from your own agency records about other contracts performed by the offeror, information from contractor performance reports generated by other agencies, and information from other federal, state, or local agencies or commercial sources such as banks, customers, and suppliers. This information can be subjective, and its validity may be questionable.

Assigning numerical scores to such a varied informational base conveys a preciseness that may be misleading. The numerical scores or color codes are only guides for the evaluators and cannot be used as the basis for decisions. Decisions are made based on the narrative explanations supporting the scores or rating assigned. Documenting an evaluation using only the wording of the definitions provided for each score or rating is not a sufficient explanation for the scores assigned. The narrative explanation must show the relationship to the specific proposal.

OFPP, in Appendix III of its May 2000 guide, *Best Practices for Collecting and Using Current and Past Performance Information*, suggests a rating system that uses five ratings—Exceptional, Very Good, Satisfactory, Marginal, and Unsatisfactory—and provides criteria for each of the evaluation categories. It should be noted, however, that this rating system provides "suggested guidelines for assigning ratings on a contractor's compliance with the contract performance, cost, and schedule goals as specified in the Statement of Work." In other words, the rating system is meant to be used in contractor performance reports (a contract administration activity) and not in evaluating past performance for source selection. OFPP does not suggest a specific rating scheme for evaluating proposals.

Color Coding Scoring Systems

Color coding scoring systems usually use five adjectival ratings: Exceptional, Acceptable, Marginal, and Unacceptable, with a color code and a definition assigned to each rating; and Neutral, for offerors with no past performance history. Color coding provides a broader evaluation range, and the absence of numbers eliminates the implied preciseness of numerical scoring.

34 PAST PERFORMANCE HANDBOOK

Color coding is more appropriate than numerical scoring in evaluating past performance, but it suffers from the need to gather a great deal of information. As with numerical scoring, documenting an evaluation using only the wording of the definitions provided for each rating is not a sufficient explanation for the scores assigned. A narrative explanation, related to the specific proposal, is required to support the rating assigned to each evaluation factor and subfactor, including past performance. For past performance, this explanation must relate the problems (or strengths) found in the past performance information to the rating assigned and its definition.

Two problems are associated with both numerical and color coding scoring systems: (1) while both systems work well in identifying poor proposals (for the competitive range determination), they do not work as well in distinguishing the best of the most highly rated proposals (for the source selection decision); and (2) there is a tendency to concentrate more on the rating categories than on the required narrative evaluation. In a properly conducted evaluation, the narrative evaluation should be developed before assigning any numerical ratings or color codes. Comptroller General decisions offer ample evidence, however, that the documentation in this area is not as good as it should be. Competitive range and source selection decisions must be based on the narrative evaluations and not the ratings assigned.

Performance Risk Assessments

Evaluating past performance separately as performance risk is probably the most effective way to evaluate past performance. The evaluation of past performance is essentially an assessment of the risk of successful performance based on an offeror's past performance history. The evaluation of performance risk uses broad ranges, such as high, moderate, and low risk, and requires a risk analysis rather than detailed scoring. The risk analysis relates the strengths or weaknesses of the offeror's past performance to the likelihood of successful performance on the prospective contract. Using broad ranges is more effective primarily because trying to rate prospective performance more closely is not realistic. A quote cited in a Comptroller General decision[12] amplifies this point:

> Past performance instills confidence that a company will probably do well but does not, in and of itself, guarantee that a company will do well, whereas, poor performance is a good indicator of performance risk.

When used, the evaluation of past performance in terms of performance risk should be kept simple, particularly for fixed-price contracts. Generally, there is no need to use multiple evaluation ratings because the degree of risk, particularly at the high and low ends, is not particularly important in distinguishing one proposal from another.

For example, in an RFP for the replacement of livestock gates (see Example 3.2), where a fixed-price award without discussions was contemplated and award would be made based on a past performance/price tradeoff, the RFP provided that all offerors would receive a performance risk assessment of: (1) exceptional/high confidence, (2) very good/significant confidence, (3) satisfactory/confidence, (4) neutral/unknown confidence, (5) marginal/little confidence, and (6) unsatisfactory/no confidence.

This performance risk assessment was more complicated than necessary for the requirement (replacement of livestock gates). The six risk ratings could have been replaced by four—*low risk* to replace the exceptional and very good ratings (is there a significant difference between an exceptional and a very good gate replacement?), *moderate risk* for satisfactory, *high risk* for marginal and unsatisfactory (would you want to award a fixed-price contract to a marginal or unsatisfactory performer?), and the *neutral* rating would, of course, be retained. While the rating system used in this procurement did not cause the agency any difficulties, it could have if, for example, the tradeoff decision turned on the difference between exceptional and very good. In terms of risk, it would be difficult to make such a distinction, particularly considering the nature of the requirement. Risk assessments should not be burdened with excessive ratings.

Both the numerical and the color coding systems try to measure how good is good and how bad is bad when really all that is needed is the identification of the good offerors and the bad offerors (risk assessment) with respect to past performance. Remember that scoring systems are only guides to evaluation decisions. The actual decisions must be based on the narratives developed during the evaluation, which should provide the basis for distinguishing the differences between the proposals, particularly with respect to supporting tradeoff and source selection decisions. However, the rating descriptors often significantly influence the evaluation narratives, even though the reverse should be true. This problem can be diminished by limiting the number of ratings and relying more on the evaluation narratives—as should be the case with performance risk assessments. Generally, developing the scoring plan is the last major preparation activity before issuing the RFP. Note that the details of the scoring plan are not part of the RFP. Scoring plans are internal agency documents and are not for release to offerors.

NOTES

[1] FAR 15.304(c)(2).

[2] FAR 15.304(c)(ii).

[3] FAR 15.304 (c)(iii).

[4] *Si-Nor, Inc.*, B-282064; B-282064.2, 5/25/99.

[5] *Power Connector, Inc.*, B-286875, B-286875.2, 2/14/01.

[6] OMV Medical, Inc.; Saratoga Medical Cntr., Inc., B-281387 et al., 2/3/99, 99-1 CPD ¶52 at 4.

[7] USATREX Int'l, Inc., B-275592; B-275592.2, 3/6/97, 98-1 CPD ¶99 at 4; Braswell Servs. Group, Inc., B-278921.2, 6/17/98, 98-2 CPD ¶10 at 6.

[8] TEAM Support Servs., Inc., B-279379.2, 6/22/98, 98-1 CPD ¶167 at 6.

[9] Advanced Data Concepts, Inc., B-277801.4, 6/1/98, 98-1 CPD ¶145 at 10.

[10] Office of Federal Procurement Policy, Best Practices for Collecting and Using Current and Past Performance Information, May 2000.

[11] Power Connector, Inc., B-286875; B-286875.2, 2/14/01, fn 2.

[12] Keane Federal Systems, Inc., B-280595, 10/23/98, GCR 110,440.

Chapter 3

Pre-Award: Obtaining Past Performance Information

by Peter S. Cole

This chapter has two parts—one directed at government personnel and the other directed at contractor personnel. The first part addresses those things government personnel should do when obtaining past performance information for evaluation purposes in a competitive acquisition. It should, however, also be of interest to contractor personnel. The second part is directed primarily at contractor personnel who will be involved in providing past performance information in response to a government solicitation. Government personnel should also be aware of those things an offeror should be doing.

FOR THE GOVERNMENT

Government personnel should direct their attention to the following areas when obtaining past performance information.

Sources of Past Performance Information

The primary source for past performance information is *the offeror*. As noted in Chapter 2, the RFP should require each offeror to provide a reference listing of past or current federal, state, local government, or private contracts for the same or similar work, including the contract number, dollar value, dates, name of the contracting agency, a contact telephone number, and a description of the work effort that demonstrates how it relates to the prospective contract.

In addition, the RFP should encourage offerors to provide information on problems encountered on the referenced contracts and to explain how the problems were corrected. Offerors should be allowed to provide information on predecessor companies, key personnel who have relevant experience, and subcontractors who will perform major or critical aspects of the requirement, when such information is relevant to the instant contract. In addition, the offeror should be encouraged to comment on the quality of its performance on the referenced contracts. This information will be a significant part of the evaluation of past performance.

38   PAST PERFORMANCE HANDBOOK

Note that while the other non-cost evaluation factors (technical, management, etc.) are evaluated solely on the information provided in the proposals, the evaluation of past performance is based on information outside of the proposals, and such information, therefore, must be verified to the extent practicable. This verification is accomplished by contacting the references provided.

Give some consideration to how you will ask the offeror to provide references. If you do not indicate the number of references to be provided, the number is up to the offerors. Some may provide a large number, and some may only provide a few. This may prove to be a problem when evaluating past performance. The May 2000 OFPP Guide[1] suggests that offerors be required to provide references to five to ten specific contracts, not more than three years old, to establish their past performance qualifications. There are, however, some problems with this suggestion.

1. You should not ask for more references than you are prepared to check. If you expect a large number of responses, five to ten references from each may exceed your ability to check them all. While the Comptroller General has ruled that you are not *required* to check all references (see Example 5.1), you can be sure that offerors will expect that any reference provided will be checked. You may generate protests if you fail to check all references, particularly if you fail to check some of the better references. You will win the protest but lose a great deal of time responding to it.

2. Asking for five to ten references may adversely affect small businesses or newly formed businesses that have not had an opportunity to perform the requisite number of contracts that are the same or similar to the work required. Even large businesses might have trouble in this area if the prospective contract is for supplies or services that are unique, innovative, or simply not often acquired. The number of references required should be realistic in relation to the kind of work required by the prospective contract. One way to avoid problems in this area is to ask for a minimum number of references and indicate that if more than the minimum number are provided, the government reserves the right to determine how many and which of those references will be checked. The minimum number should be that which you think can be checked efficiently by the evaluation resources available.

3. Generally, indicating that the references must be not more than three years old will be sufficient, but you must indicate what that means—three years old with respect to when the contract was awarded or when the contract was completed. You also should consider expanding the time period to five years or more for effort of more than one year or for supplies or services not frequently acquired. When establishing a time period, you also should consider whether there have been changes in technology or meth-

odology that might affect the relevancy of older contracts. The time period should be realistic for the kind of supplies or services being required.

Checking only the references provided by the offeror usually is not sufficient because the offeror may not identify past contracts that had serious performance deficiencies. *Checking your own agency's contract database* should be a priority because an agency is obligated to consider past performance information that is readily available (i.e., close at hand, see Examples 5.3 and 5.4). While this might require some research to identify past and current contracts of the same or similar nature, the effort is not formidable because the required reporting form (SF 279, Federal Procurement Data Systems [FPDS] Individual Contract Action Report) identifies the general nature of the work performed.

Other database sources, such as the Federal Procurement Data System or the procurement data systems of other agencies, also can be accessed to help identify an offeror's past and current contracts. These data systems all use the same input form (the SF 279) and can be entered using the offeror's name. However, because the database only indicates the general nature of the work done by specific contractors, identifying contracts of a specific nature will require additional research.

Private sector sources, such as subcontractors, suppliers, financial institutions, and commercial customers, also may be used if they can be identified (market survey information might be helpful here). When using private sector sources, ensure that written documents support any comments used in the evaluation. Written documents are particularly important where adverse comments are involved.

Surveys of end users might be useful if you can identify the appropriate end users. End users, however, are often difficult to identify to a specific contract. Generally, end user surveys are practicable only for supplies or services shipped or provided directly to the end users and that can be identified to a specific contractor.

Contractor performance reports developed by your agency or other agencies are a valuable information source. FAR 42.1503 calls for an evaluation report to be written on a contractor's performance for each contract over $100,000 once the contract work is completed, with interim evaluations, as appropriate, for contracts over one year (contractor performance reports are discussed in greater detail in Chapters 7–11). These reports must be provided to the contractor for comment and are retained on file as "source selection information." This information can only be released to other contracting officers or to the contractor whose performance was evaluated. When verifying an offeror's past performance, you should check the availability of these reports. If the offeror does not have them, the contracting agency should have them on file. Technically, it is the offeror's responsibility to obtain them for its proposal, but offerors may not know that these reports even exist or may have trouble obtaining them in time to submit the reports with their proposal. Therefore, if the offeror does not provide a report in its proposal, you can obtain the report when you conduct the reference check.

FAR 42.1503(b) also indicates that the *evaluations used in determining award or incentive fee payments* also may be used to satisfy the requirements for an evaluation of a contractor's performance. A word of caution here: Incentive fee payments are based on a mathematical formula and do not require any other analysis of contractor performance. Award fee payments do require a written analysis of contractor performance to support the amount paid, but generally do not include any contractor comments or other input. One of the key ingredients to the use of contractor performance evaluations in later source selections is the contractor's participation in the process. Generally, this is lacking in the documentation supporting incentive or award fee payments. This information should be used only if no other performance information is available.

Conducting a Reference Check

The primary purpose of a reference check is to verify the past performance information provided by the offeror in its proposal, although the term generally covers any activity related to determining how well an offeror performed on past or other current contracts.

Before contacting any reference sources, either within your agency or in other agencies, you should identify the personnel to be contacted. Your primary contact should be the individual responsible for monitoring the contract (the contracting officer's technical representative—COTR—or equivalent). This individual can address the contractor's technical performance. You also should contact the procuring contracting officer (PCO) or the administrative contracting officer (ACO), who can comment on the contractor's compliance with contractual requirements. Contracting officers have access to the official contract file, which should contain contractor performance reports and assessments made during contract performance or upon contract completion.

Next, you should decide how these persons will be contacted. You may contact them by telephone, regular mail, fax, e-mail, or any combination thereof. Getting a timely response to your query may be difficult. If you simply send out a past performance questionnaire with no advance notice, it may end up perpetually at the bottom of someone's in-basket. You should make an initial contact by telephone, speak to the person involved, and explain what you are doing. In some instances it may be possible to conduct an interview by telephone, but if adverse comments are involved the interview should be followed up with a questionnaire so that the adverse information will be in writing. If for some reason a telephone interview is not possible once the initial contact has been made, you may forward, by appropriate means, a questionnaire for the contact to complete.

When requesting information from other agencies or sources, your biggest challenge will be getting someone to respond to your query with usable information. Getting a negative response (and this is of greater interest) may be more of a problem than getting a positive response because the responder must expend more time and effort to explain why the offeror's past performance was deficient. You cannot accept "yes" or "no" responses to your questions when the response is negative. Explanations are required.

An agency's allegation of poor past performance, particularly when in conflict with reports of other agencies, should be examined closely, first to determine the accuracy of the allegation and then to determine if the reported poor past performance is likely to affect performance under the current contract.

Getting a positive response is not difficult, but you must remember to ask for identification of the contractor's strong points, too. These may prove to be important when trying to distinguish the quality of one offeror's past performance from that of another offeror.

Asking the Right Questions

Once you have determined who will be contacted, develop a list of the questions to ask. Questions should be tailored to your particular requirement and should reflect the SOW requirements, in terms of the work effort as well as how the responses will be evaluated and scored. Design the questions as though you were going to have to respond to them (i.e., keep them short and simple). You will have difficulty getting responses to long, convoluted questionnaires. Initially, you might ask general questions, such as the following:

1. *If you had a choice, would you contract with this contractor again?* If no, why not? If yes, does the contractor have any particular performance strong points?

2. *Did the end product or services meet contractual requirements,* particularly with respect to the quality provided?

3. *Did the contractor make contractual and administrative deliveries on time?* If not, why not, and what specific delivery dates were not met?

42   PAST PERFORMANCE HANDBOOK

4. *Did the contractor complete the effort within the budget?* If not, were the cost growth or other cost control problems due to contractor inefficiency or lack of expertise? (NOTE—This question does not apply to fixed-price contracts.)

5. *Were contract changes made because of the manner of the contractor's performance,* particularly with respect to delivery times and contract specifications?

6. *Was the contractor cooperative and responsive to your needs?*

7. *If there were problems, did the contractor act promptly to resolve them?*

Responses to these questions will help you assess an offeror's past performance properly. However, because past performance also will be evaluated by a comparative assessment, you are looking for points that distinguish one proposal from another—either strong points that enhance an offeror's standing or weak points that indicate potential performance problems.

With respect to past performance problems, you need to know the answers to the following questions, which can be either part of the initial questionnaire or used as follow-up questions:

1. *What went wrong and why?* An allegation of problems in past performance must be specific and supported by a written explanation.

2. *Who (government or contractor) was at fault?* Did the government contribute, directly or indirectly, to the problem?

3. *Was the problem a local one?* Was the problem related only to a particular contract, or was it the result of a higher-level corporate decision or policy? Corporate-level problems are often much more difficult to resolve and are more likely to affect the current contract than are local contract-related problems.

4. *What corrective action was taken to resolve the problem, and have any past performance problems been inadequately corrected or otherwise remain unresolved?* This includes assessing whether the corrective action was responsive and timely—and corrected the problem. Past performance problems that have been corrected or will be corrected before performance of your contract begins should not be considered germane. If the problems have not been corrected, the presumption should be that unresolved problems are likely to recur.

5. *Will contractor personnel involved with past performance problems be employed on the current contract?* This is particularly important with respect to unre-

solved problems. You cannot use blacklisting techniques (such as down-grading the proposal because of the individual's participation), but the use of such personnel on your contract should be a matter for discussions if the offeror is included in the competitive range. Do not assume that contractor personnel involved with problem contracts are responsible for the problems without discussing this with the contractor.

Getting Answers

You should consider the following problems and potential solutions when planning your approach to contacting other agencies:

1. *The contact person identified in the offeror's proposal may no longer be at the agency or may have transferred to other duties.* If the person cannot be located, ask if another COTR is involved with the contract, or ask the contracting officer for an analysis of the contract file.

2. *The contract file may not be readily available.* If the file has been retired or for some other reason is not readily available in the contracting office, you are not likely to get a timely response. An initial telephone call will help to ascertain the availability of the file.

3. *The contract file may not have been adequately documented.* There is no federal standard for documenting contractor performance. While the FAR requires a performance evaluation upon contract completion, some agencies will document contractor performance well and others will not document it at all. Even where documenting procedures exist, there is no guarantee that the documentation will have been done properly or, even if done properly, will provide the answers you seek. For example, an agency could document a contractor's performance using only the final rating without a narrative explaining the rating assigned and without the contractor's comments on the rating. A rating with no explanation or contractor comments will be of little use, particularly if the rating is low.

4. *The contact person may be too busy to respond in the detail required.* This is a particular problem with contracting personnel at the end of the fiscal year. An advance telephone call may help to get the cooperation of busy personnel.

5. *The contact person may be reluctant to be candid if the agency bears some responsibility for the problem.* Agencies tend to frown on personnel who tell other agencies of their mistakes. You may have to read between the lines to assess negative reports properly.

44   PAST PERFORMANCE HANDBOOK

6. *Past problems may be related more to personality conflicts than to a failure to meet requirements.* This is particularly true in "soft" areas, such as a contractor's responsiveness to problems. A telephone conversation can often help assess whether or not personality conflicts are part of the problem.

7. *The problems may have resulted from honest differences of opinion, such as the interpretation of specifications or other requirements.* The validity of responses in such instances often depends on the candor of the responding individual, underlining the importance of making an initial telephone call to establish rapport with the contact individual.

Making Offerors Responsible for Reference Checks

Conducting reference checks can be a time-consuming process and can generate protests if offerors do not like the way the reference checks were conducted. Some agencies have come up with a way to make this effort an offeror responsibility. First, a questionnaire is designed for use as a reference check and included in the RFP. Then offerors are instructed that it is their responsibility to provide a copy of the questionnaire to the agencies responsible for the referenced contracts and to provide the completed questionnaires with their proposals.

Offerors are told that a certain minimum number of completed questionnaires is required and that if the minimum number is not provided, they will receive a neutral past performance rating (on the premise that at least the minimum number is required to perform a valid past performance evaluation). This moves the time frame necessary to collect the information needed for the past performance evaluation from after receipt of proposals to before receipt of proposals and spreads the effort needed among the offerors rather than concentrating it with the contracting agency.

This process could significantly reduce the time required for past performance evaluations, but there are some potential problems that must be considered:

- *Can an agency make offerors responsible for the timely submission of past performance questionnaires by other government agencies?* The answer is yes. In the Thomas Brand Siding case,[2] the protester complained that it had problems getting timely responses from other agencies and therefore was not been able to produce the required number of questionnaires. The Comptroller General did not respond directly to this complaint, but there are many cases on record to the point that offerors are responsible for submitting a complete response to the RFP, and as long as the requirement is reasonable—in this case the submission of at least three completed questionnaires—the offeror must comply (see Example 3.1).

- *Can an agency assign a neutral past performance rating if the minimum number of questionnaires is not provided?* The answer is yes. As noted in the Comptroller General decision, an agency may set any evaluation requirements it deems necessary, as long as the requirement is reasonable. However, there are other past performance information sources that an agency is obligated to consider, such as information close at hand (see Examples 5.3 and 5.4), and these sources would have to be considered as part of the minimum requirement.

- *Can this potential time savings be used to decrease the time allotted for receipt of proposals?* The answer is no. A reasonable agency should recognize that obtaining responses to the questionnaires will require more time for offerors to respond to an RFP and should increase the response time accordingly. This increase should be minimal, however, because offerors can pursue past performance questionnaires independent of their other proposal preparation efforts. If offerors are to be responsible for obtaining completed questionnaires, the RFP should provide that a contractor performance report prepared on a referenced contract can be substituted for a completed past performance questionnaire. While the time allotted for proposal preparation may be increased, this increase will be offset by the decrease in the overall acquisition time.

Using Contractor Performance Reports

As noted, the primary source of past performance information is the offeror's reference listing of past or current contracts for the same or similar effort. It was also noted that FAR 42.1503 calls for an evaluation report to be written on a contractor's performance for each contract once the contract work is completed, with interim evaluations as appropriate. Contractor performance reports should be a primary source of past performance information; locating these reports will continue to be a problem, however, until all agencies have easy access to other agencies' past performance information systems and there is a standard format to such information.

Currently, the best source for contractor performance reports is the offeror. Encourage offerors to submit relevant performance reports with their proposals. If an offeror does not or cannot submit such reports on referenced contracts, you should ask the agency involved if they are available. Generally, you may accept the results of an agency's contractor performance report without further verification if it includes the contractor's comments on the report.

Because there is no federal standard for final contractor performance reports, such reports may or may not contain all of the supporting information, particularly the contractor's comments, which are required to be a part of the initial report. If the final contractor performance report does not contain the contractor comments and does contain adverse past performance information about an offeror, the information should be verified with the issuing agency. If it is determined that the offeror did not have an opportunity to comment on the adverse information, consideration should be given to permitting the offeror an opportunity to rebut such information.

Note that while the FAR requires contractor performance reports on completed contracts, the use of interim reports is voluntary, and interim performance reports may not be available when verifying an offeror's performance on a current contract. In such instances, use past performance questionnaires to obtain the necessary past performance information.

A contractor performance report containing information significantly at variance with other reports or information from other sources should be verified, particularly if the report contains adverse past performance information. A contractor's performance should be consistent, and variances should be accounted for during the evaluation.

You also should verify contractor performance reports when it appears that the contractor's comments were ignored in the final report, but only if it seems that the contractor's rebuttal was valid (a contractor is given the opportunity to comment on the initial performance report, but the final report is prepared by the government). The reasons why a rebuttal was unsuccessful could be important to your evaluation of the offeror's past performance.

FOR THE CONTRACTOR

This section is directed primarily at contractor personnel who will be involved in providing past performance information in response to a government solicitation. This information also should be of interest to government personnel.

General

OFPP has recommended that past performance be weighted at least 25 percent, or an amount equal to the total of all other non-cost evaluation factors. While some contracting officers will be more discriminating in determining the relative importance of past performance as an evaluation factor, other contracting officers simply will follow the OFPP guidance. Note, however, that the OFPP guidance also indicates that there are times when past performance could be weighted as much as 100 percent, such as when acquiring supplies or standard services on a fixed-price basis.

So, what is a contractor to do? First, you must realize that simply performing in a satisfactory manner may no longer be good enough to win a competitively negotiated government contract. When the government evaluates past performance by a comparative assessment, a contractor's past performance may have to be rated at excellent or outstanding to have a chance of being included in the competitive range. Keep in mind that the FAR now requires that the competitive range include only the most highly rated proposals. Couple this competitive range requirement with the requirement that past performance be a significant evaluation factor, and it becomes clear that the government's evaluation of contract performance has become a key competitive factor.

You also must understand what the government is supposed to do when evaluating past performance. Knowing the government's approach will help when developing a strategy to ensure a high past performance rating. A contractor's past performance is first assessed in terms of the past performance evaluation factors set forth in the RFP and then comparatively assessed in relation to other competing contractors.

Note, however, that if the solicitation indicates that award will be made without discussions, the only chance to address your past performance will be in the initial proposal, and the government is not obligated to permit you to address any adverse information provided by third parties. You have to get it right the first time.

As noted in Chapter 2, OFPP has suggested that a contractor's past performance be evaluated on the basis of:

- *Performance quality*. The emphasis here is on how well a contractor met all contract requirements during and at the end of contract performance. This evaluation will encompass more detail than a responsibility determination (which focuses only on failures), and problems other than a total failure to conform now will be significant. Performance quality also involves technical excellence (including quality awards and certificates), the accuracy of reports, rejections and reworks, and any other successes or failures with respect to the contractor's conformance to contract requirements. Your proposal should include anything related to technical excellence and explain how you corrected any problems related to performance quality on referenced contracts.

- *Schedule performance*. This involves evaluating a contractor's ability to adhere to delivery and administrative schedules. It is more than a failure to deliver end products on time. The timeliness of interim product deliveries and administrative deliveries, such as reports and other documentation, will be examined, as well as intangible deliveries, such as a contractor's ability to meet interim and final milestone schedules on a timely basis. Your proposal should explain any schedule problems on referenced contracts and highlight anything related to positive schedule performance, such as meeting rapidly changing delivery schedules.

- *Cost performance.* For other than fixed-price contracts, the contractor's record of forecasting and containing costs may be evaluated. This would involve such things as staying within budget, the relationship of negotiated costs to actual costs, and how well changes were priced during contract performance. Emphasis also will be placed on the accuracy of the contractor's initial cost estimates, but any pricing problem may be assessed, such as cost inefficiencies and a failure to provide current, accurate, and complete billing on a timely basis. Your proposal should highlight positive cost performance, such as coming in under budget, on referenced contracts and explain how any cost problems were corrected.

- *Business relations.* A contractor's history of reasonable and cooperative behavior also may be assessed. This deals with the working relationship between the contractor and the government during contract performance, such as how well the contractor responded to government requests for information and reports, how well the contractor responded to contract changes, and other areas, such as end user satisfaction, subcontract management, meeting of socioeconomic goals, and integrating and coordinating contract activities. This is a difficult area to address in a proposal because you may not be aware of how the government views your business relations. Generally, however, positive business relations are known and should be highlighted in proposals. Negative business relations in referenced contracts, to the extent known, should be identified and the corrective action taken should be explained.

Agencies may use other specific criteria to evaluate past performance. Agencies are not required to follow OFPP's suggestions, and many will develop their own past performance evaluation criteria. You are obligated to examine a solicitation closely (particularly Sections L and M) to determine how to respond to the solicitation requirements in your proposal. If you want to remain in the competition, you must respond to all of the evaluation criteria with specific information. Making generalizations or assuming that the agency will conduct research to determine your qualifications under evaluation criteria practically guarantees proposal rejection.

As a contractor, you must develop a strategy and procedures to deal with the increased emphasis on past performance. Such a strategy would involve how to describe past performance in a proposal, identifying actions to take during contract performance, how to respond to negative past performance reports during the evaluation of proposals (addressed in Chapter 5), and how to re-

Describing Past Performance in a Proposal

The RFP indicates how a proposal will be evaluated and what information it will provide. This information is found in Sections L and M of the RFP. Check the solicitation closely to ensure that you have responded to all of the solicitation requirements, particularly with respect to past performance information. The offeror bears the responsibility to provide sufficient information to enable the government to evaluate its proposal, and a failure to comply with all solicitation requirements will result in the downgrading and possible rejection of your proposal, as shown in Examples 3.1 and 3.2.

Example 3.1—A failure to comply with RFP requirements for information related to past performance can be fatal (#1).[3]

In a solicitation for one or more indefinite-delivery/indefinite-quantity contracts for heavy road construction and paving to be awarded on a best-value basis, proposals were to be evaluated on the basis of two technical considerations—experience and past performance of the prime contractor and key subcontractors on similar projects (the more important factor), and qualifications and past experience of key personnel. To demonstrate experience and past performance, offerors were required to provide information on three prior similar contracts for the prime and each key subcontractor. Similarly, under the qualifications and past experience of key personnel criterion, offerors were required to provide information on three similar projects for each key employee to show that they were qualified to perform the requirement. The agency reserved the right to evaluate proposals and award on the basis of initial offers, without conducting discussions.

After the initial evaluation, GSA made awards on the basis of the initial proposals, without discussions. GSA concluded that MDA's proposal was technically unacceptable because of a lack of information relating to the experience and past performance of both MDA and its proposed subcontractors, and because MDA's proposed key personnel lacked relevant experience in road construction. The record showed that MDA submitted information on three prior contracts it had performed, which the agency determined were not similar to the solicited requirement (the contracts were for construction management and inspection services and quality control services, as opposed to the actual performance of heavy road construction). As for its key subcontractors, MDA submitted no information whatsoever relating to its prior contracts. Finally, GSA determined that MDA's proposed key personnel, for the most part, did not have experience in performing the type of heavy road construction contemplated by the RFP.

MDA protested the award, arguing that it was improper for the agency to reject its proposal as unacceptable without first seeking to clarify its experience and past performance information, either by soliciting additional information from it or by

50 PAST PERFORMANCE HANDBOOK

consulting the agency's own records, which, MDA maintained, contained information relating to its prior contracts. MDA further argued that, even without such additional information, it was improper for the agency to rate its proposal unacceptable; it maintained that the agency was required to assign a neutral rating in the absence of past performance information.

The Comptroller General denied the protest.

The evaluation of technical proposals is a matter primarily within the discretion of the contracting agency; in reviewing challenges to an agency's evaluation, our Office does not reevaluate technical proposals but, instead, considers whether the evaluation was reasonable and consistent with the solicitation's evaluation criteria.[4] Since an agency's evaluation is dependent upon the information furnished in a proposal, it is the offeror's burden to submit an adequately written proposal for the agency to evaluate, especially where, as here, the offeror is specifically on notice that the agency intends to make award based on initial proposals without discussions. An agency may reject a proposal for informational deficiencies that prevent the agency from fully evaluating the proposal.[5]

We note that, since the record confirms that the prior contracts MDA listed to establish its past performance were not similar to the current requirement, the agency reasonably determined that MDA's prior contracts did not provide a basis for assessing the firm's past performance. However, it appears this aspect of MDA's past performance warranted a neutral, rather than an unacceptable rating; under FAR 15.305(a)(2)(iv), where an offeror does not have a record of relevant past performance, the offeror may not be evaluated either favorably or unfavorably. On the other hand, even if this were the case, and even if we also agreed with MDA that the agency should have clarified its experience or obtained additional information from its own records, as discussed below, GSA reasonably rated the proposal unacceptable based on MDA's failure to establish adequate experience and past performance for its subcontractors and key employees.

MDA's proposal generally refers to contracts which appear to be relevant and which were performed by MDA with its proposed subcontractors. However, detailed information necessary to assess the nature and relevance of those contracts was not included in the proposal. . . . such as, for example, the contract number, a contact point, and a description of the project—despite the express RFP requirement that such information be provided.

The protester states in its comments to the agency report that it did not provide information relating to the prior contracts of its proposed subcontractors because it did not want to make irrevocable commitments to any of its subcontractors in advance (planning instead to obtain proposed pricing from an appropriate subcontractor at the time when actual requirements were presented in the form of delivery orders), and consequently did not want to rely on their past experience in its proposal. This purported approach is nowhere described in MDA's proposal and, in fact, is inconsistent with the explicit terms of the proposal, which affirmatively stated that MDA will subcontract with one of its identified subcontractors based on the geographical location of the work. We conclude that the agency reasonably found that MDA's proposal failed to provide the information required by the RFP to enable it to evaluate MDA's key subcontractors.

To the extent MDA contends that GSA was required to assign a neutral rating to its proposal based on the absence of information relating to its key subcontractors, we disagree. Although FAR 15.305(a)(2)(iv) requires an agency to assign a neutral rating where past performance information is not "available," here, the protester's proposal represented that its proposed subcontractors are engaged in projects that would illustrate their performance capability. The information thus was available, but MDA chose not to present the information in its proposal, in direct contravention of the terms of the RFP. In our view, an offeror cannot simply choose to withhold past performance information—and thereby obtain a neutral rating—where the solicitation expressly requires that the information be furnished, and where the information is readily available to the offeror.

In any case, notwithstanding the evaluation under the experience and past performance factor, as noted, the agency also rated MDA's proposal unacceptable based on its determination that MDA's proposed key personnel lacked experience on projects similar to the solicited effort. MDA does not dispute the agency's conclusion, and we find nothing in the record that calls the evaluation in this regard into question.

Finally, MDA's assertion that the agency improperly failed to consider its price in connection with the award decisions is without merit. Because MDA's proposal was properly found technically unacceptable, and a technically unacceptable offer cannot properly form the basis for award, the agency was not required to further consider price or the other terms of the offer.[6]

Notes

1. MDA asserts in the alternative that GSA should have referred its technical unacceptability to the Small Business Administration (SBA) for review under that agency's certificate of competency program, citing Federal Acquisition Regulation (FAR) 15.101-2(b)(1). However, the reasons the agency found MDA's proposal unacceptable concerned only MDA's failure to submit information establishing its and its subcontractor's experience and past performance, and did not constitute a finding that MDA is not a responsible prospective contractor.

Example 3.1 presents several points of interest to a contractor preparing to submit a proposal to the government. First and foremost, if the RFP requires the submission of certain information, this information must be submitted in complete detail, as set forth in the RFP. This is particularly true with respect to experience and past performance information because the government must be able to verify this information with the contracting agencies involved. In this case, MDA *chose* not to provide the required information about its key subcontractors. While a neutral rating is appropriate where past performance information is not available, the required information was, in fact, readily available to MDA. Therefore, because subcontracting was a major consideration in this evaluation, the failure to provide the required information was sufficient to find the proposal technically unacceptable.

If the RFP has specific qualification requirements for key personnel, the proposal must clearly demonstrate these qualifications as well as the availability of these personnel for work on the proposed contract. MDA did not provide sufficient information to establish that its key personnel had the experience required by the RFP. Depending on the relative importance of the key personnel factor, a failure here could have resulted in a significant downgrading of the proposal rather than an outright rejection; but when coupled with the failure to provide sufficient information about the experience and past performance of the major subcontractors, proposal rejection was required.

Note that if a proposal is rejected as technically unacceptable, price is not a consideration; a low price cannot save a technically unacceptable proposal. In addition, in a best value procurement where proposals are evaluated by a comparative assessment, the rejection of a proposal as the result of the evaluation is not a responsibility determination and is not reviewable by the SBA.

Example 3.2—A failure to comply with RFP requirements for information related to past performance can be fatal (#2).[7]

An RFP for the replacement of livestock gates contemplated the award of a fixed-price contract based on a performance/price tradeoff (PPT) technique. The RFP provided that all offerors would receive a performance risk assessment of exceptional/high confidence, very good/significant confidence, satisfactory/confidence, neutral/unknown confidence, marginal/little confidence, or unsatisfactory/no confidence. The RFP stated that the purpose of the risk assessment was to identify and review relevant present and past performance and then make an overall risk assessment of an offeror's ability to perform the effort. The RFP required offerors to submit detailed past performance information to include aspects of the contract deemed relevant to the proposed effort. Award was to be made on the basis of initial proposals without conducting discussions.

Boland submitted the overall low price. While the ratings Boland received from its references ranged from satisfactory to very good, all of the responses involved contracts that were for landscaping projects that were valued at significantly less than the government estimate. Since Boland's prior contracts for landscaping work showed no relevance to the gate replacement work required by the solicitation, Boland's proposal received a rating of neutral/unknown confidence. Award was made to another offeror who had a slightly higher price but had received a past performance rating of exceptional/high confidence.

Boland protested, asserting that the agency had improperly evaluated its past performance. Specifically, Boland contended that the contracting officer had been verbally advised by Boland, prior to award, of the company president's experience with another firm that installed the gates that were to be replaced. Boland also argued that the simplicity of the removal and reinstallation of the gates should have been given considerable weight in the evaluation of a firm's ability to perform the requirement. Boland maintained that any construction or farm worker could perform gate replacements.

The Comptroller General denied the protest.

Notwithstanding the protester's argument that Boland verbally advised the contracting officer of its president's experience in installing the gates, the record shows that although required by the RFP to do so, the protester failed to establish in its proposal or through its past performance references that it had actual experience installing gates. The record shows that the prior contracts listed by Boland to establish past performance were all landscaping projects. In our view, the agency reasonably concluded that the landscaping contracts were not relevant to the current requirement for gate replacements. Further, the agency reports that prior to award the cognizant agency official attempted to verify the company president's prior gate installation experience under a prior contract. The agency advises that the agency official could not find that individual's name in the employment records for contracts awarded by the base for gate installation.

In sum, Boland simply did not provide in its proposal or at any time during the conduct of the procurement evidence establishing that the company had relevant past performance. While the protester argues that the requirement is simple and that any construction worker could perform it, the solicitation specifically advised offerors that award would be based on the PPT technique and that a performance risk assessment would be performed to identify and review relevant present and past performance in order to make an overall risk assessment of an offeror's ability to perform the requirement. In accordance with the solicitation, the agency performed a performance/price tradeoff and determined that the higher priced proposal of IRD, which had a better performance risk rating than the protester, represented the best value to the government. On this record, we have no basis to question the agency's evaluation of proposals or source selection decision.

You must pay attention to what the RFP says about the information that must be provided with respect to past performance. Here the RFP clearly stated that award would be made based on a performance/price tradeoff and that offerors were required to submit detailed past performance information on contracts that were relevant to the proposed effort. A failure to submit relevant information would result in a neutral/unknown confidence rating. The past performance evaluation must be conducted as set forth in the RFP and based on the information required by the RFP. Boland failed to provide relevant information and received the appropriate rating.

The fact that the requirement was not complex and that the simplicity of the effort should have been given considerable weight was not germane to the agency's decision. Based on the RFP requirements, Boland either should not have submitted a proposal (because it lacked the relevant past experience) or should have noted this lack of experience in its proposal and explained how it still had the ability to perform the requirement. Boland would probably not have received the award in any event because in the past performance/price tradeoff, its slightly lower price would not have offset its lack of experience against the awardee's exceptional past performance on exactly the same type of work.

Be particularly careful to check the definitions of prior experience and past performance (usually found in Section M of the RFP) when both are used as evaluation factors. Generally, prior experience is evaluated on the basis of an offeror's experience with the same or similar work and assessed to determine the offeror's technical expertise. Prior experience is related to whether the offeror has done such work in the past, not to how well it performed. Past performance is used to assess the quality of an offeror's past performance with respect to work of the same or similar nature and how that past performance is likely to affect the current effort. If the solicitation does not clearly define these factors, you must obtain clarification from the contracting officer before the time set for receipt of proposals. This is particularly important if it appears that prior experience and past performance have been combined into a single evaluation factor and it is not clear if they will be evaluated separately or together. If this is not cleared up before the time set for the receipt of proposals, you cannot complain (protest) about it later.

Generally, the solicitation should indicate how many references are required. It is not a good idea to provide more references than required unless the RFP only cites a minimum requirement. Be aware, however, that the government is not legally required to check all of the references provided (see Example 5.1), so citing a larger number than required may be of minimal value.

The government may use other sources (agency records, the records of other agencies, contractor performance reports, queries to your suppliers or other business contacts, etc.) to check your past performance, so not referencing a problem contract does not ensure that the contract problems will not come up— and the government will not be happy about your attempt to conceal problems. If there were problems with a referenced contract, you should identify the problems and explain how you resolved them (with specific actions taken, not rhetoric or promises). This is necessary to show that previous problems will not recur. If your explanation is not convincing, the government may choose to consider that the problems have not been resolved. Usually the solicitation will require such information, but even if it doesn't, a failure to provide information about performance problems initially could adversely affect your past performance evaluation.

Ensure that your proposal explains how each referenced contract relates to the prospective contract. Referenced contracts must be relevant, that is, for work of the same or similar nature as that required for the prospective contract (see Example 4.6). Disassociated contracts (past contracts that serve to show an offeror's overall work record) will not be accorded the same evaluation weight as relevant contracts. If you cite both relevant and disassociated contracts, be sure that you clearly identify which is which. A failure to make this distinction could be interpreted as a lack of understanding of the requirement.

If the past performance of a subcontractor is pertinent, such as when a subcontractor will perform a significant part of the contract work, you may use information about the subcontractor's past performance, but you must explain the relationship and how this information applies to the prospective contract (see Example 4.11).

As with the evaluation of prior experience, a newly formed firm or a firm lacking relevant performance history may cite the past performance of its key personnel on other contracts as a substitute for the firm's lack of past performance history. However, the proposal must show how such personnel contributed to the success of the referenced contracts and how the referenced contracts relate to the prospective effort (see Example 4.10).

You also can cite the past performance of other firms if they are team members or affiliates, but only if they will be significantly involved in the performance of the prospective contract (see Example 4.9). You must explain the relationship (shared management, workforce, facilities, or other resources that would affect contract performance) to show the extent of the other firm's involvement.

If you have agency contractor performance reports on previous contracts that are relevant, include them in your proposal. Contractor performance reports will be accorded significant weight in evaluating past performance.

If your previous work has resulted in awards or letters of commendation, be sure to include copies in your proposal. Such information can make a difference in the evaluation of your past performance, particularly in tradeoff determinations and the final source selection.

What you put in your initial proposal may be the only chance you get to explain past problems, particularly if award is to be made without discussions. When award is to be made without discussions, the government may (but is not required to) provide you an opportunity to clarify adverse past performance information to which you have not previously had an opportunity to respond (see Example 4.3). Generally, unless there is a reason to question the validity of the past performance information, the government will choose not to permit clarification. It is best, therefore, to explain past problems fully in your initial proposal submission.

If discussions are to be held, the government is required to permit offerors to address adverse past performance information to which the offeror has not previously had an opportunity to respond if the past performance information is a determining factor preventing the offeror from being placed in the competitive range. Note, however, that in a comparative assessment, past performance may not be the most heavily weighted evaluation factor. Where past performance problems only contributed to, but were not necessarily the determining factor in, a low overall rating, the government may not be required to permit the offeror to rebut the past performance evaluation, particularly if the past perfor-

56 PAST PERFORMANCE HANDBOOK

mance information was not adverse but simply not as highly rated as other offerors. All the more reason to ensure that your proposal provides clear, concise, candid, and complete past performance information.

It should be noted here that the phrase "adverse past performance information to which the offeror has not previously had an opportunity to respond" generally *excludes* instances where a contractor has been afforded an opportunity to comment on the evaluation of its contract performance prior to such information being entered into an electronic database or the preparation of a final contractor performance evaluation. You would be well advised to retain any correspondence relating to such evaluations and be prepared to explain in your initial proposal how any past problems have been corrected and will not recur under the prospective contract.

Given the requirement to prepare contractor performance reports at the end of contract performance, agencies are developing electronic databases to store past performance information and make it available to other agencies for source selection purposes. Example 3.3 shows how such databases are used in evaluating past performance.

Example 3.3—Contending with electronic databases[8]

In a fixed-price construction solicitation, the RFP listed the following technical factors to be evaluated on a "Go/No Go" basis: experience, past performance, effectiveness of management, and compliance with safety standards. Under the past performance area, the RFP also listed two subfactors: (1) timeliness and (2) quality. All factors and subfactors were of equal weight, but a rating of "No Go" under any subfactor made the proposal unacceptable. Award was to be made without discussions to the lowest-priced technically acceptable proposal.

In the past performance area, under the timeliness subfactor, offerors were to be evaluated on their success in completing construction contracts on schedule. Under the quality subfactor, offerors were to be evaluated on their success in complying with the requirements of past contracts and standards of workmanship. The RFP also stated that past performance would be evaluated by reviewing: (1) all U.S. Army Corps of Engineers' Construction Contractor Appraisal Support System (CCASS) database factors relative to Timely Performance, (2) communication with the points of contact listed by the offeror, or (3) other data available to the government pertinent to the required work.

The RFP further stated that the offerors must have received an average satisfactory performance rating on all CCASS data related to Timely Performance (Adequacy of Initial Progress Schedule, Adherence to Approved Schedule, Resolution of Delays, Submission of Required Documentation, Completion of Punchlist Items, Submission of Updated and Revised Progress Schedule, Warranty Response), with no individual factor rated at Unsatisfactory, similar supporting data in the last three years, or telephone interview reports rated satisfactory (average) or higher to receive a "Go" evaluation.

Pre-Award: Obtaining Past Performance Information **57**

TLT Construction submitted a protest before the closing date for receipt of proposals arguing, among other things, that under the RFP's evaluation approach, it would improperly be denied the opportunity to address alleged negative past performance information in the agency's electronic database. TLT also argued that this would effectively debar it from competing under this (and perhaps other) construction projects.

The Comptroller General did not agree and denied the protest.

The U.S. Army Corps of Engineers Regulation (ER) No. 415-1-17 (March 26, 1993) establishes procedures for evaluating a construction contractor's performance, and for transmitting those evaluations to the CCASS database. The CCASS is a centralized, automated database of performance evaluations on construction contractors which contains past performance information to assist federal government contracting agencies in assessing contractors' past performance. Generally the CCASS database contains past performance information for the last 6 years, starting from the time a reviewing official signs the performance rating. Final performance evaluation reports are prepared by the contracting agency which reviewed and accepted the construction firm's work within 60 days of substantial completion of the work, and are transmitted electronically to CCASS by the office that signed the evaluation. The regulation provides for each performance report to be reviewed for accuracy and fairness by an individual knowledgeable of the contractor's performance at a supervisory level above that of the evaluating official. The regulation further requires that COs provide contractors a copy of their final evaluations regardless of the rating.

If the evaluating official concludes that a contractor's performance was overall "unsatisfactory," the regulation requires that the contractor be advised in writing that a report of its unsatisfactory performance is being prepared, and the basis for that report. The regulation further requires that the contractor be afforded an opportunity to submit written comments, which the agency should address and include in the final report. The regulation also allows for unsatisfactory ratings to be amended, if warranted, to reflect changes in the performance ratings. Amendments to final unsatisfactory reports in the CCASS database are to be made in writing, explaining why a change to the rating is necessary and which elements need to be changed. The regulation further states that a contractor that receives a final unsatisfactory performance rating should be notified of its option to appeal that rating within 30 days to a level above the CO. The appeal is a written request to the CO, stating the reasons why the contractor believes a further review of its performance evaluation is justified.

In addition to the final evaluation reports described above, the database also contains "interim performance evaluations" prepared when a contractor's performance is generally unsatisfactory for a period of 3 months or longer. If a firm is assigned an "unsatisfactory" interim rating, but subsequently improves its performance to a satisfactory or better, the interim rating is removed from the database upon entry of the final rating. Interim unsatisfactory performance evaluations cannot be appealed, however.

Based on our review of the record, including the protester's arguments, the agency's explanations, and the procedures established in ER No. 415-1-17 for evaluating a construction contractor's performance, we see no basis to object to the agency's approach under this RFP. The procedures established by the regulation specifically require that contractors be notified when the agency is preparing an unsatisfactory performance evaluation, and give the contractors an opportunity to submit written

58 PAST PERFORMANCE HANDBOOK

comments on that evaluation to the agency. In fact, here, in accordance with the procedures established by the regulation, the CO informed TLT that the agency was preparing an unsatisfactory "interim" performance rating on one project—the SOF Medical Barracks, Phase II at Fort Bragg, DACA21-98-C-0046—and specifically advised the firm that the CO was "willing to consider any reasons why [the CO] should not issue this evaluation." The record further shows that by letter December 21, 1999, TLT replied to the CO's letter. Although the CO considered TLT's response, the CO concluded that issuance of the interim unsatisfactory rating was warranted.

The record also contains other correspondence dated December 1, 1998, and October 25, 1999, showing that TLT responded to the agency's interim and final negative evaluations of TLT's unsatisfactory performance on other construction projects. Thus, the protester's assertion that it has not been previously afforded an opportunity to comment on the alleged negative performance reports in the CCASS database, is simply not supported by the record. Moreover, contrary to TLT's contention that the interim evaluations are "stale," the agency asserts, and the record shows, that the interim negative ratings TLT has received are dated November 1998 (DACA21-97-D-0015 and DACA21-98-C-0046). The record thus shows that the unsatisfactory ratings concern its recent performance, and that TLT has previously been given ample opportunities to clarify allegedly adverse past performance information in the database. In sum, TLT has provided no reason to question the recency or validity of the past performance information in the CCASS database.

Given our conclusion about the reliability of the CCASS database, we see no merit in TLT's argument that the agency is required to give it a further opportunity to respond before it relies on the CCASS information in conducting the past performance evaluation. Federal Acquisition Regulation (FAR) sec. 15.306(a)(2), which addresses clarifications and award without discussions, states in relevant part that where, as here, an award will be made without conducting discussions, "offerors may be given the opportunity to clarify certain aspects of proposals (e.g., the relevance of an offeror's past performance information and adverse past performance information to which the offeror has not previously had an opportunity to respond) or to resolve minor or clerical errors." As TLT recognizes, this provision is clearly permissive. That is, while it gives COs broad discretion to declare whether to communicate with a firm concerning its performance history, it does not require that they do so in every case.[9] Here, in view of the clear evidence in the record showing that TLT has had ample opportunity to comment on its unsatisfactory performance, we think that the CO reasonably could exercise her discretion in deciding not to communicate further with TLT regarding the alleged negative past performance information in the CCASS database. Given the permissive language of FAR sect. 15.306 (a)(2), the fact that TLT may wish to rebut or provide further comments on the information in the database does not give rise to a requirement that the CO give TLT an opportunity to do so.[10]

Past performance databases are a significant factor in evaluating past performance for future contracts. The best way to counter negative past performance information already in a database is to present positive performance information on more recent or current contracts. Stellar performance on current contracts may help offset past problems. If you do have performance problems, you must ensure that the performance reports contain your comments on the evaluation. These comments must explain the specific corrective actions taken or the reasons why the performance was not unsatisfactory. Generalized comments or vague promises are not acceptable. Your response to performance evaluations may be your only chance to respond to a negative evaluation because the government is not obligated to permit you to make further comments in a later acquisition.

Any government communication during contract performance about less-than-satisfactory performance should receive a prompt and complete response. You should retain such communications with your response in your files because they may be submitted with a future proposal to demonstrate how problems were corrected on a referenced contract. This is particularly important when the RFP indicates that award will be made without discussions. Note, however, that your comments must stand alone; additional non-contemporaneous comments or justifications may be submitted but will probably be accorded little weight.

Planning for Contract Performance

Past performance will play an ever-increasing role in your ability to win future contracts. While not part of your proposal, your contract planning should consider what administrative actions you should take to improve future evaluations of your past performance.

If there are problems during contract performance and there is disagreement about factual matters, contemporaneous records of the problem are often determinative (see Examples 4.1 and 4.2). One way to defend your position is to keep an internal record or log of performance problems and what you did to correct them, particularly of any event or activity that the government might view unfavorably. Because the government may not always tell you what it considers to be problems, it might be wise to keep a contemporaneous record of all contract activity. This includes delays, conformance problems, contract changes, and any disagreements with government representatives. Record the event, the participants, the problem, and what action was or will be taken. Keep the record up to date, particularly with respect to prospective actions and the final results. You should, however, check with legal counsel to determine how to do this if the proposed contract will include FAR clause 52.215-2, Audit and Records—Negotiation. This clause gives the government the right to examine certain records, and your legal counsel will want some input as to how, or if, such records are kept.

Try to get performance feedback from government representatives during contract performance. If possible, get such feedback in writing, or at least make a note of the feedback for your records. Recording positive feedback is particularly important because such information usually will be considered a strong point in the evaluation of past performance. Negative feedback also should be recorded to ensure that action is taken to resolve the problem. Keep in mind that a problem resolved is not a problem in the evaluation of past performance—but only if the government evaluators are aware that the problem was resolved.

60   PAST PERFORMANCE HANDBOOK

You also might consider developing a past performance file or database similar to that of government agencies. This would involve developing a past performance questionnaire and requesting that the contracting agency complete it at the end of contract performance. You then can use copies of the completed questionnaires as past performance information for future procurements. This has the advantage of providing contemporaneous past performance information that might counter different information provided by the agency in response to a later past performance questionnaire by a different procuring agency. Such a file would have proved useful to FC Construction Company[11] in its protest that an agency either erroneously or intentionally misrepresented telephonic responses to queries about FC's past performance. FC alleged that the responses rated its performance higher than that recorded by the agency. FC's protest on this point was denied when it was unable to produce the individuals in question for a GAO conference. FC would not have had this problem if it could have produced contemporaneous documentation of its past performance.

As noted earlier, all federal agencies are supposed to complete a contractor performance report at the end of contract performance and provide a copy to the contractor. Your request for the completion of a past performance questionnaire would be a subtle reminder to your contracting agency of this requirement. For purposes of your past performance file, either a completed past performance questionnaire or a copy of the agency's contractor performance report would serve the purpose.

During contract performance, be sure to respond quickly and positively to government requirements or inquires. The government is your customer and as such deserves your consideration. Do not construe this as a surrender of your contract rights but as a show of respect for your customer.

If problems arise during contract performance, do not make excuses—solve problems. If the government finds fault with your contract performance and is correct, fix the problem promptly. If the government is not correct, provide a positive response that points out why the government's position is incorrect (using suitably diplomatic language) and suggest how the misunderstanding might be resolved. When addressing performance problems, do not generalize about the problem and its solution—be specific. Do not make promises that will not be kept. Such correspondence can prove to be significant when addressing past performance problems in a future proposal.

Despite the need to be cooperative and sensitive to your customer's needs, you should not surrender your contractual rights, such as making contract claims, questioning specifications, requesting contract changes, or other actions you have a contractual right to take. The Comptroller General has ruled that such actions cannot be cited as adverse past performance (see Example 4.5) during the evaluation of past performance.

It is virtually impossible to have contract performance that is completely problem-free. Contract problems can be minimized, however, through effective communication with the government. This concept is not new, but it has become even more important with the increasing importance of past performance evaluations in awarding future contracts.

Responding to adverse past performance information is critical, whether it comes up during the solicitation process or at the end of contract performance. Generally, you will get only one chance to respond. Your response to such information must be clear, concise, and, most of all, convincing. The fact that you do not agree with the adverse findings is not sufficient. It is your responsibility to successfully rebut adverse past performance information, and the agency's perception of adverse past performance will prevail if you fail to respond fully to the adverse information.

Chapter 5 discusses responding to adverse past performance information during the solicitation process in greater detail, and Chapter 10 addresses responding to contractor performance evaluations.

NOTES

[1] Office of Federal Procurement Policy, *Best Practices for Collecting and Using Current and Past Performance Information*, May 2000, p. 18.

[2] *Thomas Brand Siding Co.*, B-286914.3, 3/12/01.

[3] *Menendez-Donnel & Assoc.*, B-286599, 1/16/01.

[4] *Dual, Inc.*, B-279295, 6/1/98, 98-1 CPD ¶146 at 3.

[5] *Phantom Prods., Inc.*, B-283882, 12/30/99, 2000 CPD ¶7 at 4.

[6] *Plasma-Therm, Inc.*, B-280664.2, 12/28/98, 98-2 CPD ¶160 at 3.

[7] *Boland Well Systems, Inc.*, B-287030, 3/7/01.

[8] *TLT Construction Corp.*, B-286226, 11/7/00.

[9] *Rohmann Servs., Inc.*, B-280154.2, 11/16/98, 98-2 CPD ¶134 at 8-9.

[10] *A.G. Cullen Constr., Inc.*, B-284049.2, 2/22/00, 2000 CPD ¶45 at 5-6.

[11] *FC Construction Company, Inc.*, B-287059, 4/10/01.

Chapter 4

Pre-Award: Factors That Affect the Evaluation of Past Performance

by Peter S. Cole

A number of factors affect the evaluation of past performance.

FAR FACTORS

Past performance is one indicator of an offeror's ability to perform a contract successfully, and its importance depends on the circumstances of the procurement. The FAR[1] identifies the currency and relevance of past performance information, the source of past performance information, the context of the data, and the general trends in contractor performance as factors that should be considered when evaluating an offeror's past performance.

Currency and Relevance of the Past Performance Information

Currency means that the information is generally known and believed. Generally, there would be greater value or believability to information on more recently completed contracts, particularly where there may have been recent technological changes or innovations in methodology that apply to the goods or services being procured, than there would be for information about older contracts that may have employed different personnel and used less recent technology or methodologies.

But currency is not necessarily time-related. For example, one offeror has an excellent performance record on recent contracts for developing systems for database management, but all the systems were based on technology that is now obsolete. A second offeror has an excellent performance rating that is not as recent as the first offeror, but this offeror developed its systems for database management using innovative technology that is now considered the leading edge of current technology. The past performance information on the first offeror lacks currency because the technology used on the referenced contracts is no longer useful or acceptable. The information on the second offeror has currency because the technology it uses is still prevalent or still in use.

64   PAST PERFORMANCE HANDBOOK

Relevance means that the information must be related to the matter at hand, i.e., it must relate to the same effort or a similar one. If the past performance information relates to work of a different nature than that of the instant acquisition, the contracting officer can disregard it because it does not serve to show how well the offeror might perform under the instant acquisition, or the information might be accorded a diminished importance as only an indicator of the offeror's general trend of performance.

For example, under a solicitation for base housing maintenance and repair services, including plumbing, electrical, mechanical, and structural work, a review of one offeror's past performance revealed that it had done only painting and painting-related work in the past. It had not performed any of the other required work effort. This offeror's past performance information was not relevant because it was not for the same or a similar effort (see Example 4.6).

Source of the Past Performance Information

Some past performance information sources are better than others. Generally, contractor performance reports from your own or other agencies are of great value, particularly if the reports contain contractor comments. Information close at hand (i.e., information personally known to the contracting officer or evaluators) is also highly valuable. Responses to questionnaires sent to the references provided by the offeror are valuable, but of lesser value than the sources noted above because they may lack objectivity. Such information, if at variance with other information received, should be verified with the responding agency. If the information is negative, consideration should also be given to permitting the offeror to rebut such information. Information from commercial sources should be handled with care because while the federal government is required to maintain past performance information in its files, commercial sources may or may not routinely retain such information in a useable form. Adverse past performance information from commercial sources must be in writing.

Context of the Data

Past performance information should be examined to ensure that the narrative description of an offeror's past performance and the assigned ratings mesh. *Context* refers to the circumstances in which an event occurs. Past performance information is in context if the ratings are supported by a narrative that is related to the work to be performed and the rating assigned. It is out of context if there is no narrative or the narrative inadequately supports the rating assigned. Generally, adjectival ratings, numerical scores, color codes, or other rating indicators are of little value without a supporting narrative or description of the offeror's past performance that is in context with the assigned rating.

Context also relates to the circumstances of the work to be performed. For example, one contractor has had very successful past performance constructing roads in urban settings but has had no contracts for constructing highways. Under a solicitation for road construction throughout the state, this offeror's past performance may not be as good an indicator of the offeror's ability to perform the contract as another offeror who has had similar successful past performance in both urban and rural settings.

General Trend of Past Performance

When evaluating past performance, evaluators often focus on a single problem contract rather than looking at the general trend of the offeror's past performance. An offeror's past performance should not necessarily be downgraded because of a single problem contract, particularly if the trend of the offeror's past performance (over time or a number of other contracts) does not show such problems. Past performance evaluation is not a mathematical or mechanical exercise. Information on past problem contracts should be examined to determine its currency, relevance, and context, and then balanced with the general trend of the offeror's past performance to determine the extent to which the overall past performance is likely to affect performance on the prospective contract.

You may evaluate an offeror's performance on the preponderance of its past efforts, even when you cannot document a relationship between specific contracts and the prospective contract, to determine whether past performance deficiencies are usual or unusual in terms of the offeror's performance record. Unrelated (not relevant) past performance may be evaluated, but given lesser weight, along with relevant effort, if deemed necessary to gain a perspective on the trend of an offeror's past performance. If the preponderance of an offeror's past efforts are deficient, this fact should be treated as an unacceptable risk factor and evaluated as such. Using unrelated past performance information should, however, be a last resort effort, used only when sufficient specifically related information is not available.

OTHER FACTORS

The factors identified in the FAR are not the only factors that can affect the evaluation of past performance. In the context of the past performance subfactors set forth in the RFP (i.e., quality, schedule, cost control, business relations, other

66 PAST PERFORMANCE HANDBOOK

specific subfactors), the following should be considered when evaluating an offeror's past performance:

- Impact on prospective performance

- Extent of government's responsibility

- Relevance of past performance information

- New firms/firms with no past performance history

- Performance of other companies, key personnel, or subcontractors.

Impact on Prospective Performance

When evaluating an offeror's past performance, assess the extent to which the offeror's past performance is likely to affect its performance on the prospective contract. A demonstrable relationship should exist between the offeror's past performance and the prospective performance, particularly if there is adverse past performance information. For example, if past problems have been corrected and are not likely to recur, these problems should not be used to downgrade the offeror's proposal. Or, if the past poor performance occurred in a corporate division that will not be involved in the prospective contract, the past problems should not be counted against the offeror unless it can be demonstrated that the problems originated at the corporate level and thus, unless corrected, would be likely to affect the prospective effort adversely. On the other hand, poor past performance on an effort similar to the prospective contract, if not explained satisfactorily, is a good indicator that the performance on the prospective contract will also be poor.

Generally, using unrelated poor past performance to reject or significantly downgrade an offeror is not reasonable. The evaluation of past performance should not be used as a means to punish an offeror for unrelated past performance problems, except to the extent that they may indicate a general trend of poor performance. Poor past performance should be considered with respect to the risk that such problems will recur and adversely affect performance on the prospective contract.

When considering the impact of an offeror's past performance on prospective performance, assess the nature and severity of past problems and the effectiveness of any corrective action taken by the offeror in terms of the prospective performance. If the past problems have not been corrected, determine if they are likely to recur and if they will adversely affect the chance of successful performance. If the problems have been successfully corrected or are unlikely to recur, the past problems are not germane to the prospective contract, as shown in Examples 4.1 and 4.2.

Example 4.1 — Impact on prospective performance (#1)[2]

The Communities Group (TCG) protested that Housing and Urban Development (HUD), in rating Management Solutions' past performance, improperly failed to consider the negative past performance of the firm's subcontractor, MTB Investments, Inc. (MTB), on a current HUD contract for similar services. (The RFP stated that the past performance evaluation would consider the performance of the offeror, as well as any proposed subcontractors who would perform a major portion of the work.) TCG asserted that MTB, a major subcontractor for Management Solutions, had to replace 20 of 100 inspectors for poor performance; that as a result of this performance, MTB had to reinspect approximately 89 sites; and that MTB's rejection rate was three to six times higher than TCG's under its current contract.

The Comptroller General did not agree that the evaluation was improper.

HUD reports that MTB's past performance information was viewed favorably because the company has a significant amount of direct experience conducting HUD-certified inspections of HUD properties and that the performance problems alleged by the protester were not before the agency at the time past performance was evaluated because this matter was being investigated. Further, HUD advises that the protester's characterization of the alleged problems is inaccurate and that consideration of the matter would not have resulted in a negative past performance rating because MTB undertook prompt and appropriate remedial action. In this regard, HUD advises that it was discovered that a non-licensed individual was conducting inspections on properties using the credentials of a HUD-certified inspector employed by MTB, and that when apprised of the problem MTB took the prompt corrective action of reinspecting 83 properties, terminating the MTB employee involved, and reporting this matter to the relevant state authorities for appropriate disciplinary action.

We have reviewed the protester's allegations, as well as the agency's detailed response, and cannot say that Management Solutions' past performance rating was unreasonably high in light of MTB's past performance. As indicated, the incident had not been investigated when the past performance evaluation was done; in any event, the record indicates that TCG's version of MTB's problems is inaccurate and that HUD was favorably impressed with MTB's prompt and appropriate response when the problem was discovered. We note that under the technical evaluation plan employed to evaluate proposals under this RFP an offeror could still receive a high rating for past performance so long as problems identified during performance were handled to the satisfaction of the client.

Note that at the time Management Solutions' past performance was evaluated, the problem with its subcontractor had not been investigated, and because the facts of the matter were not known, the problem could not be considered in the evaluation. By the time of the protest, however, it was found that MTB had taken appropriate corrective

68   PAST PERFORMANCE HANDBOOK

action and the problem was not likely to recur, thus an adverse past performance finding would be inappropriate because the problem would have no effect on the prospective performance.

Example 4.2—Impact on prospective performance (#2)[3]

A NASA source evaluation board (SEB) learned that a contracting officer's representative (COR) administering another NASA contract intended to give Federal Data Corporation (FDC) a negative performance rating for its transition effort on that contract. This information was not used to downgrade FDC's past performance, and the other offeror protested that the past performance evaluation was unreasonable.

The Comptroller General did not agree.

The evaluation in this area was reasonable. After learning of the COR's potential negative rating, NASA asked FDC to respond to this information. FDC did so, both explaining its position, and sending the SEB a copy of the response it had sent to the COR. According to FDC's response, the transition effort did not go well for reasons other than FDC's actions; FDC maintained that the follow-on contractor caused many of the problems. Since the COR had not actually assigned FDC a final negative rating, the SEB considered the issue unresolved and did not use it to downgrade FDC in the past performance evaluation. We see nothing improper in the SEB's actions. Since the COR had not provided a final rating by the time the SEB was completing its past performance evaluation, and FDC provided a response in which it denied that it was responsible for the difficult transition, it was reasonable not to automatically attribute the problems to FDC. We think the SEB therefore reasonably could conclude that the information available did not support a finding of deficient past performance, and thus did not warrant downgrading FDC.[4]

As with Example 4.1, if a matter dealing with adverse past performance information is not officially resolved at the time of the evaluation, the evaluators are not required to consider it. However, if the evaluators are aware of a problem, they should allow the offeror to comment on the adverse information, and the offeror's response must be credible. If FDC had not responded with reasonable arguments, the matter might have been resolved differently.

Examples 4.1 and 4.2 involved acquisitions in which discussions were to be conducted and there was time to consider these matters before award. But what happens when award will be made without discussions and time is of the essence? The FAR[5] states that where award will be made without discussions, the agency may (but is not required to) give the offeror an opportunity to clarify adverse past performance information to which the offeror has not previously had an opportunity to respond. Example 4.3 provides some clarification on this point.

Example 4.3—Clarifying adverse past performance information where award will be made without discussions[6]

The Comptroller General made the following comment in a case involving the evaluation of past performance where award was to be made without discussions.

With regard specifically to clarifications concerning adverse past performance information to which the offeror has not previously had an opportunity to respond, we think that, for the exercise of discretion to be reasonable, the contracting officer must give the offeror an opportunity to respond where there clearly is a reason to question the validity of the past performance information, for example, where there are obvious inconsistencies between a reference's narrative comments and the actual ratings the reference gives the offeror. In the absence of such a clear basis to question the past performance information, we think that, short of acting in bad faith, the contracting officer reasonably may decide not to ask for clarifications.

Applying this standard here, we think that the contracting officer reasonably exercised his discretion in deciding not to communicate with Cullen regarding the adverse past performance information received from one of Cullen's references. There is nothing on the face of the reference that would create concerns about its validity. Given the permissive language of FAR 15.306(a)(2), the fact that Cullen may wish to respond to the reference does not give rise to a requirement that the contracting officer give Cullen an opportunity to do so.

Note that while the FAR is permissive about giving an offeror a chance to respond, the Comptroller General states that the offeror *must* be given an opportunity to respond if there is reason to question the validity of the adverse past performance information. The agency has the *discretion* to do so in all other cases.

Even if award is to be made without discussions, it is suggested that offerors be permitted to clarify adverse past performance information in *all* cases where the adverse information might be an important factor in the award decision (i.e., the offeror might otherwise be in line for award), regardless of any questions about the validity of the reference's information. Without the offeror's input, it would be difficult to assess the impact the problem might have on prospective performance. While this might add a few days to the procurement process, a protest (even a losing one) will cause even greater disruption. It should be noted, however, that this suggestion applies only where the offeror's clarification will not result in any changes to the proposal. Proposal changes are not permitted when award will be made without discussions.

Where discussions will be held, the FAR[7] states that communications *shall* be held with offerors where adverse past performance information is a determin-

70 PAST PERFORMANCE HANDBOOK

ing factor preventing them from being placed in the competitive range, and the offeror has not had a prior opportunity to respond to such information. Technically, this would not include adverse information about contracts the offeror has referenced because, theoretically, the offeror would know of any problems on these contracts and should comment on such problems in its proposal. In reality, however, an offeror does not always know how an agency has rated its past performance, particularly with respect to some of the "soft" past performance evaluation criteria, such as cost control and business relations. Contractors are not always informed of government-perceived problems during contract performance, particularly on contracts that end satisfactorily. These problems, however, may be noted on responses to a query about past performance from another agency. This information should be available through contractor performance evaluation reports, but because these reports are not completed until contract completion, which could be a year or more after contract award, such information accumulates slowly and is not necessarily available to offerors in the interim.

It would be good policy, therefore, to permit offerors to comment on *any* adverse past performance information before determining the competitive range or making an award without discussions if the adverse information might be a determining factor preventing the offeror from being included in the competitive range or considered for award. With offeror comments in hand, evaluators are better prepared to assess the impact of the problems on prospective performance. Permitting such comments might help avoid a protest.

If it is decided that an offeror is to be included in the competitive range despite some adverse past performance information, this information should be identified as a discussion question to be addressed during discussions.

In any event, if an offeror fails to provide information on past problems and the associated corrective action in its proposal, or fails to respond to questions about such problems, you may determine that the problems are not corrected and evaluate the offeror's past performance accordingly, as shown in Example 4.4.

Example 4.4—If an offeror fails to respond to questions about past problems, you may assume that the problems have not been corrected.[8]

A protester was delinquent on two contracts and, in response to direct discussion questions, did not submit any evidence to explain the delinquencies. The protester challenged the evaluation of its past performance.

The Comptroller General denied the protest.

Given the agency's discussion letter, which clearly placed Smith on notice that the firm needed to furnish additional evidence to improve its past performance rating, and Smith's failure to respond—in any fashion—to the agency's past performance con-

cerns, we think the agency reasonably found Smith's proposal marginally acceptable under the past performance factor.

While this case involved discussions after establishment of the competitive range, the ruling also would apply to an offeror who failed to respond adequately to a clarification request prior to an award without discussions or the establishment of the competitive range.

You should be careful, however, about what you evaluate as poor past performance. A contractor's exercise of its rights during contract performance, even when it annoys the government, should not be evaluated as poor performance, as noted in Example 4.5.

Example 4.5 – Filing of contract claims is not poor performance.[9]

While the claims apparently had no impact here, we agree with the protester that, absent some evidence of abuse of the process, agencies should not lower a firm's past performance evaluation based solely on its having filed claims. Contract claims, like bid protests, constitute remedies established by statute and regulation, and firms should not be prejudiced in competing for other contracts because of their reasonable pursuit of such remedies in the past.

This decision encompasses more than the taking of formal contractual actions, such as claims, disputes, and appeals. Disagreements with the government about contract administration, such as contract interpretation, do not constitute poor past performance unless they are determined to be frivolous or deliberately misleading.

Extent of Government's Responsibility

One of the more difficult past performance evaluation areas is determining the extent to which government actions may have contributed to an offeror's deficient performance. Government actions, such as faulty specifications, late delivery of government-furnished property (GFP), delivery of faulty GFP, failure to provide timely testing or other approvals, and numerous contract changes, can contribute to cost overruns and late deliveries.

When faced with an allegation of deficient performance, the contractor often will blame the government, and the government usually will deny any responsibility. Resolving these issues is not easy; nevertheless, the extent of government involvement should be assessed before any decisions are made. Keep in mind that agency comments on an offeror's past performance often reflect the respondent's subjective judgment and may even be in error. It is not reasonable to penalize a contractor for problems resulting from, or significantly affected by, government actions.

72 PAST PERFORMANCE HANDBOOK

For example, while discussing the background in a decision,[10] the Comptroller General noted that the contracting officer had asked an offeror about comments made by another agency indicating that the offeror's technical performance was considered inadequate. In response, the offeror produced a letter of commendation from the contracting agency's project manager on its performance under the contract in question, in which the project manager praised the offeror's performance as outstanding and tacitly admitted that the government was responsible for the alleged problems. Had the offeror been denied an opportunity to respond to the adverse comments, the record would have shown that the offeror had performed poorly on a contract when it actually performed in an outstanding manner.

Trying to assess the validity of an offeror's contention that the fault lay with the government is usually a matter of weighing the arguments of both sides and deciding, often subjectively, which side has the best argument. You cannot automatically side with the government, but you should assess the government's allegations of poor performance against the offeror's other references. If the other references show high performance assessments, the matter should be investigated further if a singular finding of poor performance would adversely affect the offeror's competitive position.

Relevance of Past Performance Information

Although the need for relevance has been noted earlier, this matter must be addressed in further detail because of its importance. Generally, information on past performance should not be more than three to five years old, unless it can be shown that it is still relevant to the current effort. Relevance encompasses not only similar work but also the presence of the same management or technical personnel, the use of the same technology or methodology, or other similarities between the past effort and the current effort. If you cannot make a connection between the past effort and the current effort, the past performance information is not relevant, as shown in example 4.6.

Example 4.6—Past performance information must be relevant.[11]

The RFP was for a fixed-price requirements contract for routine and emergency maintenance and repair services (including plumbing, electrical, mechanical, and structural work) for 1,769 military family housing units. Award was to be made without discussions. The only two evaluation factors were past performance and price. Offerors were instructed that information obtained from their past performance references would be reviewed to evaluate the quality and extent of the offerors' experience deemed relevant to the requirements of the RFP. Relevant contracts would include, but were not limited to, those providing housing property maintenance services or other types similar in magnitude to those required in the RFP. The two offerors in contention for award were Ostrom (the lowest price) and BMAR (the second lowest price).

Pre-Award: Factors That Affect the Evaluation of Past Performance 73

Ostrom received favorable performance ratings (of very good and exceptional) from its referenced sources; when queried, however, the references indicated that the contracts were primarily for painting-related and refinishing services. The evaluators concluded that, although Ostrom had favorable references for its painting-related work, painting was only a small portion of the current RFP's work requirements. Consequently, Ostrom's proposal received a neutral rating under the past performance factor for failure to provide sufficiently relevant past performance information for evaluation of the firm's capability to perform the RFP's overall "complex, multi-skilled" contract requirements.

Conversely, BMAR's past performance was rated as exceptional based on the exceptional performance reviews from its references for contracts involving substantially similar contracts of similar magnitude, with the same type of comprehensive housing maintenance services as those required under the RFP.

The contracting officer decided that the price difference was slight and outweighed by the benefits of BMAR's performance assurances, as shown by its past performance rating, and awarded the contract to BMAR as offering the best value.

Ostrom protested, contending that its referenced contracts demonstrated relevant, highly-rated past performance, as evidenced by the high ratings from its past performance references for those contracts. Ostrom also argued that the dollar value of its prior contracts demonstrates that they are similar in magnitude to the proposed contract and Ostrom, therefore, should have been rated as exceptional under the past performance factor and awarded the contract as the lowest-priced offeror.

The Comptroller General did not agree.

In reviewing a protest against an agency's evaluation of proposals, we examine the record to determine whether the agency's judgment was reasonable and consistent with the stated evaluation criteria and applicable statutes and regulations.[12] The protester's mere disagreement with the agency's judgment in its determination of the relative merit of competing proposals does not establish that the evaluation was unreasonable.[13] As discussed below, we find that the evaluation of the protester's past performance information and the agency's price/past performance tradeoff determination were reasonable and consistent with the evaluation criteria.

Although Ostrom contends that having performed a contract of approximately the same contract price and others of substantial dollar value shows that it can successfully perform a contract under the RFP, the RFP's past performance evaluation provisions provided for a comparative assessment of the offerors' past performance and experience in terms of "relevant contracts" for "the same or similar items." We recognize that, in describing relevant contracts, the RFP refers to contracts for "housing property maintenance services or other types similar in magnitude to those required in this solicitation." This reference, however, must be read with the purpose of the experience evaluation in mind. That purpose was to evaluate an offeror's capability to perform the requirements of the RFP, which, as described above, called for multiple, distinct services and capabilities. Accordingly, we think it clearly was reasonable and consistent with the RFP for the agency to consider "relevant" only those prior contracts involving services that are the same as or similar to those called for under the RFP.

Our review of the record supports the reasonableness of the evaluators' determination that Ostrom's past performance information, at best, indicated that the firm had

74 PAST PERFORMANCE HANDBOOK

successfully performed only a small portion of the current RFP's requirements. None of the protester's past performance information, for example, demonstrated experience providing services in the areas of plumbing, electrical, and mechanical repair services. We therefore find reasonable the evaluators' conclusion that the limited scope of that experience did not demonstrate the firm's capability to perform the full range of services required under the current RFP.

[And in a footnote] Ostrom also generally challenges the agency's failure to hold discussions with the firm or request clarifications regarding the relevance of its past performance information. Where, as here, the RFP advised offerors that the agency did not intend to conduct discussions,[14] there generally is no obligation to conduct discussions.[15] With regard to seeking clarifications on this issue from Ostrom, FAR 15.306(a)(2) provides that when an award is to be made without discussions, an offeror may be given the opportunity to clarify certain aspects of its proposal such as the relevance of its past performance information. Here, we cannot see any basis to conclude that the agency was required to issue clarification requests, given that the past performance information it obtained from the protester regarding the scope of its prior contracts was clear and was confirmed by the firm's references.[16]

This case demonstrates the importance of carefully wording the description of the past performance evaluation factor in the RFP. In this case, the wording properly wrapped prior experience and past performance together to ensure that any referenced contracts will show that the past performance being rated is relevant to the current effort in terms of the varied work requirements in the statement of work. This example also demonstrates the need not only to check the reference's rating of an offeror's past performance, but also to verify that the work under the referenced contract is relevant to the work under the prospective contract.

When award is to be made without discussions, any clarifications permitted must be explanatory in nature, clarifying information already submitted in the proposal. Additional information, such as other references, would constitute a change in the proposal, —which is not permitted. Ostrom's references clearly demonstrated that its past performance did not meet the requirements of the RFP. Because there was nothing to clarify (such as the validity of adverse past performance information), the contracting officer properly did not seek clarifications. See also Example 4.3.

New Firms/Firms with No Past Performance History

The evaluation of past performance must provide for newly formed firms that lack a history of relevant past performance or firms for which there is no pertinent past performance information available (i.e., an established firm desiring to expand into new areas). The FAR[17] states that firms without a past performance record or for whom past performance information is not available may not be evaluated favorably or unfavorably on past performance. In effect, you are to give such a firm a neutral rating, which, in theory, does not affect its competitive position. The concept of "neutral" ratings is not new, as shown in Example 4.7.

Example 4.7—Evaluating offerors with no past performance history (#1)[18]

In a 1996 decision, the Comptroller General discussed the use of neutral ratings in a protest where both offerors received a green/low risk past performance rating, so award was made to the lowest-priced offeror. The protester argued that the awardee's past performance should have been given an insufficient data (neutral) rating because the awardee had never produced the item before, and the protester should have received award because its higher past performance rating and the minimal difference in price made it the best value.

In a best value procurement, price is not necessarily controlling in determining the offer that represents the best value to the government. Rather, that determination is made on the basis of whatever evaluation factors are set forth in the RFP, with the source selection official often required to make a cost/technical tradeoff to determine if one proposal's technical superiority is worth the higher cost that may be associated with that proposal. In this regard, price/past performance tradeoffs are permitted when such tradeoffs are consistent with the RFP evaluation scheme.[19] Thus, where an RFP identifies past performance and price as the evaluation criteria and indicates that an offeror with good past performance can expect a higher rating than an offeror without such a record of performance, proposals must be evaluated on that basis, and ultimately the selection official must decide, if the offeror with the better past performance rating is not the low-cost offeror, whether the more costly offeror represents the best value to the government in light of the better past performance rating.

In general, we do not view RFP evaluation schemes that specify a "neutral" rating for vendors with no past performance record[20] as precluding this same type of source selection decision-making. That is, we think that the use of a neutral rating approach, to avoid penalizing a vendor without prior experience and thereby enhance competition, does not preclude, in a best value procurement, a determination to award to a higher-priced offeror with a good past performance record over a lower-cost vendor with a neutral past performance rating [And in a footnote here—It does, however, preclude evaluation scoring that penalizes an offeror for receiving neutral ratings.[21]] Indeed such a determination is inherent in the concept of best value.

So, does the protester win? Not in this case, as the Comptroller General goes on to explain.

Here, however, the Navy explains that its evaluation scheme does not call for rewarding a vendor with good past performance over a vendor with no relevant past performance. Rather, the Navy further explains, its evaluation scheme is intended to differentiate between those with good past performance and those with differing degrees of less than good performance. In other words, the Navy's position is that under the RFP an offeror with a green rating is superior to an offeror with a red or yellow rating but not to an offeror with a neutral insufficient data rating.

We have no basis to disagree with the Navy. In fact, we have previously recognized that this very evaluation scheme contemplates that "a green rating [is] to be given greater weight in the evaluation only when compared to a red or a yellow rating," and that an offeror's green rating is "not to be given greater weight in the evaluation when compared to an offeror[s] . . . insufficient data rating," so that in the circumstances here the agency is to compare the competing proposals "based on price."[22]

Accordingly, we conclude that even if Condor's green rating is changed to an insufficient data rating the award decision would not change.

The Comptroller General denied this protest because the RFP clearly stated that offerors receiving insufficient data classifications "shall be evaluated solely on the basis of price [and that] [p]ast performance shall not be a consideration in their evaluation." This meant that a comparative assessment of past performance would be made only among those offerors with a past performance record, and then the offerors, including those with insufficient data ratings, would compete on the basis of price alone.

The RFP's explanation of how the past performance of new firms or those with no past performance history will be evaluated must be worded carefully to express clearly the purpose of the evaluation. In Example 4.7, the Navy was clear as to how neutral past performance would be evaluated; but what happens when the award turns on a tradeoff between price and past performance and the two lowest priced offerors have no past performance history? This can make things difficult, as shown in Example 4.8.

Example 4.8—Evaluating offerors with no past performance history (#2)[23]

In a procurement for insecticide, offerors were to be evaluated on the basis of price and past performance and award was to be made on a best-value basis. Past performance was scored using an Automated Best Value Model (ABVM) that combined each offeror's delivery and quality scores. Offerors with no past performance history with the agency were to be given a neutral (unscored) past performance rating.

The two lowest-priced offerors had no performance history. The third lowest-priced offeror had an excellent past performance rating and a price that was within 5% of the two lower-priced offerors. The contracting officer found that the item was currently out of stock and that there were outstanding backorders. The contracting officer therefore concluded that the third lowest-priced offeror's price was worth the reduced risk of non-performance (as evidenced by its excellent past performance rating) in light of the high demand for items already in a back-ordered inventory position, and awarded to Amjay, the third lowest-priced offeror, as the best value.

Phillips Industries, the lowest-priced offeror, protested that it should have been awarded the contract under an evaluation scheme that provided for a neutral rating for an offeror with no performance history.

The Comptroller General did not agree.

We think the agency's decision to award to Amjay was reasonable and consistent with the RFP. Here, the RFP established that price and past performance would be the factors for award among the technically acceptable firms. The ABVM clause stated how past performance would be rated based on ABVM scores, that a lack of perfor-

mance history would not disqualify a firm, but that, among other things, the offeror could be considered less favorably than an offeror with a favorable performance history. The clause further provided for a comparative assessment of offers and stated that "[w]here the offeror with the best performance history has not also offered the lowest price, the Government will determine the appropriate tradeoff of price for past performance."

The RFP listed certain factors, including delivery schedule/inventory status, which could affect the tradeoff determination. Here, the contracting officer decided, given the high demand and the backlog status for the item, that award to a slightly higher-priced firm which had an excellent performance history was justified to ensure timely delivery and represented the best value to the government. This was entirely consistent with the RFP evaluation scheme and the discretion afforded the contracting officer in making the tradeoff decision.[24]

As we stated in Excalibur,[25] the use of a neutral rating approach, to avoid penalizing a vendor without prior experience and thereby enhance competition, does not preclude, in a best value procurement, a determination to award to a higher-priced offeror with a good performance record over a lower-cost vendor with a neutral past performance rating. Indeed, such a determination is inherent in the concept of best value.

The decision in this case turned on a bona fide need to ensure timely delivery because of the high demand and backlog status of the item being procured. This is what tradeoffs are all about—deciding, after the evaluations are completed and based on the circumstances of the instant procurement, which of the proposals offers the best value to the government.

Note that while a best-value determination may favor a higher priced offeror with a favorable past performance rating over a lower-priced offeror with a neutral past performance rating, the *evaluation scoring* cannot penalize an offeror for its neutral rating.

The OFPP Guide[26] suggests that when scoring an offeror with no past performance history, the offeror should be given the middle rating in whatever rating system is used (e.g., 50 on a 100-point scale, 3 on a 5-point scale, a satisfactory rating on an adjectival scale, or the middle color on a color rating scale). Although the OFPP guide indicates that this should happen rarely, proposals from new firms or firms with no pertinent past performance history are not that unusual. Giving a middle rating ensures that the offeror is not penalized for its neutral rating and is probably better than not scoring past performance at all (by avoiding possible confusion)—unless, of course, the situation as set forth in Example 4.7 applies. Pay careful attention to the wording of the evaluation scheme with respect to offerors with no performance history to ensure that the rating scheme itself does not work to downgrade new firms or offerors with no performance history.

Performance of Other Companies, Key Personnel, or Subcontractors

The FAR[27] provides that the evaluation should take into account past performance information regarding predecessor companies, key personnel who have relevant experience, or subcontractors who will perform major or critical aspects of the requirement when such information is relevant to the instant acquisition. The application of this FAR provision, however, can be problematic if the RFP does not explain how this will be done and what documentation or explanations the offeror should provide in its proposal. This is particularly important when the RFP provides that prior experience or key personnel are separate technical evaluation factors in addition to past performance.

It should be noted, however, that when past performance and pricing are the only evaluation factors, the difference between prior experience and past performance tends to blur if past performance is not clearly explained. One way to handle this is to explain that the contracts referenced for past performance purposes must be relevant, that is, the work must be of a similar nature and scope as the requirements contained in the RFP (prior experience), and that the contracts will be evaluated on the basis of the quality (past performance) of the work accomplished, i.e., make the definition of past performance include both prior experience and past performance, rather than treating them as separate parts of the overall past performance evaluation factor.

Generally, the need to evaluate the past performance of other companies, key personnel, and subcontractors comes into play with newly formed firms or firms with little or no relevant past performance history. This does not, however, change the need to explain clearly how the past performance will be evaluated in such instances.

Performance of Other Companies—You may consider the past performance of other companies when they are team members, affiliates, or significant subcontractors, as shown in Example 4.9.

Example 4.9—When should one company's past performance be attributed to another?[28]

A protester argued that GSA improperly evaluated the awardee's past performance by considering the contracts of the awardee's parent company. The record showed that the awardee, Service Star USA, Inc., performed only one of its five referenced contracts. In fact, although not made clear by the awardee in its written proposal, four of the five contracts listed were performed by two subsidiaries of Service Star's parent company, Service Star International, Inc.

The agency responded that it properly considered the parent company's and its other subsidiaries' contracts in its evaluation, citing FAR 15.305(a)(2)(iii) as the basis for its decision to consider these contracts. This FAR reference provides, in essence, that a past performance evaluation should consider information regarding predecessor companies, key personnel, or subcontractors that will perform major or critical aspects of the requirement when such information is relevant.

The Comptroller General did not agree with GSA's position.

We have stated that in determining whether one company's performance should be attributed to another, an agency must consider the nature and extent of the relationship between the two companies—in particular, whether the workforce, management, facilities, or other resources of one may affect contract performance of the other. In this regard, while it would be inappropriate to consider a company's performance record where that record does not bear on the likelihood of successful performance by the offeror, it would be appropriate to consider a company's performance record where it will be involved in the contract effort or where it shares management with the offeror. See NAHB Research CTR and Fluor Daniel.[29] In these decisions, the proposals clearly showed that the affiliate or other company had meaningful involvement in the performance of the contract. Here the awardee's proposal does not establish this fact. We conclude that the agency did not reasonably evaluate the relationship of the companies for purposes of attributing the past performance of the parent company or its other subsidiaries to Service Star USA, Inc., and therefore could not consider four of the five contracts referenced by Service Star USA, Inc. in evaluating its past performance. . . More specifically, there is no indication from the awardee's proposal that the parent company intends to use its workforce, management, facilities, or other resources in performing this contract.

While a firm may not have a past performance history of its own, it still can have a performance history through other companies, as long as the other companies will be significantly involved in performing the prospective contract. In this case, however, GSA went beyond what was in the written proposal and either assumed performance by these other companies or simply ignored the fact that the proposal did not demonstrate the participation by these other companies. Therefore, the Comptroller General sustained the protest.

The point here is that while the performance of other companies may be used to demonstrate an offeror's past performance, this can be done only when the proposal clearly explains how these other companies will be significantly involved in the proposed contract. It might be beneficial to explain this in the RFP's description of how past performance will be evaluated. Otherwise this information might not be provided in an offeror's proposal.

Performance of Key Personnel—The FAR permits the evaluation of past performance to be broadened to include the experience of a firm's key technical and management personnel. This can be important to new firms or firms with no past performance history because they can attribute their past performance to the experience of their key personnel. This is an interesting concept because it equates prior experience to past performance without explanation. Note, however, that this evaluation should involve how well the key personnel performed under the referenced contract, not simply that they had worked (i.e., had experience) under the particular contract.

This concept assumes that if the referenced contract was performed successfully, the success is imputed to the named key person for purposes of the evaluation of past performance. This may present problems, however, if the contract was not performed successfully or if the reference's response was otherwise negative. Downgrading an offeror under the past performance factor solely because some of its proposed key personnel were involved with a past problem contract might be difficult to justify without some evidence that the subject personnel were responsible for the problems. To presume that particular individuals are responsible for past problems requires definitive evidence. There are many reasons why a contract has problems that may be beyond the control of the responsible contractor personnel. Note, however, that the presence of such individuals, if they were deemed responsible for the problems on the referenced contract, could be determined to be a performance risk and evaluated as such.

The relationship of a key person to the performance of a past contract with respect to the evaluation of past performance, as noted above, has yet to be specifically addressed by the Comptroller General. However, offerors should be advised to establish clearly a proposed key person's *contribution* to the success of the referenced contract when relying on that person's prior experience under the past performance evaluation factor. A failure to establish this relationship could result in a finding of insufficient information and a neutral past performance rating.

Evaluating the past performance of key personnel can get complicated, as shown in Example 4.10.

Example 4.10—Evaluating the past performance of key personnel[30]

In an Air Force solicitation for mess attendant services, award was to be based on best value, and the only evaluation factors were past performance and price. The past performance factor was to be evaluated on the basis of the quality of service, management, and compliance with contract requirements. Offerors were to submit relevant past performance information, including a list of at least five contracts performed within the last five years and all current contracts.

The RFP provided that past performance would be considered relevant if the services provided were of a similar nature and scope as the requirements contained in the solicitation and that past performance, for the purpose of satisfying the requirement, meant that the quality, quantity, and level of work must be essentially comparable to the current requirements. Offerors having no relevant past performance would be given a neutral rating for past performance.

SWR submitted seven past performance references, all of which rated its performance as exceptional or very good under each past performance subfactor. The agency, however, found that the referenced contracts were not similar in nature and

Pre-Award: Factors That Affect the Evaluation of Past Performance **81**

scope to the RFP requirements and therefore were not relevant. SWR's proposal thus was rated neutral overall for past performance. Award was made to another offeror.

SWR protested the award on the basis that its neutral past performance rating was not proper. SWR acknowledged that it had no history of providing the identical services required but argued that the agency was required—under the terms of the RFP and the FAR—to consider the experience of its proposed project manager, a key employee, who had worked in the same capacity for the incumbent contractor for three years. SWR concluded that had the agency considered the project manager's past performance, SWR would have received a higher rating and, based on its lower price, its proposal would have been determined to be the best value to the government.

The Comptroller General denied the protest, but not because the proposed project manager did not have the requisite experience.

SWR is correct—and the agency does not dispute—that the RFP indicated that the past performance evaluation would include key personnel. In this regard, the RFP stated under the heading "Past Performance Procedures" that "[i]nformation will also be considered regarding any significant subcontractors and key personnel records." The RFP also referenced FAR 15.305(a)(2) which states in relevant part, that the agency should consider past performance information concerning "key personnel who have relevant experience . . . when such information is relevant to the instant acquisition."

SWR's proposal indicated that the individual it was proposing as project manager was not a current SWR employee, but was employed as the project manager for the incumbent contractor. In order to establish that the individual intended to be employed by SWR, the firm included in its proposal a letter, purportedly from the individual, that reads as follows:

"If upon successful Award of the Food Services contract with your Company and Moody Air Force Base, Valdosta, Georgia. Please accept this letter as my intent to continue employment as Project Manager at that facility for as long as the contract is in force."

The typed name of the project manager appears in the signature block, but the letter is unsigned. The letter is addressed to "To Whom this may concern," and there is no reference in the letter to SWR or any SWR employee.

The agency takes the position that the letter from the proposed individual did not reliably convey that she would, in fact, perform as project manager for SWR, and that it therefore reasonably did not attribute her experience to SWR. We agree. The possibility that, due to unforeseen circumstances, a proposed key individual may not be hired by the offeror, is an appropriate consideration for an agency in deciding whether the individual's experience should be imputed to the offeror for evaluation purposes.[31] The letter included in SWR's proposal established no commitment on the part of the proposed individual to work for SWR and, indeed, did not even refer to SWR, and there was nothing else in the proposal indicating that SWR and the individual had even discussed specific employment terms. We think the agency reasonably could decline to impute the proposed individual's experience to SWR based on the absence of stronger evidence of an employment commitment, or other evidence that the individual would in fact be employed by SWR.

82 Past Performance Handbook

SWR asserts that the absence of a firm employment commitment should not be relevant, since the RFP did not require firm letters of commitment from proposed employees. However, our above conclusion is not dependent upon such a requirement; rather, it is based on the inherent rationality of an agency's assessing whether a proposed individual will be employed by an offeror before it imputes that employee's past performance to the offeror. The fact that letters of commitment were not required did not preclude the agency from making this assessment based on all relevant consideration.

Example 4.10 contains lessons for both government and contractor personnel. For the government it shows that an RFP should always require firm letters of commitment from key personnel who are not currently employed by an offeror. The RFP also should explain that at a minimum, the letter should be signed by the individual concerned and should show a firm commitment to be employed by the firm. Requiring valid letters of commitment can help avoid protests such as the one in Example 4.10.

Contractor personnel also should be aware of the need for a valid letter of commitment from proposed key personnel not currently employed by an offeror. Contractor personnel should be aware of the need to recheck the validity of the letters of commitment when there is a significant period of time between the submission of the proposal and the time set for the submission of the final proposal revisions. It is the offeror's responsibility to ensure that the key personnel proposed will be available for contract performance.

Both parties should be aware of the importance of relevancy to evaluating past performance. Government personnel must be aware of the need to look closely at relevancy during the evaluation, and contractor personnel must understand the need to establish clearly the relevancy of past performance references in their proposals.

Note that a lack of relevancy is not considered to be adverse past performance information, and the government is not required to communicate relevancy questions to an offeror while evaluating past performance.

Performance of Subcontractors—The past performance of proposed subcontractors may be evaluated if the subcontractors will perform major or critical aspects of the requirement and if the past performance is relevant to the current requirement. Example 4.11 deals specifically with evaluating the past performance of subcontractors.

Example 4.11—Evaluating the past performance of subcontractors[32]

Can subcontractors be listed as past performance references? Here is what the Comptroller General said.

With regard to its claims regarding Porton's work on two of the contracts, Battelle is essentially arguing that the only entity that may properly list a prior contract for purposes of past performance evaluation is the concern which actually performed the work relevant to that covered in the solicitation. We disagree. The general rule is that the prime contractor under a government contract is responsible for the performance of its subcontractors.[33] Further, subcontractors and joint venturers perform various portions of contracts and accordingly may obtain experience useful in predicting success in future contract performance. George A. and Peter A. Palivos[34] (experience of a proposed subcontractor may be considered in determining whether an offeror meets a past performance requirement in a solicitation).[35] Where an offeror was involved as a subcontractor or joint venture in performing work under a prior contract similar to work to be included under the instant contract, such experience may properly be considered in assessing that offeror's past performance.[36]

The key to evaluating a subcontractor's past performance is relevancy. The government must look for it, and the offeror must clearly demonstrate it in the proposal. Keep in mind, however, that what is to be evaluated is how well the subcontractor performed the referenced contracts, not simply that it performed similar work.

NOTES

[1] FAR 15.305(A)(2).

[2] *The Communities Group*, B-283147, 10/12/99, 99-2 CPD ¶101 at 5,6.

[3] *Dynacs Engineering Co., Inc.*, B-284234; B-284234.2; B-284234.3, 3/17/00.

[4] *The Communities Group*, B-283147, 10/12/99, 99-2 CPD ¶101 at 5,6.

[5] FAR 15.306(a)(2).

[6] *A.G. Cullen Construction, Inc.*, B-284049.2, 2/22/2000.

[7] FAR 15.306(b)(1)(i).

[8] *Smith of Galeton Gloves, Inc.*, B-271686, 7/24/96, GCR 109,568.

[9] *Amclyde Engineered Products Co., Inc.*, B-282271; B-282271.2, 6/21/99, 99-2 CPD ¶5, n.5.

[10] *Columbia Research Corp.*, B-247073; B-247073.2, 4/23/92, GCR 106,570.

[11] *Ostrom Painting & Sandblasting, Inc.*, B-285244, 7/18/00.

[12] *Support Servs., Inc.*, B-282407, B-282407.2, 7/8/99, 99-2 CPD ¶30 at 3.

[13] *Hard Bodies, Inc.*, B-279543, 6/23/98, 98-1 CPD ¶172 at 3.

[14] FAR 52.212-1(g), 52.212-2(a)(6).

[15] *Inland Serv. Corp.*, B-282272, 6/21/99, 99-1 CPD ¶113 at 4.

[16] *A.G. Cullen Constr., Inc.*, B-284049.2, 2/22/00, 2000 CPD ¶45.

[17] FAR 15.305(a)(2)(iv).

[18] *Excalibur Sys., Inc.*, B-272017, 7/12/96, 96-2 CPD ¶13 at 3.

[19] *Dragon Servs., Inc.*, B-255354, 2/25/94, 94-1 CPD ¶151.

[20] See, e.g., *Quality Fabricators, Inc.*, B-271431; B-271431.3, 6/25/96; *Caltech Serv. Corp.*, B-261044.4, 12/14/95, 95-2 CPD ¶285.

84 Past Performance Handbook

[21] See *Inlingua Schools of Languages*, B-229784,4/5/88, 88-1 CPD ¶340.

[22] *Espey Mfg. & Elecs. Corp.*, B-254738.3, 3/8/94, 94-1 CPD ¶180.

[23] *Phillips Industries, Inc.*, B-280645, 9/17/98, 98-2 CPD ¶74 at 5.

[24] *Excalibur Sys., Inc.*, B-272017, 7/12/96, 96-2 CPD ¶13 at 3.

[25] *Excalibur*, supra at 3.

[26] Office of Federal Procurement Policy, *Best Practices for Collecting and Using Current and Past Performance Information*, May 2000, p. 24.

[27] FAR 15.305(a)(2)(iii).

[28] *Universal Building Maintenance, Inc.*, B-282456, 7/15/99.

[29] *NAHB Research Ctr., Inc.*, B-278876.2, 5/4/98, 98-1 CPD ¶150 at 4; *Fluor Daniel, Inc.*, B-262501; B-262501.2, 11/21/95, 95-2 CPD ¶241 at 12.

[30] *SWR Inc.*, B-286044.2; B-286044.3, 11/1/00.

[31] *Pacific Architects & Eng'rs, Inc.*, B-262243; B-262243.2, 12/12/95, 95-2 CPD ¶253 at 7-8.

[32] *Battelle Memorial Institute*, B-278673, 2/27/98.

[33] *Neal R. Gross & Co., Inc.*, B-275066, 1/17/97, 97-1 CPD ¶30 at 4.

[34] *George A. and Peter A. Palivos*, B-245878.2; B-245878.3, 3/16/92, 92-1 CPD ¶286 at 10.

[35] See also *Commercial Bldg. Serv.*, B-237865.2; B-237865.3, 5/16/90, 90-1 CPD ¶473 at 6.

[36] *Phillips Nat'l, Inc.*, B-253875, 11/1/93, 93-2 CPD ¶252 at 6.

Chapter 5

Pre-Award: Evaluating Past Performance

by Peter S. Cole

Evaluating past performance differs from evaluating the other quality evaluation factors (such as technical, management, and prior experience), which are evaluated in accordance with the criteria set forth in the RFP, based only on what the offeror has stated in its proposal. If something is not in the proposal, it is not evaluated (except for prior experience, where the evaluators may check the referenced contracts to verify the type of work done, generally by a telephone call).

Past performance, however, while evaluated in accordance with the criteria set forth in the RFP, is based on information gathered from sources outside of the proposal. While the offeror is required to provide references to past contracts in its proposal and to explain how the work under the referenced contracts relates to the proposed effort, the primary information-gathering emphasis is on reference checking to verify the offeror's claims about its past performance and queries to other sources regarding the offeror's past performance.

Section M of the RFP sets forth the criteria to use in evaluating past performance. These criteria should be applied considering the factors that affect a contractor's performance as explained in Chapter 4. However, when conducting the evaluation, a number of specific areas concerning the evaluation warrant particular attention. These areas have been the subject of numerous protests, and both government and contractor personnel should be aware of the potential pitfalls and how to avoid them. They are:

- Checking references

- Using information close at hand

- Using personal knowledge

- Allowing offerors to rebut adverse past performance information

86 PAST PERFORMANCE HANDBOOK

- Applying rating systems

- Documenting the evaluation findings.

CHECKING REFERENCES

Evaluators cannot simply accept the offeror's word on its past performance without some kind of verification. Generally, this involves contacting the past performance references provided by the offeror and verifying the information, as well as checking other available sources. Chapter 3 addresses the process of checking references; this section addresses some of the problems encountered and suggests possible solutions.

Checking past performance references provided by offerors is time-consuming. You must contact the references, ask questions, receive the answers, and sort it all out. This process can be facilitated by limiting the number of references offerors must provide or simply by not contacting all of the references. Will you get in trouble if you fail to contact all of the references? That depends on the circumstances outlined in Example 5.1.

Example 5.1 — Must all past performance references be checked?[1]

The Comptroller General has consistently ruled that there is no requirement that an agency contact all the references an offeror provides.

The protester objects to the agency's inability to contact the two other references. The agency, however, is only required to make a reasonable effort to contact the references, and it is not objectionable to evaluate an offeror's past performance on less than the maximum possible number of references the agency could have received. See IGIT, Inc.[2] (although agencies are required to evaluate the past performance of all offerors on the same basis, there is no general requirement that an agency contact all of an offeror's references, or contact the same number of references for each offeror).

Note that in Example 5.1, the Comptroller General indicated that an agency must make a reasonable effort to contact references and that there is no requirement to contact all references. This should be taken to mean that: (1) if an agency makes a reasonable attempt to contact a reference but with no success, the agency is not *required* to make repeated attempts or to take unusual steps to contact the reference; and (2) an agency may check some, but not necessarily all, references provided by an offeror.

The key to an acceptable past performance evaluation is not how many references are checked, but how well the evaluation is conducted, i.e., the evaluation process must result in a well-informed and reasonable evaluation of an offeror's past performance. The Comptroller General's position on the requirement to check all references is probably best summed up by following:[3]

> There is no legal requirement that all past performance references listed in an offeror's proposal be checked or included in a valid review of past performance.[4] Rather, what is critical is whether the evaluation is conducted fairly, reasonably, and in accordance with the stated evaluation criteria, and whether it is based upon relevant information sufficient to make a reasonable determination of the offeror's overall past performance rating, including relevant information close at hand or known by the contracting personnel awarding the contract.[5]

While there is no *requirement* that all references be contacted, an allegation of poor past performance is a sore point with contractors and a protest is likely if an offeror feels that it was not treated fairly in the past performance evaluation. A good-faith effort should be made to contact as many references as possible, considering the evaluation resources available.

Evaluating past performance for a comparative assessment ordinarily requires more information than required when evaluating past performance in terms of responsibility. Responsibility determinations center on negative areas (such as late deliveries, a failure to deliver, and a failure to meet contract requirements) that generally can be assessed objectively. Evaluating for a comparative assessment requires more detail, such as the reasons that problems occurred and whether they have been corrected, and focuses on both positive and negative areas. Generally, the procedure for checking references involves sending questionnaires to the contracting agencies referenced. Example 5.2 addresses what happens when the questionnaires are not returned.

Example 5.2—What happens when past performance questionnaires are not returned?[6]

The RFP required offerors to identify past contracts for review, but offerors were told not to provide general information about their performance of the contracts, as the agency would obtain this information directly from the references. The awardee referenced three prior DOE contracts, and all of the references returned the past performance questionnaires. The protester referenced two current DOE contracts and one from another agency. When none of the protester's references returned the past performance questionnaires, the protester was awarded a neutral past performance rating (this was provided for in the RFP); however, the evaluation panel later converted the neutral rating to a score of 8 out of 10 possible points.

Despite ADC's arguments to the contrary, there is no legal requirement that all past performance references be included in a valid review of past performance.[7] For our Office to sustain a protest challenging the failure to obtain or consider a reference's

88 PAST PERFORMANCE HANDBOOK

assessment of past performance, a protester must show unusual factual circumstances that convert the failure to a significant inequity for the protester.[8] . . . In short, without a showing that the DOE evaluators here should have been aware of the assessments that would have been received, and without some other showing that an agency's evaluation was unreasonable, we deny this protest ground.

So, in general, if past performance questionnaires are not returned, the offeror is out of luck. However, this case presents some issues that, while dismissed in this instance, warrant some thought: (1) should DOE have refused to permit offerors to comment on their performance of the referenced contracts? and (2) should DOE have compelled the return of the questionnaires from at least the DOE components?

DOE prohibited offerors from commenting on their performance of the referenced contracts because it planned to obtain this information itself. DOE attempted to obtain the information from the protester's references, but none of them replied, thus giving the protester a neutral past performance rating as provided for in the RFP.

The protester argued that the neutral rating was unreasonable because FAR Subpart 42.15 requires agencies to share past performance information, and DOE should have taken action to compel return of the questionnaires. The Comptroller General dismissed this argument on the grounds that one of the references was an agency not covered by the FAR and the other two references were current DOE contracts for which no interim past performance reports had been completed. Because the completion of interim reports was voluntary, there was no requirement for such information to be available.

The Comptroller General's finding is correct, but it begs the question of whether an agency should do more to obtain responses from within the agency. This is not a question for the Comptroller General to decide. What was involved here was not whether an interim contractor performance report was required, but whether a response to an interagency past performance questionnaire should have been required. There is no indication that the DOE contracting component tried very hard to compel the return of the questionnaires. It is suggested, however, that contracting officers ought to be more aggressive when dealing within their own agency. Possibly the evaluators thought so, too, because they later translated the protester's neutral rating to a favorable score of 8 out of 10 available points. This eliminated any possible harm to the protester in evaluating the past performance evaluation factor.

Should an agency prohibit offerors from commenting on the quality of their performance on referenced contracts? It is suggested that offerors should be encouraged, not discouraged, to make such comments (except perhaps when the offeror is submitting relevant contractor performance reports that contain the offeror's contemporaneous comments). One of the best indications of a problem is when the offeror and the responding agency differ significantly in their assessment of the offeror's past performance. In these situations, the responding agency should be queried again to validate its initial response. Here, DOE deprived itself of this information. The result was a protest, and, although the agency won, it still had to devote time and resources to respond to the protest.

To gather sufficient information to evaluate past performance properly, the RFP should require offerors to: (1) show how the referenced contracts relate to

Pre-Award: Evaluating Past Performance   **89**

the current effort, (2) identify any problems with the referenced contracts, (3) show how these problems were or will be corrected, and (4) otherwise indicate how well they performed. This information is directly relevant to evaluating past performance and provides a basis for the verification.

USING INFORMATION CLOSE AT HAND

Don't get complacent—the fact that you are not required to check all references does not let you off the hook if there is other information "close at hand," as shown in Example 5.3.

Example 5.3—You must consider past performance information close at hand (#1).[9]

While agencies generally need not evaluate all past performance references or those not reflected in the proposals, our Office has recognized that in certain limited circumstances an agency evaluating an offeror's past performance has an obligation (as opposed to the discretion) to consider "outside information" bearing on an offeror's past performance.[10] Where we have charged an agency with responsibility for considering such outside information, the record has demonstrated that the information in question was "simply too close at hand to require offerors to shoulder the inequities that spring from an agency's failure to obtain, and consider, the information.[11] See GTS Duratck, Inc.[12] (agency should have considered offeror's past performance of a prior contract where the contract discussed in the offeror's past performance proposal was so relevant as to have served as the basis for the government estimate for the subject solicitation, and the contracting officer's technical representative for the contract was a member of the technical evaluation team for the subject solicitation); G. Marine Diesel[13] (contracting officer that was personally aware of the awardee's continuing difficulties in performing a contract for services related to the subject solicitation, and considered the performance difficulties relevant to the extent that the contracting officer determined not to exercise the options in the contract awarded under the subject solicitation, erred in not considering the awardee's performance difficulties when determining whether the contract under the subject solicitation had been properly awarded); G. Marine Diesel; Phillyship[14] (agency should have considered awardee's prior experience under a directly relevant contract where the contract was referenced in the awardee's proposal and the agency personnel were familiar with the awardee's performance). However, the "close at hand" information in these cases generally concerned contracts for the same services with the same procuring activity, or at least information personally known to the evaluators.[15]

An agency cannot overlook past performance information that is "close at hand." This term refers to information that is, or should be, known personally by the contracting officer or the evaluators. While an agency *may*, at its discretion, query outside sources about an offeror's past performance, it is *obligated* to review information close at hand.

90 PAST PERFORMANCE HANDBOOK

Note that in the Comptroller General quotation immediately following Example 5.1, the Comptroller General said, "What is critical is whether the evaluation is conducted fairly, reasonably, and in accordance with the stated evaluation criteria, and whether it is based upon relevant information sufficient to make a reasonable determination of the offeror's overall past performance rating, *including relevant information close at hand or known by the contracting personnel awarding the contract.*" If the RFP requires a minimum number of references and an offeror fails to provide the minimum, you must look to information close at hand or known by the contracting or evaluation personnel before downgrading or rejecting the proposal because the minimum number of references was not provided.

Example 5.4 illustrates the problems that arise when a contracting officer fails to consider past performance information close at hand simply because administrative procedures were not followed.

Example 5.4—You must consider past performance information close at hand (#2).[16]

A Veterans Administration (VA) RFP stated that award was to be made to the technically acceptable proposal determined to be most advantageous to the government based on price and past performance. Award was made to an offeror with an excellent past performance rating and the lowest price. The award was protested on the grounds of an unreasonable past performance evaluation. The protester argued that the awardee did not have the direct experience required to earn an excellent past performance rating.

In preparing a response to the protest, the contracting officer reevaluated the awardee's past performance and discovered that the protester was right—the awardee did not have any direct experience. The contracting officer took corrective action, giving the awardee a neutral past performance rating.

While reevaluating the protester's past performance, the contracting officer identified two VA references directly applicable to the solicitation. She considered only one of them, however, because the individual responsible for responding to the other past performance questionnaire failed to complete and return the questionnaire.

The contracting officer then compared the protester's good rating with the awardee's neutral rating and decided that both proposals were essentially equal in past performance. Because the awardee offered the lowest price, the contracting officer concluded that the initial award was proper. The protester argued that its past performance evaluation was improperly conducted because the contracting officer did not consider both references.

The Comptroller General agreed with the protester.

Where an RFP identifies past performance and price as the evaluation factors and indicates that an offeror with a better past performance record than that of another offeror can expect a higher past performance rating, proposals must be evaluated on that basis. The selection official, however, has the discretion to decide the appropriate tradeoff between past performance and price in determining which proposal represents the best value to the government.[17] Such a tradeoff is not precluded under an evaluation scheme specifying a "neutral" rating for vendors with no past performance record.[18]

Our disagreement with the agency springs from its overly mechanical application of its procedures for evaluating past performance. While the VA is correct in its view that there is no legal requirement that all past performance references be included in a valid review of past performance,[19] some information is simply too close at hand to require offerors to shoulder the inequities that spring from an agency's failure to obtain, and consider, the information.[20]

Here, the record shows that IBSI's proposal clearly identified a recent contract involving the same agency, the same services, and the same contracting officer, and asked that its performance of this contract be considered as part of its evaluation, as the solicitation anticipated and required. The record shows that the contracting officer was aware of IBSI's performance of this contract and had termed it "exemplary" in a letter to the SBA written barely 4 months before the award decision here. Under these circumstances, we conclude that the agency unreasonably failed to consider IBSI's performance on its earlier contract simply because an individual in the agency did not complete the assessment required. See G. Marine Diesel; Phillyship[21] (protest sustained where the Navy elected not to consider unsatisfactory past performance of awardee involving similar services and the same command because awardee did not include the controversial contract on its list of references for the past performance review).

In this case, the Comptroller General found that had the agency considered the second referenced contract, which was rated as "exemplary" performance," the contracting officer might not have found the two offerors essentially equal with respect to past performance and the tradeoff between price and past performance might have had a different result. The Comptroller General recommended that the agency redo the evaluation properly.

Examples 5.3 and 5.4 illustrate that there is no excuse for ignoring information close at hand. Note, however, that "close at hand" refers to information that the contracting officer knew about on a first-hand basis. A contracting officer is not expected to know about every contract the agency awarded. However, checking your own agency records to see if an offeror had previous contracts with your agency and how well such contracts were performed would be a sound practice.

USING PERSONAL KNOWLEDGE

Close-at-hand information is the personal knowledge of personnel involved in the evaluation process. This would include the personal knowledge of the assigned evaluators. Can an evaluator use his or her own personal knowledge

92 PAST PERFORMANCE HANDBOOK

about an offeror when evaluating past performance? The answer is yes—under certain circumstances—as illustrated in Example 5.5.

Example 5.5—An evaluator's personal knowledge may be used.[22]

A protester maintained that its proposal was improperly downgraded under past performance based on the undocumented personal knowledge of the evaluators. This allegation was based on narrative comments contained in the evaluation score sheets for two of the three evaluators, which stated, "info provided was responsive, but personal experience resulted in lower score."

The Comptroller General did not agree with the protester.

An evaluator's personal knowledge of an offeror may properly be considered in a past performance evaluation.[23] More specifically, where the solicitation provides for references to be used in the evaluation, as here, the agency may consider the unsatisfactory past performance of an offeror under a recent contract with the agency, thus, in effect, furnishing its own reference.[24] In an evaluation which takes into account the agency's own knowledge of offerors, the fundamental requirement that evaluation judgments be documented in sufficient detail to show that they are reasonable and not arbitrary still must be met.

Based on these numerous documented complaints about Omega's past performance, which were the basis of the personal knowledge of two of the evaluators, and which are undisputed by the protester, we have no basis to question the downgrading of Omega's proposal under past performance.

Evaluators may use their personal knowledge when evaluating past performance, but this must be documented sufficiently to show the origin of the information and the basis for the findings. An evaluator cannot, however, assume something based on third-party knowledge (i.e., other people said this firm performed poorly on some other contracts). Likewise, past performance evaluations cannot be based solely on a firm's reputation (i.e., this is a successful company, so it must be a good performer). You can use personal knowledge only when it is first-hand and can be documented.

An agency may base an evaluation of past performance on its reasonable perception of inadequate prior performance, regardless of whether the offeror disputes the agency's interpretation of the facts. If this is the case, the evaluators may downgrade the offeror's proposal and eliminate the offeror from the competitive range, as shown in Example 5.6.

Example 5.6—An agency's perception of poor past performance prevails when supported by sufficient evidence.[25]

The evaluators concluded that an offeror had a series of performance problems under prior contracts. The offeror was excluded from the competitive range and protested that the past performance evaluation was unfair.

The Comptroller General did not agree.

An agency's evaluation of past performance may be based upon the procuring agency's reasonable perception of inadequate prior performance, regardless of whether the contractor disputes the agency's interpretation of the facts.[26] This record affords us no basis upon which to object to the Navy's conclusion regarding QFI/Hampton Roads's past performance—that it produced some items of poor quality under prior contracts and could not, or would not, manufacture certain items which are the subject of this solicitation. While QFI offers explanations and interpretations of the record that provide a more favorable picture of its performance history than drawn by the agency, this does not alter the fact that there was sufficient evidence for the agency to conclude that the firm had a series of performance problems under its prior contracts.

We also conclude that QFI's proposal was reasonably excluded from the competitive range. Under the solicitation, past performance was considered significantly more important than price, and the agency was permitted to award to other than the lowest-priced offeror. Under this evaluation scheme, which placed paramount importance on past performance, it was a reasonable exercise of the agency's discretion to decide that a firm with an exceptional performance history (based on very favorable references and no deficiency reports) and a relatively low price would be the only firm with a reasonable chance for award when all other offerors had significantly higher prices and/or less attractive performance histories. This is particularly true since the agency's assessment of Tri-Way's past performance as exceptional is unchallenged. Since the agency reasonably concluded that QFI had no reasonable chance for award, the exclusion of its proposal from the competitive range is not legally objectionable.[27]

The protester, citing our decisions holding that agencies have the discretion to eliminate from the competitive range proposals which do not include information required by the solicitation,[28] suggests that agencies are required to eliminate such proposals from the competitive range. We disagree. The fact that an agency may eliminate a proposal from the competitive range for failure to include within the proposal information required by the solicitation does not mean the agency would be acting improperly if it included the proposal in the competitive range.[29]

This case makes two points about an agency's discretion. First, the agency has the discretion to eliminate an offeror from the competitive range if it determines that the offeror's past performance is so poor that it should not be included in the competitive range, even if the offeror disagrees with the determination. Second, the agency has the discretion to include an offeror in the competitive range if it determines that information deficiencies in the offeror's proposal are not so great as to warrant rejection. The agency must, however, have documented its determinations sufficiently to show that it has not abused its discretion.

Do not let the evaluation of past performance become a mechanical process—simply checking the boxes on a questionnaire or adding up scores. A respondent's report on past performance can be subjective and sometimes self-serving. Checking more than one or two references will provide a broader picture of an offeror's ability to perform. There is, of course, a practical limit on the number of references that you can effectively check during the evaluation process. If you have multiple offerors with multiple references, the past performance evaluation is going to bog down and adversely affect the efficiency of the evaluation process. So, what to do? As noted earlier, one solution is to establish a minimum number of references to be provided (generally at least three references per offeror) and indicate that excess references may or may not be checked. In such instances you should make a good-faith effort to check at least the minimum number of references. Or, as noted in Chapter 3, you could establish a minimum number of references to be submitted and make the offerors responsible for conducting the reference check and submitting the completed past performance questionnaires with their proposals.

In the initial evaluation, negative past performance information generally draws more attention than positive information. However, you need to ensure the validity of the negative reports before making any decisions.

ALLOWING OFFERORS TO REBUT ADVERSE PAST PERFORMANCE INFORMATION

An agency's report on an offeror's past performance can be subjective and sometimes addresses adverse information not known to the offeror. You can level the playing field, however, by providing offerors an opportunity to rebut adverse past performance information, whether the information originates from the references provided or from other sources.

With respect to the pre-award evaluation of past performance, the FAR does not use the term "rebut"; it uses instead the terms "clarify" and "comment." When award will be made without discussions, the FAR[30] states that offerors may be given the opportunity to *clarify* adverse past performance information to which the offeror has not previously had an opportunity to respond. With respect to competitive solicitations where discussions will be held, the FAR[31] states that communications shall be held with offerors whose past performance information is a determining factor preventing them from being placed in the competitive range when the offeror has not had a prior opportunity to *comment* on such information.

The term "rebut" is used here because it more clearly expresses what an offeror must do in response to adverse past performance information. If an offeror is not able to rebut or otherwise account for the adverse information, its chance for award is diminished significantly.

What the Government Should Do

Offerors are reluctant to accept a determination that they are poor performers. Likewise, government officials may be reluctant to admit to another government agency that their actions contributed to an offeror's poor performance. A finding of poor past performance can easily degenerate into a dispute over facts and result in a protest that the offeror has not been treated fairly.

The likelihood of such protests might be minimized, however, if offerors are notified of adverse past performance information and allowed to rebut it when the adverse information might be an important factor in an award without discussions or a competitive range decision. While this might add a few days to the procurement process, a protest (even when the agency wins) will cause even greater disruption.

Note that rebuttals of adverse past performance information do not involve any changes to the proposal but merely the provision of explanatory information. The offeror is given one chance to reply in writing, and these comments must be considered in any decisions to be made. No discussions, proposal changes, or submittal of new references are allowed.

When using past performance as an evaluation factor first became a preferred practice and protests mounted, the Comptroller General ruled that when adverse past performance information was received from a reference that the offeror had provided in its proposal, the government had no obligation to permit the offeror to comment on the adverse information. The Comptroller General viewed such information as historical in nature, and the protester would be unlikely to be able to make a significant contribution to its interpretation, as shown in Example 5.7.

Example 5.7 — Past performance viewed as historical in nature[32]

To the extent Centrex objects to the downgrading of its proposal based on unfavorable information obtained from Centrex's references, where, as part of the technical evaluation of offers, offerors have been required to furnish references on prior experience and are aware that these references may be contacted, the contracting agency may consider the replies of the references without being required to seek the offeror's comments concerning the information. We view this information as essentially historical in nature and protester is unlikely to be able to make a significant contribution to its interpretation.[33]

Note that this decision is itself historical in nature because the FAR 15 rewrite[34] now *permits* offerors to be notified of adverse past performance information if award is to be made without discussions and *requires* such communications before establishment of the competitive range when discussions will be held. The Comptroller General has not objected to the FAR coverage.

Example 5.7 makes the point that while poor past performance is indeed a historical matter and cannot be changed, the cause of the poor performance is subject to interpretation. Even a late delivery, which is a factual matter, can be interpreted as excusable under certain circumstances. To assume that poor past performance information is not subject to interpretation misses the point of the evaluation of past performance. The fact of a problem is important, but just as important is why it happened, if it was corrected, and if it is likely to affect the prospective performance. It is not a good practice to accept negative past performance information without looking at the circumstances, particularly when other sources have provided positive past performance information.

Generally, it is not a good idea to refuse an offeror the opportunity to rebut adverse past performance reports found during the initial evaluation when the adverse information may have a significant effect on the offeror's competitive position. FAR 15.306(b)(4) recognizes this in part in its statement that communications (before the establishment of the competitive range) shall address adverse past performance information to which the offeror has not previously had an opportunity to comment.

This FAR reference could be interpreted to mean that the contracting officer does not have to address adverse information from references provided by the offeror (particularly if the RFP has requested that offerors comment on any performance problems involved in the referenced contracts) because the offeror has already had a chance to comment on such problems in its proposal. However, despite the requirements of FAR 42.15 (which requires reports on a contractor's performance), an offeror does not always know how an agency has rated its past performance. Contractors are not necessarily informed of all problems, particularly if the contract is satisfactorily completed. These problems may, however, be mentioned in response to later queries about the contractor's performance. Permitting offerors to rebut adverse information may well avoid a protest on these grounds.

It should be noted here that there is a potential problem with the use of contractor performance reports as source selection information. Lacking a standard government-wide reporting form, agency contractor performance reports may vary significantly in the amount of information provided. In addition to a contractor's performance rating, there are two other requirements for a valid contractor performance report. One is a narrative explanation supporting the rating assigned, and the other is the contractor's comments on the initial evaluation. A contractor performance report without this information would require the evaluators simply to accept the agency's assigned rating on its face value. It is not clear how the Comptroller General might rule on a protest that a contractor performance report with only a rating and no supporting information lacks a sufficient basis for use in evaluating a contractor's past performance. The OFPP guide,[35] however, provides a sample form for the contractor performance evaluation report that could be used to avoid this potential problem.

When offered the opportunity to respond to adverse past performance information, the offeror is responsible for providing a successful explanation of the poor past performance. If the offeror fails to do this, you are not required to pursue the matter further, as shown in Example 5.8.

Example 5.8—Offeror must successfully rebut adverse past performance information.[36]

An award was made to the offeror with the lowest performance risk because the technical and management ratings were equal and the lower performance risk offset the relatively small difference in price.

The protester listed three contracts to support its performance record. For two of the contracts, the past performance reports indicated good performance, but there were no specific strong points to report. The other contract was with an Army installation that responded with a negative report.

After receiving the negative performance report, the contracting agency permitted the protester to submit a rebuttal. The protester responded, but only with general allegations of corrective action. The protester failed to provide specific information about the nature of the deficiencies or their resolution. The contracting agency contacted the Army installation three more times in an attempt to reconcile the differences between its report and the protester's response. The Army installation's replies did not bring up any significant new information, and the protester was not advised of these contacts.

The protester argued that its proposal was not fairly evaluated because it was not informed of these additional contacts and permitted to comment on what the Army installation had said.

The Comptroller General did not agree.

While Dragon offers general denials of the statements made by Fort Bragg contracting officials, as well as explanations and interpretations of the record that provide a more favorable picture of Dragon's activities than drawn by the Army, this does not alter the fact that there was sufficient evidence for the Army to conclude that the firm had a series of performance problems under the Fort Bragg contract. An agency's evaluation of past performance may be based upon the procuring agency's reasonable perception of inadequate prior performance, even where the contractor disputes the agency's interpretation of the facts. [37]

In this case the contracting agency went out of its way to ensure a fair evaluation, as evidenced by the fact that after the initial negative response, the agency contacted the Army installation three more times in an attempt to reconcile its negative report with the response by the protester. The Army installation did not change its position, so the evaluators were faced with one negative performance report and two positive reports. In light of the negative report (and no information from the protester indicating that the problems were resolved), the agency could not reasonably rate the performance as

98   Past Performance Handbook

low risk, and the two positive reports (one on a current contract) precluded a rating of high risk. A rating of moderate risk was the only reasonable choice. With technical and management equal and a minimal price difference, award was properly made to another offeror on the basis of lowest performance risk.

The real problem in this case was that when given the opportunity to rebut the initial negative findings, the offeror failed to respond fully. If the offeror fails to respond appropriately, the evaluators are not required to pursue the matter further.

It is the offeror's responsibility to support its proposal fully. When adverse comments are made about an offeror's past performance, the offeror must completely rebut such comments with proof, not generalized, self-serving statements. The offeror must show how the adverse comments are not applicable or that the problems have been resolved and will not recur. If the offeror fails to do this in its response to the notification of adverse past performance information, you should consider the problem unresolved and downgrade the proposal accordingly.

What The Offeror Should Do

When the government identifies negative past performance information, you must respond with positive information, not generalizations, excuses, or promises. You must specifically address each negative comment. Generally, you will be afforded only one opportunity to explain past problems, so you need to get it right the first time.

If the Adverse Information Is Correct

If the adverse information is correct, your response must show how the problems have been or will be corrected, or, if applicable, how the reported problems will not affect the prospective performance. (This might apply, for example, if the problems involved a part of your company that will not be involved with the prospective contract.) If the problems have been corrected, you must explain what corrective action you took and how such action ensures that the problem will not recur (see Examples 4.1 and 4.2).

If you fail to show in your initial rebuttal that the problems were corrected (either through communications before the establishment of the competitive range or discussions after establishment of the competitive range), the government has no choice but to consider the problem unresolved and likely to recur. Contemporaneous documentation showing how the problem was, or will be, resolved (such as records you kept during contract performance or letters from government personnel involved with the contract and written during contract performance) will bolster your rebuttal significantly.

If the Adverse Information Is Not Correct

If you disagree with the adverse past performance information or feel that the government was directly or indirectly responsible for the problems, you must prove your case with facts, not allegations or generalized statements. In particular, do not allege bias on the part of government personnel unless you can prove it with evidence sufficient to take to court. It is important that you address each allegation of poor past performance. Any point not addressed will be considered a tacit admission that the allegation is correct.

You must show that the allegations were incorrect or that the problems were beyond your control (caused by third parties, the government, acts of God, etc.) and should not be considered adverse past performance information. Again, contemporaneous documentation that supports your position would be of significant help. If you cannot provide contemporaneous documentation to prove your case, you are less likely to prevail. However, in the absence of contemporaneous documentation, a fact-based argument supported by written statements from personnel involved in the performance of the contract can help make your case.

APPLYING RATING SYSTEMS

Chapter 2 addresses some of the considerations related to selecting a rating or scoring system to use in evaluating past performance. Applying the rating systems during the evaluation is another matter. The evaluation of an offeror's past performance is not so much an assessment of how the offeror performed as an assessment of how the offeror's performance was viewed by the contracting agencies for whom the offeror performed past contracts.

Initially, what you will see is an evaluation of an offeror's past performance as viewed by a third party. Past performance information comes in the form of statements and references provided by the offeror (which must be verified), contractor performance reports from other agencies, information close at hand or other information from within your agency, and responses to questionnaires sent to other contracting agencies or commercial sources doing business with the offeror, requesting information on the offeror's performance.

This information must be reviewed, assessed, queried as necessary, and consolidated into whatever rating system you are using. As noted in Chapter 4, you must assess the currency and relevance of the information, weigh the source of the information, examine the context of the data, and assess the general trend of the offerors' performances. You should not simply accept the ratings or evaluations of third parties without examining the accompanying evaluation narratives to ensure that they are in context with the assigned ratings. If they are not in context or are otherwise questionable, go back to the respondent and question the rating. If no evaluation narratives are provided, you should verify the ratings assigned. Keep in mind that you must consider the general trend of an offeror's past performance; a single negative report on an offeror with an otherwise good record should be questioned to determine the degree to which this report should affect your overall assessment of the offeror's performance.

For example, an offeror has one negative report because of a late delivery; the other reports indicate superior performance. Instead of automatically lowering this offeror's past performance rating, you should examine the circumstances of the negative report to determine the likelihood of a recurrence of the delivery problem. If the problem is recent and uncorrected, this could have a significant affect on your evaluation. If the problem is not recent and, even if uncorrected, is not likely to recur, then it should not have a significant effect on the evaluation. Past performance evaluations made by third parties are not necessarily equal in importance. Your evaluation should be a considered assessment centered on the likelihood of recurrence, not simply a mathematical exercise.

The following quotation from a Comptroller General decision[38] points out the requirement to examine the circumstances related to past performance and not to rely simply on numbers or scores:

> It is undisputed that more weight was to be accorded more recent competitive ranking data and that OSI's most recent CPCS ranking trended downward, and it is undisputed that OSI's performance was erratic over the course of the contract based upon its CPCS rankings. However, the agency's reliance on these rankings to argue that OSI has not been prejudiced perpetuates the central flaw in this past performance evaluation: the agency's failure to review relevant performance data in its possession and to make reasoned judgments as to its value to arrive at an accurate assessment of each offeror's past performance. Since the agency's past performance evaluation did not comply with the stated evaluation terms, the CPCS scores alone are an inadequate indicator of overall past performance without consideration of the circumstances and underlying performance data; the agency has not adequately supported its past performance evaluation of offerors, both on an individual and a relative basis; since OSI has otherwise very high scores and a positive evaluation, we conclude that the source selection cannot be viewed as reasonable and that the protester was prejudiced by the agency's actions.

In the case cited, the agency not only failed to follow the RFP's evaluation scheme, but it relied on a rating system that was designed for other purposes and not for the evaluation of overall past performance. A past performance evaluation that does not consider the circumstances of poor past performance and their implications in relation to the prospective performance is not likely to be considered reasonable.

While past performance evaluations initially concentrate on negative findings, do not lose sight of the need to identify positive aspects of an offeror's past performance. Such information could be a deciding factor in a tradeoff determination when making the final source selection. Queries to third parties should always solicit comments on the positive aspects of an offeror's past performance.

The information collected must be evaluated in accordance with whatever scoring or rating system you have elected to use. The three most commonly used rating schemes are: numerical systems, color coding systems, and performance risk assessments.

Numerical Systems

If a numerical rating or scoring system is used, guidance must be provided to the evaluators on how to apply the system. Generally, numerical systems are established with a scoring range, an adjectival rating for that range, and a narrative description or standard to be met to get a score within that range. Figure 5.1 is an example of how this might be done.

Figure 5.1 Numerical Scoring

90–100	Excellent—Met or exceeded all requirements, provided improved performance/quality results. Timely or accelerated delivery. Contractor exceptionally cooperative. Only minor problems, which were quickly corrected in a responsive and highly effective manner. Effective cost control, came within or underran budget. No significant cost issues.
80–89	Very Good—Met all quality and delivery requirements. Contractor highly cooperative. Any problems corrected in a responsive and effective manner. Effective cost control, came within budget, quickly resolved cost issues.
70–79	Good—Met basic quality and delivery requirements. Contractor reasonably cooperative. Satisfactory correction of problems. Satisfactory cost control and resolution of cost issues.
50–69	Fair—Did not meet all requirements, quality/delivery performance barely acceptable. Contractor not always responsive to problems. Some problems not effectively corrected. Cost control barely satisfactory, cost issues not effectively resolved.
0–49	Poor—Did not meet basic quality/delivery requirements, performance considered unsatisfactory. Contractor not cooperative or responsive to problems, major problems remain unresolved. Cost control inadequate, cost problems not satisfactorily resolved.
—	Neutral—No past performance history

---

102 PAST PERFORMANCE HANDBOOK

Rating systems are established before issuing the RFP and should address only those past performance subfactors cited in the RFP. In the Figure 5.1 example, the rating descriptions address the four basic past performance evaluation areas—quality, schedule, cost control, and business relations. So, this should work well, right? Well, not necessarily.

First, there is the problem of varying sources of information that may or may not be in a format that would allow for an analysis of each evaluation area, i.e., the information received may not address all of the subfactors used in the current RFP. Also, if the past performance information does not contain an evaluation narrative with details necessary to support the assigned ratings, it will be difficult to translate this information into your rating system.

In addition, assigning numerical scores to varying information sources conveys a preciseness that may be misleading; for example, what is the real difference between a score of 88 and a score of 90? Numerical scores are only guides for the evaluators to point out differences between proposals and cannot be used as the basis for decisions. Decisions must be made based on the narrative explanations supporting the scores or rating assigned. It should be noted that documenting an evaluation using only the wording of the definitions provided for each score/rating is not a sufficient explanation for the scores assigned. The narrative explanation must show its relationship to specific proposal information (or lack thereof). Without a definitive narrative, numerical scoring may be difficult to apply.

A numerical scoring system works adequately when used to identify poor past performance, but it does not work as well in distinguishing the most highly rated proposals. In evaluating past performance, is it necessary to identify the best of the best? Superior past performance is only an indicator, not a guarantee, that an offeror will perform as well on the prospective contract. A rating system that attempts to distinguish between Exceptional, Very Good, and Good, based on an evaluations by third parties may be assigning more significance to the adjectival ratings than warranted.

The numerical system demonstrated by Figure 5.1 is not the only numerical system available. For example, GSA used a different type of system in its evaluation of past performance in a solicitation for landscape maintenance services.[39] GSA contacted the references provided by the offerors and asked them seven questions, four of which were past performance questions dealing with: (1) overall rating of performance on a 1 (poor) to 5 (excellent) scale, (2) timeliness of performance, (3) any problems with performance, and (4) positive or negative performance factors regarding personnel qualifications and performance. When evaluating the responses, GSA used the same numerical scale as used on the questionnaires (1 = poor to 5 = excellent). In applying this scale, GSA rated positive comments such as "good employees, responsive" and "good personnel," as well as affirmative responses regarding timeliness and absence of performance problems as 5s. To arrive at a final numerical score for each offeror, the scores for each of the performance questions were averaged. This was a simple but effective scheme.

While the numerical scoring system in Figure 5.1 might look good on paper, its practical value is questionable, particularly if the past performance information comes from a variety of sources using differing formats and providing different information. Note that the GSA scheme mentioned above worked because the only sources used were the responses from its questionnaires, which required narrative responses. It is not certain how well the scheme would have worked had the information come from disparate sources that did not address all of GSA's questions.

Generally, the value of a numerical system depends on the agency's ability to control the information sources and receive responses to uniform questions. This may be difficult, however, when dealing with contractor performance reports from different agencies that use varying evaluation criteria.

Color Coding Systems

As with numerical scoring, when a color coding system is used, guidance must be provided to the evaluators as to how to apply the system. A color coding system is similar to a numerical system in that it uses a color code (instead of a numerical range), an adjectival rating for that code, and a narrative description or standard to be met to receive each color code. Figure 5.2 offers an example of how this might be done.

Figure 5.2 Color Coding

Blue = Exceptional—Met or exceeded all requirements, provided improved performance/quality results. Timely or accelerated delivery. Contractor exceptionally cooperative. Only minor problems, which were quickly corrected in a responsive and highly effective manner. Effective cost control, came within or underran budget. No significant cost issues.

Green = Acceptable—Met quality and delivery requirements. Contractor reasonably cooperative. Satisfactory correction of problems. Satisfactory cost control and resolution of cost issues.

Yellow = Marginal—Did not meet all requirements, quality/delivery performance barely acceptable. Contractor not always responsive to problems. Some problems not effectively corrected. Cost control barely satisfactory, cost issues not effectively resolved.

Red = Unacceptable—Did not meet basic quality/delivery requirements, performance considered unsatisfactory. Contractor not cooperative or responsive to problems, major problems remain unresolved. Cost control inadequate, cost problems not satisfactorily resolved.

Gray = Neutral—No past performance history.

In Figure 5.2 the narrative description for each color code addresses the four basic past performance subfactors, but as with the numerical system, only descriptors related to the actual subfactors cited in the RFP should be used. Color coding provides a broader evaluation range (four instead of five evaluation areas, not including the required neutral rating), and the absence of numbers eliminates the implied precision of numerical scoring. The major difference is that this system does not try to identify the best of the best; on the plus side, really good past performance gets an exceptional rating, and the rest are simply acceptable. This is good.

However, on the minus side, color coding systems usually use both marginal and unacceptable color codes, and the utility of having two ranges below acceptable is questionable with respect to past performance. In terms of being eligible for award, what is the real difference between marginal and unacceptable? It would probably be more effective to eliminate the unacceptable code and simply evaluate offerors with less than acceptable past performance as marginal (a rating that might be more acceptable to offerors than unacceptable). Where past performance is a significant evaluation factor, an offeror with marginal past performance is not likely to be considered among the most highly rated proposals.

Color coding is more appropriate in the evaluation of past performance than numerical scoring but still suffers from the need to gather a lot of information, which may or may not be available from the third-party sources. Both the numerical and the color coding systems suffer from another problem: The third party sources may have used different scoring systems, which will have to be translated into the system you are using.

As with numerical scoring, evaluation narratives are required to support the color ratings assigned. The narratives must relate the problems (or strengths) found in the initial past performance evaluation to the rating assigned and its definition. An evaluation narrative using only the wording of the definitions provided for each rating is not a sufficient explanation for the rating assigned.

Performance Risk Assessments

Evaluating past performance as performance risk is an effective evaluation technique. Performance risk relates to the evaluation of an offeror's current and past performance to assess the degree of confidence to be accorded to the offeror's ability to perform a prospective contract successfully. Performance risk is inherent in the evaluation of past performance and could be evaluated even if not listed as a specific evaluation factor. With respect to evaluating third party evaluations, the broad range of the risk evaluation lends itself to the assessment of varying information sources. Figure 5.3 shows how performance risk might be evaluated.

Figure 5.3 Performance Risk

High Risk—Significant doubt exists, based on the offeror's performance record, that the offeror can perform the proposed effort.

Moderate Risk—Some doubt exists, based on the offeror's performance record, that the offeror can perform the proposed effort.

Low Risk—Little doubt exists, based on the offeror's performance record, that the offeror can perform the proposed effort.

Unknown—No performance history.

Generally, performance risk is evaluated using only three broad rating ranges (plus an unknown or neutral rating). These ranges lend themselves to a risk analysis rather than detailed scoring. A risk analysis relates the strengths or weaknesses of the offeror's past performance to the likelihood of successful performance on the prospective contract. Performance risk analysis should consider the number and severity of problems, the effectiveness of corrective action taken, any demonstrated strengths, and the offeror's overall work record. The assessment of performance risk is not a simple arithmetic function of an offeror's performance on a list of contracts, but should focus on the information deemed most relevant and significant to the offeror's likely performance on the prospective contract.

As noted earlier, the primary virtue of a performance risk analysis is that it is not impeded by varying information sources. Each source can be evaluated based on the information provided without having to contend with differing

106 PAST PERFORMANCE HANDBOOK

scoring systems. Basically, all a contracting officer really needs to know is: (1) which offeror's past performance is rated as high risk (generally eliminated in the competitive range determination) and (2) which are low or moderate risk (generally dealt with in tradeoffs to determine the best value). Trying to identify the best of the best with respect to past performance is not a productive exercise (see Example 6.1).

DOCUMENTING THE EVALUATION FINDINGS

The need to document fully all evaluation activity cannot be stressed enough. The initial evaluation findings by the individual evaluators and the evaluation team's consensus evaluation findings that provide the basis for the competitive range determination, the competitive range determination itself, and the final evaluations that support the evaluators' award recommendation must be documented and retained in the contract file. This documentation provides an audit trail to the factors that support the decisions made during the initial and final evaluation process and serves as the basis for the source selection official's tradeoff and final award decisions.

Proper documentation is particularly important with respect to the evaluation of past performance because much of the information used comes from sources outside of the proposal itself. Past performance information provided by the offeror must be verified, agency contract records must be checked, contractor performance reports from other agencies must be examined, and, when appropriate, third parties must be queried about an offeror's past performance. All of this must be fully documented and retained in the contract files.

Instances of poor performance as well as strong performance should be recorded. Documenting poor performance is important in determining the competitive range. Documenting strong points is important for tradeoff decisions and the source selection decision, where the strong points of an offeror's past performance may be a significant discriminator in determining the best value. Note that tradeoff decisions are made based on the narrative evaluations, not adjectival ratings, numerical scores, or color codes—all the more reason to document fully the evaluation, regardless of the scoring system used.

When evaluating a best-value procurement, you are always subject to unintended consequences. The least important evaluation factor may become the deciding factor if all of the other factors are rated as essentially equal. The best way to deal with this potential problem is to ensure that the evaluation results are fully documented, particularly with respect to the evaluation of the differences between the proposals. The differences between proposals, or lack thereof, are often the basis for identifying the proposal offering the best value.

AVOIDING PROBLEMS

There is no sure way to avoid problems when evaluating an offeror's past performance. Offerors are not likely to simply accept a report of poor past performance if this is the primary factor in their exclusion from the competitive range or failure to receive the award. The following, however, may help minimize problems with offerors when evaluating past performance.

1. The RFP should warn offerors that they must address instances of performance problems in referenced contracts and explain how these problems were resolved. Indicate that a failure to explain past performance problems satisfactorily will have an adverse effect on the evaluation of past performance.

2. The RFP also should advise offerors to submit information on any awards or commendations received regarding their past performance, as these could have a positive effect on the past performance evaluation.

3. Adverse past performance information identified during the initial evaluation—both that concerning referenced contracts and that identified by other sources—should be revealed to the offeror if the adverse information might affect the offeror's competitive standing. The offeror should be afforded the opportunity to rebut such information before an award without discussions or the establishment of the competitive range, even though this is not required by the FAR.

4. Past performance problems not resolved before establishment of the competitive range should be treated as significant weaknesses and addressed during discussions.

5. All past performance evaluations must be fully documented. Make note of any strong points found, as well as any adverse past performance information and the offeror's response to such information.

6. It is not necessary to open another round of discussions to address past performance problems first identified during discussions. You should advise offerors to address such issues in their final proposal revisions.

7. If offerors do not satisfactorily explain how past performance problems were resolved in their final proposal revisions, you should consider the problems to be unresolved and likely to recur.

8. Do not reopen discussions to address past performance problems first revealed in an offeror's final proposal revisions. The receipt of final proposal

108 PAST PERFORMANCE HANDBOOK

revisions marks the end of discussions. Reopening discussions after receiving the final proposal revisions is done only in extreme circumstances to avoid making an improper award.

NOTES

[1] *Universal Building Maintenance, Inc.*, B-282456, 7/15/99, fn 2.

[2] *IGIT, Inc.*, B-275299.2, 6/23/97, 97-2 CPD ¶7 at 6.

[3] *U.S. Technology Corp.*, B-278584, 2/17/98.

[4] *Dragon Servs., Inc.*, B-255354, 2/25/94, 94-1 CPD ¶151 at 8; *Questech, Inc.*, B-236028, 11/1/89, 89-2 CPD ¶407 at 3.

[5] *Int'l Bus. Sys., Inc.*, B-275554, 3/3/97, 97-1 CPD ¶114 at 5.

[6] *Advanced Data Concepts, Inc.*, B-277801.4, 6/1/98, GCR 110,318.

[7] *Dragon Servs., Inc.*, B-255354, 2/25/94, 94-1 CPD ¶151 at 8; *Questech Inc.*, B-236028, 11/1/89, 89-2 CPD ¶407 at 3.

[8] *International Bus. Sys., Inc.*, B-275554, 3/3/97, 97-1 CPD ¶114 at 5, GCR 109,877.

[9] *TRW, Inc.*, B-282162; B-282162.2, 6/9/99.

[10] *International Bus. Sys., Inc.*, B-275554, 3/3/97, 97-1 CPD ¶114 at 5, GCR 109,877.

[11] Ibid.

[12] *GTS Duratck, Inc.*, B-280511.2; B-280511.3, 10/19/98, 98-2 CPD ¶130 at 14.

[13] *G. Marine Diesel*, B-231619.3, 8/3/89, 89-2 CPD ¶101 at 4-6.

[14] *G. Marine Diesel; Phillyship*, B-232619; B-232619.2, 1/27/89, 89-1 CPD ¶90 at 4-5.

[15] *Morrison Knudsen Corp.*, B-280261, 9/9/98, 98-2 CPD ¶63 at 5-6.

[16] *International Bus. Sys., Inc.*, B-275554, 3/3/97, 97-1 CPD ¶114 at 5, GCR 109,877.

[17] *Excalibur Sys. Inc.*, B-272017, 7/12/96, 96-2 CPD ¶13 at 3.

[18] *Engineering and Computation Inc.*, B-275180.2, 1/29/97, 97-1 CPD ¶47 at 4-5; *Excalibur Sys. Inc.*, supra.

[19] *Dragon Servs., Inc.*, B-255354, 2/25/94, 94-1 CPD ¶151 at 8; *Questech Inc.*, B-236028, 11/1/89, 89-2 CPD ¶407 at 3.

[20] *G. Marine Diesel*, 68 Comp. Gen. 577 (1989), 89-2 CPD ¶101 at 5-6; *New Hampshire-Vermont Health Serv.*, 57 Comp. Gen. 347 (1978), 78-1 CPD ¶202 at 12-13; *Continental Maritime of San Diego, Inc.*, B-249858.2; B-249858.3, 2/11/93, 93-1 CPD ¶230 at 6-8; *G. Marine Diesel; Phillyship*, B-232619; B-232619.2, 1/27/89, 89-1 CPD ¶90 at 4-5; *Inlingua Schools of Languages*, B-229784, 4/5/88, 88-1 CPD ¶340 at 5.

[21] *G. Marine Diesel; Phillyship*, supra.

[22] *Omega World Travel, Inc.*, B-271262.2, 7/25/96, GCR 109,579.

[23] *TRESP Assoc., Inc.; Advanced Data Concepts, Inc.*, B-258322.5; B-258322.6, 3/9/95, 96-1 CPD ¶8.

[24] *G. Marine Diesel; Phillyship*, B-232619; B-232619.2, 1/27/89, 89-1 CPD ¶90.

[25] *Quality Fabricators, Inc.*, B-271431; B-271431.3, 6/25/96, GCR 109,553.

[26] *Otto Einhaupl*, B-241553 et al., 2/20/91, 91-1 CPD ¶192.

[27] *Counter Technology Inc.*, B-260853, 7/20/95, 95-2 CPD ¶39; *Engineering & Computation Inc.*, B-258728, 1/31/95, 95-1 CPD ¶155.

Pre-Award: Evaluating Past Performance **109**

[28] *Panasonic Communications & Sys. Co.*, B-239917, 10/10/90, 90-2 CPD ¶279.

[29] *Intermagnetics Gen. Corp.—Recon.*, 73 Comp. Gen. 333 (1994), 94-2 CPD ¶119.

[30] FAR 15.306(a)(2).

[31] FAR 15.306(b)(1)(i) and (4).

[32] *Centrex Construction Co., Inc.*, B-238777, 6/14/90, GCR 104,470.

[33] *Saturn Constr., Co., Inc.*, B-236209, 11/16/89, 89-2 CPD ¶467, GCR 104,470.

[34] FAR 15.306(b)(1)(i) and (4).

[35] Office of Federal Procurement Policy, *Best Practices for Collecting and Using Past Performance Information*, May 2000, Appendix I.

[36] *Dragon Services, Inc.*, B-255354, 2/25/94, 94-1 CPD ¶151, GCR 108,099.

[37] *Pannesma Co. Ltd.*, B-251688, 4/19/93, 93-1 CPD ¶333; *Firm Otto Einhaupl*, B-241533 *et al.*, 2/20/91, 91-1 CPD ¶192.

[38] *OSI Collection Services, Inc.*, B-286597, 1/17/01.

[39] *Professional Landscape Management Servs., Inc.*, B-286612, 12/22/00.

Chapter 6

Pre-Award: Past Performance and Source Selection

by Peter S. Cole

The source selection official (usually the contracting officer, but may be another appointed official for major acquisitions) makes the final award decision based on the accumulated evaluation information developed during the course of the acquisition process (the initial evaluation report supported by the individual evaluators' comments, documentation of the competitive range determination, the final evaluation report with its supporting documentation, and the award recommendation). While the source selection official may follow the results and advice of the initial and final evaluations, he or she is not required to do so. Evaluation results are considered to be advisory only, and the source selection official, after examining the evaluation results, may come to a different conclusion and make award to an offeror other than that recommended by the evaluators.

The source selection decision must represent the source selection official's independent judgment. This decision must be fully documented and include the rationale for any tradeoffs or business judgments made, including the benefits associated with additional costs. The rationale should address the relative differences between the competing technical proposals, including their relative strengths, deficiencies, significant weaknesses, and risks, and how these differences would have an impact (positive or negative) on performance of the prospective contract. This does not involve changing assigned ratings but is an assessment of the relative value of the technical proposals. The rationale must then show how the source selection official balanced these differences with the proposed cost or price in making the source selection decision. Note that tradeoffs are based on the evaluated pricing (proposed pricing plus or minus any adjustments made as a result of cost or price analysis and cost realism analysis) rather than the pricing proposed in the offeror's proposal.

Some source selection decisions are fairly straightforward, such as when the RFP calls for award to be made to the lowest-priced, technically acceptable proposal. In this type of acquisition, the relative quality of the competing proposals is not considered. The proposals only have to meet the minimum technical requirements; quality above the minimum is not germane. Therefore, once the evaluators have identified the technically acceptable proposals, the final decision is based on the lowest evaluated price. While the source selection official has the authority to disagree with the selection of the technically acceptable proposals or with the determination of the lowest evaluated price, and change these results, generally this does not happen. However, should such an occasion arise, the source selection official would be required to document fully the reasons for the changes.

When awarding on the basis of best value, the source selection decision is more complicated. Here the relative quality of the competing proposals is a primary consideration, and award may be made to other than the lowest evaluated price. The source selection official must first examine the results of the technical evaluation to determine if the differences between the proposals actually represent technical differences in terms of contract performance. (It should again be noted that the scores or ratings assigned by the evaluators are only guides to point out the differences between proposals. Decisions are made based on the technical evaluation narratives that serve as the basis for the assigned scores or ratings.) The source selection official then examines the evaluated cost or price and, if appropriate, makes a tradeoff to determine which proposal offers the best value.

In a best value procurement, the RFP should indicate that the government reserves the right to award to other than the lowest priced proposal. This gives the government the flexibility to balance the value of the technical aspects and the evaluated cost or price of the competing proposals and make a tradeoff to determine which proposal offers the best value to the government. If the highest technically rated proposal also has the lowest evaluated cost or price, and the source selection official agrees with the evaluation findings, the source selection decision is relatively easy. The source selection official merely has to show why he or she agrees with the evaluation findings. This requires more than a simple "I agree," however—every source selection decision must be a stand-alone document with the award rationale fully addressed.

If the highest technically rated proposal does not offer the lowest evaluated cost or price, the source selection decision is more difficult. To justify an award to the highest technically rated proposal, the source selection decision must show how such an award is worth the price premium to be paid. Conversely, to justify an award to a proposal that is not rated the highest technically but offers the lowest price, the source selection decision must show how award to the highest technically rated proposal is *not* worth the price premium to be paid. In short, all source selection decisions must show how the source selection official balanced the technical and pricing aspects of the competing proposals and why a particular proposal was selected for award.

There are times, however, when using multiple non-cost evaluation factors can produce unintended results. For example, an RFP called for the evaluation of technical, management, and past performance, with past performance having the least weight in the evaluation. The evaluation found the technical and management factors of the competing proposals to be roughly equal (they do not have to be determined to be exactly equal, only close enough that one could not reasonably be considered to be better than the other). In such an instance, past performance would become the primary discriminating factor, and the award would have to be made on the basis of past performance and price regardless of the original intent of the evaluation. The source selection decision would have to show how the technical and management factors were determined to be roughly equal and how the tradeoff between past performance and price was made.

PAST PERFORMANCE TRADEOFFS AND SOURCE SELECTION DECISIONS

Because the competitive range consists of only the most highly rated proposals, most offerors with serious past performance problems will be eliminated before discussions begin. This does not mean, however, that past performance is no longer an issue. In acquisitions where past performance is an evaluation factor, it can play a significant role in the source selection decision.

Some of the more common problem areas in making a source selection decision when past performance is a significant, or the only, non-cost evaluation factor are:

- Determining which proposal offers the best value

- Making tradeoffs between past performance and price

- Properly documenting the source selection decision.

Determining Best Value

Determining which proposal offers the best value can be an exercise in determining the best of the best, because only the most highly rated proposals remain after discussions and the final evaluation are completed. Past performance may still be an issue when determining which proposal offers the best value, even though the proposals with serious performance problems have been eliminated from the competition. But there are limits in determining the best of the best, as shown in Example 6.1.

Example 6.1—Determining the best of the best[1]

An incumbent (AWV) and another offeror (DynCorp) both received the highest past performance rating of exceptional/high confidence. When it did not receive the award, AWV protested that it possessed vastly more relevant experience than DynCorp, such that the agency could not reasonably assign the same past performance rating to both offerors. The Comptroller General found that both offerors had received a valid past performance rating and denied the protest.

We recognize that, as asserted by AWV, that company possesses extensive, relevant experience. For example, AWV is not only the incumbent Air Force WRM contractor in Southwest Asia; it has also provided base operations and maintenance services for Air Force bases in Turkey; training, logistics and related support to the Saudi Arabian National Guard; and personnel support services for United States personnel in Egypt. However, AWV received the highest possible rating under this factor, reflecting the high quality and relevance of its past performance, and the agency was not obligated to reduce the rating reasonably assigned to DynCorp even if, as AWV contends, AWV's past performance was even better. Agencies are not required to give evaluation credit for proposal features it determines will not contribute in a meaningful manner to better satisfying the agency's needs.[2] Here, given DynCorp's highly-rated relevant past performance, it is unclear how AWV's additional relevant past performance would contribute to better satisfying the agency's stated needs so as to warrant a significantly higher rating under the past performance factor.

Here the protester argued that its proposal should not have received the same past performance rating as the awardee because it had the better past performance and, therefore, the awardee's past performance rating should be lowered and the protester should receive the award. However, where two offerors are given the highest past performance rating possible, the fact that one might have even a better past performance record than the other is not material unless it can be shown that there is a clear benefit to be gained by awarding to the offeror with the better past performance record (the best of the best).

In this case there was no clear benefit, and based on the past performance evaluation, both proposals represented the same low risk. Past performance ratings and the other non-cost evaluation ratings are assigned independently of other proposals and generally are not changed as a result of a comparative assessment. However, while the assigned ratings are not changed, the relative value of a particular evaluation factor in one proposal when compared to another proposal can be a discriminator during a tradeoff determination to decide the best value. In this case, however, the value of past performance was not a discriminating factor; the award decision turned on the fact that the awardee's technical proposal was rated higher than the protester's proposal and was lower priced.

Even if past performance had been the only non-cost evaluation factor, the protester's argument would have been invalid. Because the past performance of both offerors was evaluated as exceptional/high confidence, the award would have been based on price alone, and the award decision would have remained the same.

Past performance can be a point of contention right up to the source selection decision, even when all proposals are highly rated for past performance. It should be noted here that the decision reached in Example 6.1 was based on a fully documented record that showed how the past performance ratings were established. Good decisions require good documentation.

Making Past Performance/Price Tradeoffs

Even if not originally intended, past performance may become the determinative factor if all other technical evaluation factors are evaluated as roughly equal. If the offeror with the best past performance rating is not also the lowest-priced offeror, the source selection official must make a past performance/price tradeoff to determine which proposal offers the best value. Any award to other than the lowest-priced offeror must be supported by a tradeoff rationale showing that the benefits of the higher-priced award are worth the price premium to be paid. Past performance/price tradeoffs are often required when the only evaluation factors are past performance and price, as shown in Example 6.2.

Example 6.2—Past performance/price tradeoffs[3]

In a solicitation that cited price and past performance as the only and equally weighted evaluation factors, the agency selected the offeror with the low performance risk rating instead of the lower-priced offeror with a reasonably based moderate performance risk rating. The lower-priced offeror's moderate risk rating was based on prior contract delinquencies, while the higher-priced offeror received a low performance risk rating because of its early or timely performance under its contracts. The lower-priced offeror protested that its risk rating should have been better and that it should have received the award.

The Comptroller General did not agree and denied the protest.

In a best value procurement, price is not necessarily controlling in determining the offer that represents the best value to the government. Rather, that determination is made on the basis of whatever evaluation factors are set forth in the RFP, with the source selection official often required to make a cost/technical tradeoff to determine if one proposal's technical superiority is worth the higher cost that may be associated with that proposal. In this regard, price/past performance tradeoffs are permitted when such tradeoffs are consistent with the RFP evaluation scheme.[4] Thus, where, as here, an RFP identifies past performance and price as the evaluation criteria and indicates that an offeror with good past performance can expect a higher rating than an offeror without such a record of performance, proposals must be evaluated on that basis, and ultimately the selection official must decide whether or not a higher-priced offeror with a better past performance rating represents the best value to the government.[5] Further, in reviewing an agency's evaluation of an offeror's performance risk, we will examine it to ensure that it was reasonable and consistent with the solicitation's stated evaluation criteria.[6]

116 PAST PERFORMANCE HANDBOOK

Proposals must be evaluated to the criteria set forth in the solicitation. And as stated earlier, in a best value procurement, award may be made to other than the lowest-priced offeror, but only if a tradeoff determination clearly demonstrates the benefits to the government of such an award. Note that the reverse also is true. If award is to be made to the lowest-priced offeror, where the technical factors (including past performance) were cited as being equal to or more important than price, a tradeoff determination must be made to demonstrate that the higher technical/higher-priced proposal is not worth the price premium to be paid.

One of the more difficult tradeoff areas is a past performance/price tradeoff between a firm with a neutral past performance rating and an established firm with an excellent past performance rating. Such tradeoff determinations usually involve more than just a simple comparison of offerors' past performance, as shown in Example 6.3.

Example 6.3—Using past performance to evaluate new firms or firms with no performance history—making price/past performance tradeoffs[7]

Award was made to a higher-priced proposal with a good performance record over a lower-priced proposal with no performance history. The unsuccessful offeror protested that the contracting officer did not make a proper price/past performance tradeoff.

The Comptroller General sustained the protest.

In a recent case involving DLA's use of ABVM scoring, we concluded that the use of a neutral rating approach to avoid penalizing a vendor without prior experience does not preclude a determination to award to a higher-priced firm with a good past performance record over a lower priced vendor with a neutral past performance rating. Indeed, such a determination is inherent in the concept of best value. In Phillips,[8] the contracting officer's determination to select a higher priced vendor with an excellent ABVM score, rather than a new supplier with a neutral rating, was reasonable where the record in that case showed that the agency had backorders for the item and timely delivery was critical. Nonetheless, we expressed concern that the vendor without a performance history not be disqualified for award merely because it lacked a performance history; we pointed out that such an approach would be inconsistent with the FAR and the DLA ABVM clause. As DLA recognized in that case, FAR 15.305(a)(2) provides that in the case of an offeror without a record of relevant past performance or for whom information on past performance is not available, the offeror may not be evaluated favorably or unfavorably on past performance.[9] The ABVM clause states that lack of performance history is not grounds for disqualification for award.

There is nothing in the record to show that the contracting officer performed a comparative assessment of the vendors. The contracting officer merely checked a box on a form indicating that National was not selected because its 999.9 ABVM score was based on insufficient information and therefore, was not a true indicator of its capabilities. Nor is there any indication that the contracting officer performed a tradeoff that considered the significant price premium in ordering from Tara, or that the contracting officer considered in her decision that National quoted a significantly shorter delivery time and confirmed that the metal sheets were in stock. Unlike in Phillips, there is no indication that the item was in backlog or high demand status or that timely delivery was critical and worth the price premium to avoid the risk of using a vendor with no performance history. We conclude that the contracting officer failed to make a meaningful best value determination consistent with the SPA to justify paying a price premium to Tara. As a result, DLA's decision was tantamount to rejecting National's quotation based on its lack of performance history, which is inconsistent with 41 U.S.C. sect. 405(j)(2), FAR 15.305(a)(2), and the clauses which implement the ABVM program, as discussed in the Phillips decision.

In this example, a protest of an award to a higher-priced proposal, arguing that the price/past performance tradeoff was not made properly, was sustained because the contracting officer failed to make a tradeoff determination showing that the award was worth the price premium. This had the effect of rejecting the protester because it lacked any performance history.

In this instance, the contracting officer simply wasn't paying attention. Any attempt to make a tradeoff determination would have shown that National's proposal offered the best value. National's proposal offered the lowest price and a shorter delivery time and stated that it had the required material in stock. Under these circumstances it would have been difficult to justify an award to Tara if the source selection decision had been done properly.

Note that in the Phillips case (see Example 4.8), the decision was exactly the opposite. An award to the higher-priced offeror with an excellent performance history over a lower-priced offeror with no performance history was justified because of the need for timely delivery. The difference between these two cases is that in the Phillips case the tradeoff determination provided a justification for the price premium to be paid (out-of-stock, backlogged orders and a need to ensure timely delivery), while in National not only was there no tradeoff determination, but there also was no pressing need to assure timely delivery and thus no justification for paying a price premium.

Assigning a neutral rating to new firms or firms with no performance history (i.e., an established firm trying to enter a new market or in circumstances where it was not possible to verify an offeror's past performance with any of the references provided) is done to avoid penalizing an offeror with no past performance history, thus enhancing the competition. This applies only to the rating approach, however, to avoid an otherwise arbitrary rejection of an offeror's proposal. A tradeoff determination that results in an award to a higher-priced offeror with a good past performance record over a lower-priced offeror with a neutral past performance rating, because the higher-priced offeror represents the best value to the government, demonstrates the basic concept of best value.

The decision to award to the higher-priced offeror, however, must be documented to show that such an award is worth the price premium to be paid—for example, by showing that timely and effective contract performance must be

118   PAST PERFORMANCE HANDBOOK

assured to meet the government's needs and that this assurance, based on past performance history, is found in an award to the higher-priced offeror.

Documenting Tradeoff Determinations and Source Selection Decisions

As noted earlier, the source selection decision, supported by any tradeoffs made, must be documented showing the rationale and basis for the decisions made, including the benefits associated with additional costs.[10] When tradeoffs are performed, this documentation must include an assessment of each offeror's ability to meet the technical requirements and a summary, matrix, or qualitative ranking with an appropriate supporting narrative related to each of the RFP's evaluation factors. A failure to meet this requirement could result in a successful protest and a requirement to redo all or part of the competition or, in extreme cases, a directed award. While development of the appropriate documentation can be a chore, particularly when there is no disagreement between the source selection official and the evaluators, it is better and less time-consuming to do the job correctly in the first place than to risk a successful protest and a requirement to do it all over again.

When making a source selection decision involving past performance (or any other non-cost evaluation factor), the source selection official's assessment of the competing proposals often must go beyond just the assigned ranking and supporting narrative. It must be based on an assessment of the differences between the competing proposals and the source selection official's judgment concerning the significance of the differences in light of the RFP's evaluation scheme. With respect to past performance, this assessment includes a comparative assessment of the relative complexity of offerors' past efforts when determining which proposal offers the best value to the government. This judgment must be fully documented and show that it was reasonable and adequately justified. This is particularly important when award will be made be to other than the low-priced offeror. When the source selection official fails to do this, the Comptroller General is likely to sustain a protest of the award, as shown in Example 6.4.

Example 6.4—When evaluating past performance, the comparative assessment of complexity cannot be superficial.[11]

While contract size may be relevant to contract complexity,[12] evaluating "complexity" of contract requirements based on size alone, without considering such other indicators of complexity may not yield a meaningful conclusion about an offeror's probability of future success. An increase in the amount of waste to be disposed of under a contract, for example, or the number of pick-up locations are factors to be considered, but it does not follow that the complexity of the requirement has increased merely because of increases under these factors. In other words, if a contractor that has successfully disposed of 200,000 or 600,000 pounds of specific waste—as PMT has done under two prior contracts—now must dispose of 2 million pounds of waste, it may simply have to make more pick-ups using the same procedures and similar resources. On the other hand, the contractor may have to do considerably more, such as develop new procedures for handling hazardous waste with which it has no experience, provide more trucks and drivers, and coordinate the additional resources committed to the effort. The point to be made on the record is that one cannot simply say that because the size of the contract has increased, its complexity has also increased.

There has been absolutely no showing on this record that what is primarily a two-location requirement is more complex than the one-location requirement PMT previously serviced. In this regard the agency's evaluation did not identify any types of waste, handling procedures, staffing requirements, or quantity and management resources which could make this RFP work meaningfully more complex than that performed under the Tooele contract. In sum, on this record, we cannot say that an agency's reliance on the size and number of waste generation locations reflects a reasonable analysis of PMT's prior contracts and, in the absence of a meaningful distinction in the complexity of this work as compared to PMT's previous work, that the agency's evaluation of PMT's past performance as "marginal" is reasonably based.

Although the SSA discounted the number of waste generation locations in increasing Moheat's past performance rating, the record shows that the SSA did not similarly consider the immateriality of those locations to PMT's rating. To the contrary, PMT's lack of experience with multiple locations under a single contract was a specific concern stated by the SSA in his selection decision.

The SSA selected Moheat for award after determining that the evaluated difference in the firms' past performance justified a more than one million dollar (49 percent) price premium. This tradeoff decision, however, is based upon an inadequate evaluation of PMT's past performance. Until there is a proper assessment of PMT's past performance, the SSA cannot reasonably determine whether Moheat's past performance is worth the 49 percent price premium.

In this case, the SSA simply accepted the evaluation results without a careful review of the basis for the evaluation results. The SSA then compounded the problem by treating the offerors differently with respect to the number of waste generation locations. The fact that the basic evaluation was superficial and not well thought out escaped everyone's attention. The concept that the contract was bigger and, therefore, more complex, was accepted without sufficient analysis. Had the SSA attempted to document the source selection decision properly, the documentation process might have revealed the problems with the award decision. The Comptroller General pointed out what should have been considered and why an award could not be made on the stated basis.

Example 6.5 provides another example of how a lack of proper documentation can derail a procurement.

Example 6.5—Past performance/price tradeoffs must be fully documented.[13]

In a solicitation for a fixed-price requirements contract for refuse collection and disposal services, offers were to be evaluated on the basis of two evaluation factors,

120 PAST PERFORMANCE HANDBOOK

past performance/experience and price/cost, which were to be approximately equal in weight. Past performance and experience also were approximately equal in weight. Award was to be made on a best value basis.

The two primary contenders were Si-Nor and Eagle. Both proposals were rated low risk for experience; however, Si-Nor's proposal was rated only satisfactory for past performance, while Eagle's was rated outstanding. Eagle's evaluated proposal price was $858,656.80 higher than Si-Nor's evaluated price. Despite the price difference, the source selection official determined that Eagle's proposal represented the best value, primarily because of its outstanding past performance rating as compared to Si-Nor's satisfactory rating.

Si-Nor protested on the grounds that the agency failed to document why any advantage reflected in Eagle's higher past performance rating warranted payment of an $858,636.80 premium. Si-Nor argued that its lower evaluated price warranted a determination that its proposal represented the best value to the government.

The Comptroller General agreed and sustained the protest.

Source selection officials in negotiated procurements have broad discretion in determining the manner and extent to which they will make use of the technical and price evaluation results.[14] Price/technical tradeoffs may be made, and the extent to which one may be sacrificed for the other is governed only by the tests of rationality and consistency with the established evaluation criteria.[15] In deciding between competing proposals, the propriety of such a tradeoff turns not on the difference in technical scores or ratings per se, but on whether the selection official's judgment concerning the significance of that difference was reasonable and adequately justified in light of the RFP evaluation scheme.[16] In this regard, where a price/technical tradeoff is made, the source selection decision must be documented, and the documentation must include the rationale for any business judgments and tradeoffs made, including the benefits associated with additional costs.[17]

Based on our review of the record, we conclude that the determination to award to Eagle was not adequately justified. The tradeoff rationale set forth in the new selection official's revised source selection decision stated as follows:

"I have determined [Eagle]'s proposal to be of better value than [Si-Nor]'s proposal. Both offerors received a low risk rating for experience. However, [Eagle] received an outstanding past performance rating based on their past performance record, meeting all contract requirements and exceeding some of the contract requirements, compared to the satisfactory rating given [Si-Nor]. . . . I believe that [Eagle]'s outstanding past performance outweighs the lower price offered by [Si-Nor], a difference of $858,636.80 for the total cost."

This determination—as well as the record as a whole—includes no explanation for the agency's conclusion as required by FAR 15.308. While the record clearly sets forth the agency's conclusion that Eagle's past performance rating was worth an $858,636.80 price premium, it includes no documentation, evidence or explanation of the benefits that the agency associated with Eagle's superior past performance rating which would outweigh the additional price. This lack of documentation is significant in light of the fact that price was essentially twice as important as past performance under the stated evaluation scheme.

[And in a footnote—Since past performance/experience and price/cost were to be given approximately equal weight, each was worth approximately 50 percent of the overall rating; since, within past performance/experience, each of the two components was approximately equal, past performance was worth approximately 25 percent of the overall rating.]

Absent a more detailed rationale, there is simply no way to determine whether the agency in fact accorded price this substantially greater weight. . . . We conclude that the record does not establish that the Air Force's tradeoff decision was reasonable, and sustain the protest on this basis.

This is a good example of the need to consider and document tradeoff decisions carefully. Note that this decision did not turn on the price difference itself but on the failure of the selection official to document specifically the reasons why Eagle's superior past performance was worth the price premium to be paid.

This example also shows the need to analyze the evaluation scheme before issuing the RFP. When developing their evaluation scheme, the agency failed to realize that by citing past performance and experience as a combined evaluation factor equal in weight to price, they were diminishing the value of past performance in the evaluation (from 50 percent to 25 percent). Fortunately (perhaps) for the agency, the Comptroller General recommended that the agency perform and document a proper tradeoff analysis rather than make award to the protester. The agency must now show how the superior past performance of Eagle is worth a roughly 10 percent price premium. This might be justified on the basis of environmental, sanitation, or even operational needs, but the rationale also must overcome the disparity in the evaluation weights, for example, "price may be twice as important as past performance, but the lower risk of Eagle's performance is critical because [insert reason] and therefore worth the roughly 10 percent price premium to be paid."

Proper documentation, whether of evaluation findings, tradeoffs, or source selection decisions, is critical to a successful acquisition. In the event of a protest, the quality of decision-making is immaterial if the record is not fully documented. The need for full documentation starts with the initial evaluation and continues throughout the acquisition process. Making and documenting a proper source selection decision is difficult if the evaluation process itself was not adequately documented and retained in the contract file. Note that some agencies have a practice of eliminating some documentation, such as the individual evaluation narratives for the initial evaluation, when assembling the official contract file. This is a mistake—having a skinny contract file is not worth the aggravation of a successful protest because of the lack of contemporaneous documentation.

EVALUATING PAST PERFORMANCE IS NOT EASY

Evaluating past performance in a competitive environment is not easy. In a comparative assessment, the informational requirements encompass both negative and positive information, and both must be well-documented. Positive information (proposal strong points) is usually easier to obtain and is as important as negative information, particularly when making tradeoffs between past performance and other factors. Negative information is harder to deal with because it must be documented in greater detail. A comparative assessment requires sufficient information to enable evaluators to compare one proposal to another to determine the most highly rated proposals for inclusion in the competitive range and later for the source selection official to determine which proposal offers the best value to the government.

While the current emphasis on using past performance as an evaluation factor was introduced as a way to make acquisition more efficient and effective and to promote competition, in fact, it often becomes a bureaucratic problem spawning more paperwork and effort than it is worth. Complicated questionnaires, the need to resolve differing responses, and the different methods of scoring or grading offerors' past performances have made this process more difficult than was originally envisioned.

One way to simplify the past performance evaluation process would be to evaluate past performance only as a risk factor. After all, evaluating past performance is essentially assessing an offeror's past performance to determine its ability to perform the proposed effort successfully. The broader scoring range for performance risk (low, moderate, high) could allow the minimization of the number of questions to be asked. Note that scoring systems often drive the evaluation—the more scoring ranges, the greater the detail required. Assessing performance risk generally requires less detail than an assessment using a numerical or color-coded scoring system. Chapter 3 suggests seven questions, with six follow-up questions if the responses are negative. The OFPP Guide[18] suggests 16 questions. However, for a risk assessment, the initial questions could be reduced to three questions:

1. If the offeror did not perform well, what were the problems, and how poor was its performance?

2. If there were problems, were they satisfactorily corrected?

3. If the offeror performed well, were there any particular strong points?

In the initial evaluation of past performance, the emphasis should be on identifying those offerors with poor past performance histories so they can be eliminated from the competition. The first two questions address poor past performance. Because only the most highly rated proposals are included in the competitive range, the final evaluation of past performance would involve a comparative assessment of offerors' strong points, which is addressed by the third question. While this suggestion may be an oversimplification, the emphasis should be on simplifying the evaluation process by seeking only that informa-

Pre-Award: Past Performance and Source Selection   **123**

tion needed to make a reasoned decision and eliminating the gathering of unnecessary details.

The bureaucratic problems with evaluating past performance are merely growing pains, however, and over time contracting personnel and contractors will learn how to focus on those things that are worthwhile and efficient and to ignore the rest. Eventually the evaluation of past performance will realize its goal—focusing contractors' attention on providing effective performance and permitting the government to eliminate from consideration those contractors who fail to provide effective performance.

Note that one of the key factors in focusing a contractor's attention on providing effective performance is the requirement for contractor performance reports. These reports are a key source of past performance information and an important consideration in awarding new contracts. While using contractor performance reports does not eliminate the need to verify information provided by the offeror, i.e., contract references, and the requirement to consider information close at hand, the availability of these reports will greatly simplify the evaluation process.

Chapters 7 through 12 address the post-award evaluation of a contractor's performance and the development and use of contractor performance reports.

NOTES

[1] *Airwork Limited-Vinnell Corp. (a Joint Venture)*, B-285247; B-285247.2, 8/8/00.

[2] *Consolidated Eng'g Servs., Inc.*, B-279565.5, 3/19/99, 99-1 CPD ¶76 at 3-4; see Tecom Inc., B-275518.2, 5/21/97, 97-1 CPD ¶221 at 7 (agency reasonably concluded that offeror was not entitled to higher rating where requirements were not exceeded in a manner that would increase benefit to the agency); *Computer Sys. Dev., Corp.*, B-275356, 2/11/97, 97-1 CPD ¶91 at 7-8.

[3] *H.F.Henderson Industries*, B-275017, 1/17/97, GCR 109,802.

[4] *Excalibur Systems Inc.*, B-272017, 7/12/96, 96-2 CPD ¶13; Dragon Servs. Inc., B-255354, 2/25/94, 94-1 CPD ¶151.

[5] *Excalibur Systems Inc.*, supra.

[6] *Dragon Servs. Inc.*, supra.

[7] *National Aerospace Group Inc.*, B-281958, 5/10/99.

[8] *Phillips Indus., Inc.*, B-280645, 9/17/98, 98-2 CPD ¶74 at 5.

[9] 41 U.S.C. sect 405(j)(2) (1994).

[10] FAR 15.308.

[11] *PMT Services, Inc.*, B-270538.2, 4/1/96, GCR 109,639.

[12] *Chem-Servs. of Indiana, Inc.*, B253905, 10/28/93, 93-2 CPD ¶262.

[13] *Si-Nor, Inc.*, B-282064; B-282064.2, 5/25/99.

[14] *DynCorp*, B-245289; B-245289.2, 12/23/91, 91-2 CPD ¶575 at 6.

124   Past Performance Handbook

[15] *TRW, Inc.*, B-234558, 6/21/89, 89-1 CPD ¶584 at 4.

[16] *DynCorp*, supra.

[17] FAR 15.308; *Opti-Lite Optical*, B-281693, 3/22/99, 99-1 CPD ¶61 at 5.

[18] Office of Federal Procurement Policy, *Best Practices for Collecting and Using Past Performance Information*, May 2000, Appendix IV, p. 36.

Chapter 7

Post-Award: Contractor Performance Evaluations

by Joseph W. Beausoleil

> *. . . Agencies shall prepare an evaluation of contractor performance for each contract . . . at the time the work under the contract is completed. In addition, interim evaluations should be prepared . . . to provide current information for source selection purposes, for contracts with a period of performance exceeding one year.[1]*

The effective use of past performance as an evaluation factor in source selection depends on the availability of past contractor performance information on contracts with requirements similar to the requirement of the solicitation. The most important source of past performance information is performance evaluations conducted during and upon completion of contract activities. Thus, the FAR, in requiring that past performance be used as an evaluation factor in source selection,[2] also requires that contracts be evaluated to provide information for source selection purposes.[3]

LOW COMPLIANCE

Compliance with the requirement to conduct evaluations upon completion of contract activities has been poor. As a result, past performance has not proven to be an effective evaluation factor in source selection. The reasons explaining the low compliance are many. Contracting officers complain that they do not have the time to conduct the evaluations; therefore, many evaluations are never initiated. Of those evaluations that are initiated, many are not completed because the technical offices are reluctant to participate, often because they see the evaluation process as too time-consuming. Others are reluctant to participate because they see no purpose in evaluating the contractor after the contract is completed. Of those performance evaluations that are completed, the assessment is often incomplete because the government officials are disinclined to say anything negative about a contractor with whom they have had close contact and would like to maintain good relations.

126 Past Performance Handbook

The result is that most contracts are not being evaluated, and of those that are, the usefulness of many of the evaluations is questionable. This would not be so, however, if contractor performance evaluations were understood correctly. Contractor performance evaluations can be done expeditiously and are actually easy to conduct. What is most important is that they can provide a fair and accurate assessment of a contractor's performance.

Since contracting officers are responsible for administering the evaluation, the guidance in this chapter is primarily directed at them. The information is useful, however, to all who participate in the process, particularly the government technical personnel who monitor contractor performance. It is also useful information for contractors whose performance is evaluated and who are given the opportunity to review the evaluation before final assessment is made.

PURPOSE OF THE EVALUATIONS

Contractor performance evaluations are conducted on contracts upon completion of activities. Contracts with a period of performance exceeding one year should be evaluated on an interim basis. The purpose of contractor performance evaluations is to provide information that can be used in future source selection. It is important to keep the purpose in mind since it affects how the evaluations are conducted and how the results are maintained.

Contractor performance evaluations are not meant to correct current performance. Correction of current performance is achieved primarily through monitoring actions by the government acquisition team member responsible for a particular aspect of the contract (e.g., technical, financial, legal). Nor are contractor performance evaluations contractually required. They are requirements for the agency but not for the contractor. Unlike evaluations that are contractually required (e.g., evaluations used in determining incentive or award fees), the results of contractor performance evaluations do not affect payments to contractors. Contractor performance evaluations simply record how contractors performed.

Although they do not affect the contract directly, they can affect future contracts if the award of those contracts is based on past performance. Contractor knowledge of this fact serves to motivate contractors to optimum performance. In this sense, contractor performance evaluations are considered effective tools of contract administration. This does not imply that contractor performance evaluations should be used during execution of the contract to evaluate performance. The purpose of contractor performance evaluations is to obtain performance information, and the only time that a contractor performance evaluation is conducted, other than upon completion of activities, is when there is a need to provide current information for source selection purposes on a contract where the period of performance exceeds one year.[4] This means that only one contractor performance evaluation need be conducted in a year on any single contract.

CONTRACTOR PERFORMANCE EVALUATIONS

Contractor performance evaluations are required for almost all contracts. The only contracts that are exempt from this requirement are those with Federal Prison Industries, Inc.,[5] and with nonprofit agencies employing people who are blind or severely disabled.[6] FAR Subpart 42.15 applies to all other contracts in excess of $100,000, except for construction and architect-engineer contracts.[7] Construction contracts are evaluated in accordance with FAR 36.201, and architect-engineer contracts are evaluated in accordance with FAR 36.604.

Although annually evaluating all contracts in excess of $100,000 appears to be an enormous task, it does not necessarily mean increased work for contracting officers. It does, however, require modifying some contract administration procedures.

Not a Complex Procedure

To begin, evaluating contractor performance is not a complex procedure. The evaluations focus on performance issues, such as quality, timeliness, cost control, or business relations. The targets to be met, i.e., the requirements, have been stipulated in the contract. The assessment is based on the performance standards that have been established for each requirement.

Performance Evaluations Are Based on Current Information

Performance evaluations document, at a point in time, actions that have been taken by members of the government's acquisition teams who have been monitoring performance as part of their responsibility or involvement in contract administration. The actions are with respect to the contractor's performance in meeting the requirements either stipulated or referenced in the contract. They include determinations regarding the contractor's conformance to specifications or performance standards, adherence to schedules, forecasting and control of costs, adherence to schedules, and compliance with the administrative aspects of the contract.[8] The evaluations do not ask open-ended questions, nor do they require essay-type answers. The questions are limited to the requirements of the contract, and the answers assess how well the contractor performed in meeting the particular requirements. The result of the evaluation is a contractor performance report.

Report Cards for Contractors

Performance reports are for contractors what reports cards are for students. Teachers monitor students' performance against the curriculum goals. They observe classroom participation, note completion of assignments, and give periodic and final exams. At the end of the term, they give a report card based on performance during that period. Contracting officers monitor contractors' performance against the contract. The contracting officer determines whether the contractor met the requirements stipulated in the contract. When the contract is completed, the contracting officer prepares an evaluation, rating the contractor's performance.

Evaluating versus Accepting/Rejecting Performance

Evaluating contractor performance is a new, but not necessarily an additional, contract administration responsibility for contracting officers. It is a different way of fulfilling the responsibility to see that the contractor complies with the requirements of the contract. Evaluating goes beyond accepting or rejecting the contractor's performance. It requires an assessment or appraisal of the contractor's performance in delivering the product or service. It does not change contract administration procedures during the course of contract execution. The contracting officer continues to make accept/reject decisions based on contractors' performance in meeting contract requirements. It is only upon completion of activities or, in the case of an interim evaluation, completion of a year, that the contracting officer is required to assess and record how well the contractor met the contract requirements.

Evaluating rather than merely accepting or rejecting performance is similar to a teacher giving a grade to students rather than making a pass/fail determination. Contracting officers are now required to grade the contractor's performance on delivery of the product or service, rather than simply accepting or rejecting the product or service. A pass/fail determination suffices to recognize that the student has met the class requirements. An accept/reject determination suffices to authorize payment to a contractor. Grades, however, provide a basis for comparing the qualifications of students applying for higher education. Rating a contractor's performance provides a basis for comparing the qualifications of offerors submitting proposals.

The only additional work for a contracting officer is rating the contractor and recording those ratings annually. The effort expended, however, can be more than compensated for by the benefits derived. Contract administration is improved, and future source selection decisions, which make use of past performance information obtained from performance evaluations, are more efficient and effective.

Shared Responsibility

Although the contractor is responsible for evaluating contractors' performance, he or she relies on the acquisition team to provide information about that performance. The acquisition team consists of the procurement personnel and the customers they serve.[9] Each member of the acquisition team has specific responsibilities and periodically updates the contracting officer regarding contractor performance. Based on this information, the contracting officer or the authorized representative of the contracting officer (contracting officer's representative—COR—or contracting officer's technical representative—COTR) makes decisions and judgments during the period of performance. Upon completion of activities, the contracting officer accepts or rejects the contractor's performance.

The contracting officer now must evaluate the contractor's performance. He or she uses the same information to evaluate the contractor's performance that was used to accept or reject it. If the contracting officer needs to verify or supplement a specific aspect of a contractor's performance, he or she can turn to the member of the acquisition team who has been monitoring that aspect of the contract. Before making a final determination, the contracting officer allows the contractor to review the preliminary findings. The contractor's comments, additional information provided, or rebutting statements are taken into consideration before making the final rating of performance.

TIMING/FREQUENCY

The FAR requires that the evaluations be conducted upon completion of activities. This is the obvious time to do the evaluation, considering that the purpose is to obtain performance information on the contractor. It is important to do this before the contract acquisition team takes on new duties—the sooner the better because memory of details fades with time. Interim evaluations should not be done on contracts with a period of performance exceeding one year until sufficient time has elapsed to allow the contractor to demonstrate its performance potential. Thus, interim evaluations generally are not performed more frequently than once a year.

This is not to imply that contracts with a period of performance in excess of one year must be evaluated annually. Each agency may specify the frequency of interim evaluations. Since the purpose of an interim evaluation is to provide performance information for use in source selection, interim evaluations need to be conducted only on repetitive-type contracts, not on unique-type contracts—that is, on contracts that could be listed by an offeror as contracts similar to the requirements of the solicitation. There is no need to conduct an interim evaluation on a unique contract that will not be repeated.

Many consider annual or more frequent evaluations of multiyear contracts to be good contract administration practice. Contractor performance evaluations are designed to assess performance, not to correct it. If evaluations are critical for effective contract administration, they should be tailored to the particular needs of the contract. The same can be said for using contractor performance evaluations to make a decision whether to exercise an option year on a contract. A more focused evaluation can be a more effective and efficient way of making this decision. Contract performance evaluations have a specific purpose—collecting past performance information—and should not be used for purposes other than for which they have been designed.

Contractor performance evaluations are not substitutes for other types of evaluations that are required for a particular contract. On the other hand, evaluations that are required as part of a contract's post-award administration can help to satisfy the requirement to prepare contractor performance reports. For example, evaluations to determine incentive or award fee payments provide some, if not all, of the contractor performance information that is collected in a contractor performance evaluation. In conducting a contractor performance evaluation of an incentive or award fee contract, the contracting officers should begin with a review of the information available from completed incentive or award fee evaluations. This not only facilitates the process[10] but also ensures consistency between evaluations.[11] The same can be said for evaluations that are part of quality assurance surveillance plans for performance-based contracts. If the agency is using earned value management systems to monitor contract performance, the systems reports should serve as a basis for the contractor performance evaluations.[12]

CONTENT

Because the purpose of the evaluation is to obtain performance information for use in source selection, the content of the evaluations is limited to collecting information on a contractor's performance,[13] that is, information that is an indicator of an offeror's ability to perform the contract.[14] That information falls under the following categories:

- **Quality**—Information on conformance to contract technical requirements or to standards of good workmanship. It is an indicator of an offeror's technical ability.

- **Timeliness**—Information on adherence to contract schedules, such as milestones, delivery dates for interim or final products, or reporting requirements. It is an indicator of an offeror's reliability.

- **Cost Control**—Information on forecasting and controlling costs, submitting reasonably priced change proposals, and providing current, accurate, and complete billings. It is an indicator of the offeror's financial management capability.

- **Business Relations**—Information on the working relationship between the contractor and the government's acquisition team. It is an indicator of an offeror's management philosophy and practice.

DISTINGUISHING FEATURES OF CONTRACTOR PERFORMANCE EVALUATIONS

The timing, the rating system, and the contractor's participation in the evaluation distinguish contractor performance evaluations from other types of performance evaluations. The timing of the evaluation can affect its accuracy. Rating the performance improves the quality of the information obtained. Finally, contractor participation in the evaluation adds to its fairness. The result is that contractor performance evaluations are the best source of past performance information.

- **Timing**—Conducting the evaluation during or upon completion ensures that those who have been intimately involved with the contract are available to provide input regarding the contractor's performance. The contracting officer, the members of the acquisition team, and the end users are available to provide input. Past performance information obtained through a timely evaluation is superior to past performance information obtained through reference checks after the fact. Interviews or questionnaires, for example, sent to the contacts listed by the offerors to collect performance information have limitations with respect to the informants and are not timely. They may reach one or two individuals who were involved with the contract and are done months or even years after the contract is completed.[15]

- **Rating Performance**—Rating performance as opposed to accepting or rejecting it provides information that can be used to compare and discriminate among offerors in source selection. Past performance information that accepts or rejects the contractor's performance—confirming that the contractor was successful or unsuccessful—serves only to distinguish the good performers from the bad.

- **Contractor Review**—Having the contractor review and respond to an initial assessment of performance adds legitimacy to the evaluation. It ensures that the final assessment is not just the government's perspective, but the contractor's as well.

DIFFERENT APPROACH, ADDED VALUE

Compliance with the requirement to evaluate contractors' performance can be accomplished with minimal changes in contract administration procedures. The evaluation is made only on the contractor's performance in complying with requirements contained in the contract. The contracting officer bases his or her assessment of the performance on information provided by the members of the acquisition team who have responsibility for monitoring the contractor's compliance with contract requirements. Rather than simply accepting or rejecting the contractor's performance, the contracting officer now rates it.

The contracting officer does not have to conduct the evaluations more than annually. The added work amounts to sharing the preliminary assessment with the contractor and preparing an evaluation report. The report has value to the government in that it is an indicator of a contractor's ability to perform a contract and can be used in making future source selection decisions regarding similar contracts.

NOTES

[1] FAR 42.1502, Policy.

[2] FAR 15.304(c)(2)(ii). "[P]ast performance shall be evaluated in all source selections for negotiated competitive acquisitions issued on or after January 1, 1999, for acquisitions expected to exceed $100,000."

[3] FAR 42.1502(b). "[A]gencies shall prepare an evaluation of contractor performance . . . and for each contract in excess of $100,000 not later than January 1, 1998 (regardless of the date of contract award), at the time the work under the contract is completed."

[4] FAR 42.1502(a). "In addition, interim evaluations should be prepared as specified by the agencies to provide current information for source selection purposes for contracts with a period of performance, including options, exceeding one year."

[5] Federal Prison Industries, Inc., is a self-supporting, wholly owned government corporation of the District of Columbia that provides training and employment for prisoners confined in federal penal and correctional institutions through the sale of its supplies and services to government agencies. FAR 8.6 details the rules and regulations governing these acquisitions.

[6] The Javits-Wagner-O'Day Act requires the government to purchase supplies or services from nonprofit agencies serving people who are blind or severely disabled. FAR 8.7 details the rules and regulations governing these acquisitions.

[7] FAR 42.1502(b). "Agencies shall evaluate construction contractor performance and architect/ engineer contractor performance in accordance with 36.201 and 36.604 respectively."

[8] For an illustrative list of relevant past performance information, see FAR 1501.

Post-Award: Contractor Performance Evaluations **133**

[9] FAR 1.102(c). "The acquisition team consists of all participants in government acquisition, including not only representatives of the technical, supply, and procurement communities but also the customers they serve and the contractors who provide the products and services."

[10] FAR 42.1503(b)."Evaluations used in determining award or incentive fee payments also may be used to satisfy the requirement of this subpart."

[11] Although evaluations for determining fees under award or incentive fee contracts and contractor's performance evaluations are different, "the fee amount paid to contractors should be reflective of the contractor's performance, and the past performance evaluation should closely parallel the fee determinations." See FAR 42.1500.

[12] Office of Federal Procurement Policy, *Best Practices for Collecting and Using Current and Past Performance Information*, May 2000, p. 8.

[13] FAR 42.1501.

[14] FAR 15.305(a)(2).

[15] Note that a reference check performed on a current contract listed by the offeror does not present the problem of contacting those who are intimately involved with the contract. Rather than interviewing or sending a questionnaire to the contacts identified by the offeror, it would be preferable to ask the cognizant contracting officer to conduct an interim evaluation in accordance with established procedures.

Chapter 8

Post-Award: Designing a Contractor Performance Evaluation System

by Joseph W. Beausoleil

The content and format of performance evaluations shall be established in accordance with agency procedures and should be tailored to the size, content, and complexity of the contractual requirements.[1]

Although discretion is given to each agency regarding the content and format of performance evaluations, there needs to be some commonality both in content and in format in all contractor performance evaluation systems used throughout the federal government. Otherwise, it will be difficult, if not impossible, to compare past performance information collected by one agency with that collected by other agencies. Every agency's contractor performance evaluation system should collect information on the same basic assessment areas,[2] and the outline or organization of the evaluation should ensure that prescribed procedures are followed.[3]

This chapter is directed primarily at agency procurement analysts who can affect policy. The following section offers guidance in designing a contractor performance evaluation system to meet specific agency needs.

CONTENT

The content of contractor performance evaluations may differ from one agency to another. For the past performance information obtained by the evaluations of one agency's system to be useful in source selection for other agencies, however, every contract performance evaluation should collect past performance information in four basic assessment areas—quality, timeliness, cost control, and business relations.[4] Agencies can add to this list, describe the areas differently, or subdivide the assessment areas according to their particular needs. In addition, all agencies should use a system for rating the assessment areas that has the same number of values with comparable weights.

Basic Assessment Areas

The assessment areas that were originally considered indicators of an offeror's ability to perform a contract successfully were quality of product or service, timeliness of performance, cost control, business practices, customer (end user) satisfaction, and key personnel past performance.[5] These six areas have been reduced to four[6] and are described as follows:

- **Quality of Product or Service**—An assessment of the contractor's performance in making sure that the product or service conforms to specifications or performance standards.

- **Timeliness**—An assessment of a contractor's reliability. It encompasses the contractor's adherence to contract schedules, such as milestones, delivery dates for interim or final products, or reporting requirements.

- **Cost Control**—An assessment of a contractor's performance with respect to forecasting costs, controlling costs, submitting reasonably priced change proposals, and providing current, accurate, and complete billings.

- **Business Relations**—An assessment of the contractor's business management philosophy and practice that includes both the external relations of the contractor with the government's acquisition team and internal relations with its own staff and subcontractors.

Additional Assessment Areas

Adding assessment areas is at the discretion of the agency. Adding areas creates more work for the evaluators, but should result in the improved quality of the past performance information obtained.

Some agencies have added an assessment area for collecting information on compliance with subcontracting plan goals for small disadvantaged business concerns. The justification for adding this assessment area is that, for solicitations involving bundling that offer a significant opportunity for subcontracting, the FAR now requires a factor to evaluate the past performance of offerors in complying with subcontracting plan goals.[7] Making a separate assessment area for this does not seem to be necessary considering that subcontracting with small disadvantaged businesses relates to a limited number of contracts. Furthermore, subcontracting information is already collected under the business relations assessment area.[8] Rather than add this area, it is preferable to incorporate compliance with subcontracting goals when evaluating contracts with these types of requirements.

Another assessment area that some agencies have added is management of key personnel.[9] Assessing a contractor's performance regarding the management of key personnel should be limited to assessing compliance with key personnel requirements stated in the contract. For example, did the contractor replace key personnel in a timely manner with equally qualified professionals? Because management of key personnel is already being assessed under business relations, it is preferable to evaluate it that way than to create a separate assessment area.

Always keep in mind that the purpose of the evaluation is to obtain information that will be useful in source selection. The purpose is not to evaluate the contractor's progress (i.e., what the contractor is doing), but how well it is doing it. Piggybacking on a contractor performance evaluation to accomplish this only makes additional work for the contracting officer and can distract from the primary objective of the evaluation.

Tailoring Content to Contractual Requirements

The evaluation's content can be tailored to an agency's specific needs by subdividing the four basic assessment areas. An example of this is the Department of Defense's (DOD's) performance assessment elements for large systems acquisitions. DOD has four major assessment areas that are referred to differently but are essentially the same as the four basic assessment areas mentioned above: technical (quality of product), schedule, cost control, and management. Technical subelements are product performance, systems engineering, software engineering, logistic support/sustainment, product assurance, and other technical performance. Management subelements are management responsiveness, subcontractor management, program management, and other management.[10]

Areas Not Assessed

Some areas should not be evaluated separately. Contractor performance evaluations should not be used to evaluate end user satisfaction, the performance of key personnel, or the performance of subcontractors.

- **End Users**—Input from end users of the product or service should be obtained, if appropriate, in evaluating contractor performance. This does not mean that an assessment of end user satisfaction should be made separately from the other assessment areas. Input from end users of the product or service may be an appropriate source of information regarding the contractor's performance in meeting the quality, timeliness, cost, or business relations requirements of the contract. End user satisfaction is a concern when the end user is the primary customer. End user satisfaction is not usually relevant when the end users are different from the primary customer—for example, the participants of a training course contracted at the request of the agency's personnel office. Here the primary customer is the personnel office, and the ultimate users are the trainees. If the contractor met the requirements for the training course and the end users were not satisfied, the contracting entity is responsible, not the contractor.

On the other hand, a contract may require a level of end user satisfaction. In this case, it would be subsumed under or assessed as a subcategory of the quality assessment element. If there are a large number of end users, the assessment of satisfaction may require a separate evaluation or survey. The cost for conducting the survey should be included in the contract.

- **Key Personnel**—The evaluation should not be used to evaluate key personnel, but should focus on the contractor's performance. The contractor is responsible for the key personnel's performance. If key personnel were responsible for missing a schedule event, this fact will be reflected in the assessment of timeliness. If key personnel made a significant contribution to the quality of a product or service, this will be reflected in the assessment of quality. If the contractor failed to replace key personnel in a timely manner, this will be reflected in the assessment of business relations. Experience has shown that when key personnel have been evaluated, the assessment has little value. Obtaining information on key personnel is usually difficult because of the infrequency of contacts with the key personnel. When there is a close working relationship between a member of the government's acquisition team and his or her contract counterpart, there is a propensity to be positive and a reluctance to be negative. The result is that the evaluation of key personnel is either subjective or ambiguous.

- **Subcontractor Performance**—The evaluation should not be used to evaluate subcontractor performance. As with key personnel, the prime contractor is responsible for the subcontractor's performance. The successes and failures of the subcontractor are the successes and failures of the prime contractor. The evaluation is of the prime contractor's performance—either directly with its own staff or indirectly with the subcontractors.

Rating Principles

Because the past performance information will be used by other agencies, it is essential that the rating system be comparable to other rating systems throughout the government. The basic element of the rating system is to have the middle value equivalent to meeting standards. The range should be at least three values, with an equal number of values above and below the middle value. Numerical, adjectival, or color-coded denominations can be used to express the scale values. The two standard evaluation forms that have been in use by the government—SF 1420 for evaluation of construction contracts and SF 1421 for evaluation of A&E contracts—use three ratings, with one rating above and one below the middle value. The ratings have adjectival denominations.

The rating system adopted by most agencies has a five-point scale, with the middle value being equal to meeting the standard or satisfactory. The advantage of the five-point scale is that it provides a wider range. With two values above the satisfactory level, it allows for discriminating among the good performers. With a three-point scale, all good performers are above and all poor performers below.

With a five-point scale, each value must be described in a way that clearly distinguishes it from the next higher or lower value. This is important so that those making the ratings, i.e., the acquisition team, and those receiving the rating, i.e., the contractors, interpret the rating in the same way.

For shorthand purposes, the value should have a numerical and adjectival denomination. Using numbers to designate the value facilitates entering the rating on a report form. Numerical values also are useful for statistical purposes. For consistency, the highest rating should correspond with the highest number. Suggested denominations for the five-point scale are: outstanding or exceptional, excellent or very good, satisfactory or good, marginal or poor, and unsatisfactory. Remember that denominations serve to identify the value. The important thing is that the rating has been described so that it is clearly distinguishable from the next higher or lower value.

Narrative Supporting Ratings

A narrative summary provides the rationale for the rating. A narrative must justify a rating higher than three and explain a rating lower than three. If the score is three, a narrative is optional because the contractor has met the requirements for the assessment area. A narrative may be needed, however, to explain why a higher score was not given. Comments on a score of three, however, are recommended on interim evaluations to motivate a contractor to optimal performance.

FORMAT

Like the content, the format is established in accordance with agency procedures. There are, however, several procedures required by the FAR that agencies must take into consideration when establishing an agency-specific format for the performance evaluations. For example:

- The evaluations shall provide for input from the technical office, contracting office and, if appropriate, end users of the product or service.[11]

- The contractor shall be provided the opportunity to review the evaluation.[12]

- Agencies shall provide for review at a level above the contracting officer to consider disagreements between the parties regarding the evaluation.[13]

- Evaluations shall be shared with other agencies.[14]

A basic evaluation format or outline that would ensure the incorporation of all the above-cited FAR requirements would be:

- **Background Information**—consists of the name, address, and location of the issuing activity; the contract number; the date of the award; a brief description of the item or service; the name and complete address, including an electronic address, of the contractor; and the name and title of the person who signed the award for the contractor and the contracting officer who signed the contract. This information can be provided by making a copy of the face sheet for the contract. In addition, information on key personnel and major subcontractors should be included.

- **Description of Supplies or Services and Prices/Costs**—includes incidental deliverables, such as manuals and reports. A copy of Section B of the contract schedule will suffice if the uniform contract format has been used. If the contract were for a commercial item and Standard Form (SF) 1447 was used, the description of the supplies or services and price/costs would already be included in the background information section above.

- **Initial Evaluation**—an initial evaluation of the contractor's performance in each of the assessment areas prepared by the contracting officer after consultation with the acquisition team. Each assessment area would contain a score and a narrative summary justifying that score.

- **Contractor Review**—contains any comments, additional information, or rebuttals received from the contractor.

- **Upper-level Review**—reports on a review at a level above the contracting officer when there are disagreements between the contractor and the contracting officer.

Post-Award: Designing a Contractor Performance Evaluation System **141**

- **Final Evaluation**—the final ratings with supporting narratives, incorporating the response of the contractor and the resolution of disagreements between the contracting officer and the contractor.

- **Evaluation Report**—form or report card containing the final ratings and narratives for each of the assessment areas. Using a report card facilitates the maintenance of the past performance information in an automated system, which is indispensable if it is to be accessible to source selection authorities in other agencies.

Note that a paper version of the evaluation report is kept in the contract evaluation folder along with the contractor response and review comments. Keeping all this information in an automated system is not necessary—only the report card is maintained in the agency's automated performance information system. A copy of the evaluation report should be mailed to the contractor as soon as it is finalized.

USING A FORM

A form is an essential element of performance evaluation systems. It summarizes the results of the evaluation and facilitates maintaining and accessing the past performance information.

Design of a Form

The form should be designed to minimize the recording burden placed on the contracting officer. The purpose of the evaluation is to collect performance information; therefore, space should be provided to rate and to comment on the rating of the assessment areas. Background information should be limited to identifying the contract, the contractor, and the period covered by the evaluation. There is no need to specify the value of the contract, the type of contract, or the award or completion date. This information is available elsewhere and only adds to the contracting officer's recording burden. Providing a summary description of the requirement serves no purpose, as the evaluations of the performance areas are against the specific requirements for each assessment area as stipulated in the contract. Nor is there need to state the specific requirements for each assessment area, as the evaluator and the contractor know what the requirements are. The form should require only information that is necessary to identify the contract and the contractor.

Standard Forms for Evaluating Contractor Performance

The SF 1420 and the SF 1421 are two forms for evaluating contractor performance that predate the new requirement that all contracts are to be evaluated

142 PAST PERFORMANCE HANDBOOK

on completion. These forms are used for construction and architect-engineer contracts, respectively. All agencies are required to use these forms when evaluating construction or architect-engineer contracts. There are no standard forms for evaluating other categories of contracts.

Sample Form in OFPP Guide

While a standard form is not required for evaluating other categories of contracts, every agency should have a form to record relevant past performance information that has been obtained by evaluating contractor performance. Agencies should develop a form that meets their particular needs. The sample form found in the OFPP guide is a good place to begin. The sample form, however, is a guide and is not meant to be replicated in its entirety.

Using the sample form ensures the commonality in content and format essential for using past performance information throughout the federal government. The form allows for rating the four basic assessment areas and provides space for a narrative assessment supporting the ratings. It also verifies that the contractor had an opportunity to review the initial assessment and, if disagreement resulted, that an agency review took place. The sample form collects information on subcontracting, teaming, and joint venture partners and collects information on key personnel—names and titles, employment dates, and comments on up to three individuals. Two questions on the form require a "yes" or "no" answer but not a statement or comment supporting the response. The form records contract value, award date, type of contract, and description of requirement—information that is available elsewhere.

The sample form has a serious flaw: It allows for a reassessment of the ratings after the contractor or agency review but does not provide space for revising the supporting narrative. Thus, if a rating was changed after the contractor review, there is no space provided to explain why. Even if the rating is not changed in the final assessment, the supporting narrative of the initial assessment may have to be changed due to information provided by the contractor.

The argument could be made that the contractor's comments are attached to the form and that changing the supporting narrative is therefore unnecessary. This means that the source selection official will have to read the contractor's comments to understand the rating changes in the final assessment or to know if the contractor provided additional information that would have changed the supporting narratives for the initial assessment. Having to read the contractor comments is inefficient. When a review was performed at a higher level, the contractor's comments as well as the agency's comments should be incorporated into the narrative in the final report. This is a standard operating procedure in preparing evaluation re-

Post-Award: Designing a Contractor Performance Evaluation System **143**

ports for construction contracts.[15] It not only makes it easier for the source selection official but also obviates the need to attach the contractor's response or the agency review to the form. In developing their evaluation forms, agencies should provide space for a supporting narrative for each final rating.

Proposed Sample Form

The simpler the evaluation form, the better. It should be easy for the contracting officer to fill out, providing only relevant past performance information. The basic form should cover the following fields:

- Name and address of the contractor

- Contract number

- Contract date

- Summary description of the requirement

- Rating and narrative supporting the rating for the four assessment areas

- Verification that the contractor was given the opportunity to review the assessment

- Verification that an agency reviewed disagreements between the contractor and the contracting officer

- Signature of the contracting officer

- Date the evaluation was entered into the agency's past performance information system and a copy given to the contractor.

The form should not contain information on subcontractors, teaming, or joint venture partners. This just adds to the reporting burden of the contracting officer. If this information is needed during source selection, it can be obtained by contacting the agency. The same can be said regarding the listing of key personnel. The occasional need to verify, in source selection, that a particular firm was a subcontractor or that an individual was a key employee on a contract, does not justify including this information on the report form.

There is no need to include in the evaluation form the question of whether the rating officer would select the firm again. This is the kind of question that would be asked in making a responsibility determination because it elicits an accept or reject answer and not an opinion of how well the contractor performed. It distinguishes between good and bad performers and does not provide information that is helpful to discriminate among good performers.

Asking the question regarding the contractor's commitment to customer satisfaction is redundant because it is already covered under business relations. Addressing customer satisfaction again with a "yes/no" answer and without a supporting statement adds nothing to the evaluation. There does not appear to be any justification for treating customer satisfaction as a separate assessment area. Without a rating and supporting narrative, this information is of little value in source selection.

Other than the contractor's name and the contract number, the forms need not contain contract data that can be obtained easily from other sources. The form, however, should contain information so that the source selection committee can make a judgment regarding the similarity of the requirements of the evaluated contract and the solicitation. Similarity is usually defined in terms of content, but it also can include size and complexity. Space then should be provided on the form for a summary description of the requirement, the value of the contract, and the award date and completion dates. The type of contract is not necessary, as this does not affect the evaluation. Including other fiscal data or significant dates would be at the discretion of the agency. The guidance here is to limit the reporting burden for the contracting officer to information that is needed by source selection officials.

AUTOMATION

Automation is essential for maintaining and making past performance information available, but it is not necessary for collecting past performance information. In many cases, using an automated system for collecting past performance information can be a constraint. Automation should be used for preparing the evaluations only to the extent that it facilitates the process.

For an automated system to work efficiently, all the participants in the process must have compatible hardware and know how to use the software required. The participants involved in evaluating contractor performance include, at a minimum, the contracting officer, at least one representative of the technical office, and the contractor. In some cases, the participation of the end users is appropriate, and, if there is a review to resolve differences between the contrac-

Post-Award: Designing a Contractor Performance Evaluation System **145**

tor and the contracting officer, the participation of someone at a higher level than the contracting officer is required. If one participant does not have the hardware or does not know how to use the software, the evaluation becomes stalled and may never be completed.

Automated systems for collecting performance information tend to be mechanical, resulting in the mere filling in of blanks rather than conducting a thoughtful evaluation. This can happen unintentionally when input is required from a member of the acquisition team who is unfamiliar with the software. The concern for entering the information distracts from the content of the information.

With input required from so many participants, it is suggested that the person charged with preparing the evaluation collect the information using the most expedient communication technology that the respondent is familiar with and has access to. Once the information is obtained from the acquisition team, reviewed by the contractor, and the final assessment is made, it is entered into an automated system. Thus, the preparer would use phone, fax, and e-mail to collect information from the acquisition team, to obtain the contractor's review, and to resolve disagreements. The preparer would enter the information into the automated system once the final assessment was made.

Phone, fax, and e-mail are used in the private sector when information is required from many respondents. For example, a physician doing a diagnostic examination of a patient bases his or her findings on information obtained from other specialties (e.g., laboratory work, x-rays). This information is communicated to the physician by fax, phone, e-mail, or regular mail. The last thing is entry into an automated system, and this is usually limited to billing, not findings.

Technology is available that allows for full automation of the system. Experience, however, has shown that full automation at this time is a constraint to completing the evaluations. The objective should be to get the evaluations completed in a timely manner using communication technology with which the respondents are most comfortable. E-mail may be the preferred way of communicating within the agency, but contractors may prefer to use regular mail, even when they have access to the Internet. Faxing the form with the initial assessment of performance may be acceptable to some contractors and objectionable to others. As a general rule, use the same means of communicating with the acquisition team for preparing the evaluation as you have used for communicating with the team on other contract administration matters.

SIGNATURES

The contracting officer should sign the evaluation only after the contractor has had an opportunity to review it and all differences have been resolved. In signing the evaluation form, the contracting officer attests that all agency policies and procedures have been followed. The name of any person who provided information regarding the contractor's performance should not appear on the evaluation report.

NOTES

[1] FAR 42.1502(b).

[2] Office of Federal Procurement Policy, *Best Practices for Collecting and Using Current and Past Performance Information*, May 2000, p. 9.

[3] FAR 42.1503, Procedures.

[4] FAR 42.1501, General.

[5] OFPP, supra, p. 13.

[6] Ibid., p. 10.

[7] FAR 15.304(c)(3)(iii).

[8] OFPP, supra, Appendix 3, Rating Guidelines.

[9] DOD, *A Guide to Collection and Use of Past Performance Information*, Appendix D.

[10] Ibid.

[11] See FAR 42.1503(a).

[12] See FAR 42.1503(b).

[13] Ibid.

[14] See FAR 42.1503(c).

[15] FAR 36.201(a)(3).

Chapter 9

Post-Award: The Initial Evaluation of Contractor Performance

by Joseph W. Beausoleil

Agency procedures for the past performance evaluation system shall generally provide for input to the evaluations from the technical office, contracting office and, where appropriate, end users of the product or service.[1]

CONTRACTING OFFICER'S RESPONSIBILITY

The contracting officer is responsible for preparing contractor performance evaluations.[2] The contracting officer, however, depends on other members of the acquisition team to provide input,[3] specifically those who have been monitoring contractor performance. For those contracts in which the contractor has had direct contact with the end users of the product or service, the contracting officer also may need to contact end users regarding the contractor's performance.

For small contracts, the contracting officer may be able to prepare the evaluation with the help of a representative of the technical office. As contracts become larger and more complex, the contracting officer will have to contact more members of the acquisition team to obtain a fair and accurate evaluation of performance. The time needed to conduct the evaluation, however, will not necessarily increase proportionally to the increase in the contract size or complexity if the members of the acquisition team understand their respective roles and responsibilities. This chapter is directed not just at the contracting officers but at the entire acquisition team. Understanding one's role and responsibilities is the key to conducting the contractor performance evaluations efficiently.

FORMAT, NOT FORM

Some agencies use a form for conducting the evaluations. The contracting officer initiates the process by sending the form to the technical person who has been monitoring contractor performance. This person is requested to make an initial assessment of the contractor's performance regarding four or more assessment areas. The assessment includes scoring each assessment area and providing a supporting narrative for the score given. The form is then returned to the contracting officer, who reviews the initial assessment, makes appropriate changes, and sends a copy of the form with the initial assessment to the contractor for review.

Using a form, however, may not be the most efficient way to collect the past performance information. A form does not provide sufficient space to address issues thoroughly, particularly for large or complex contracts or when problems have arisen. A form limits input to one respondent, usually the technical officer, to the exclusion of other members of the acquisition team. The contracting officer has to review the assessment of the technical officer and add his or her perspective. This usually means revising the form. The contracting officer then sends the form to the contractor for review. The comments of the contractor may require further revision to the form.

A form can serve as an outline of the evaluation to ensure that all the required assessment areas are covered and the required procedures followed. It should not be used as an instrument for collecting the information if it limits input from the acquisition team. This input must be analyzed and the preliminary findings shared with the contractor. The form should not be used until a response has been received from the contractor and disagreements resolved. This recommendation is consistent with the way that evaluations are conducted on construction and A&E contracts.

For evaluations of construction and A&E contracts, standard forms[4] are used to report the findings of the evaluations. If, in preparing the report, the evaluation official finds performance to be unsatisfactory, the contractor is advised in writing. If the contractor responds, the evaluator includes the comments in the report, resolves any alleged factual discrepancies, and makes appropriate changes.[5] In evaluating construction or A&E contracts, a distinction is made between the evaluation as a process and as a report. The same distinction should be made when evaluating other types of contracts.

USE A FORM TO RECORD INFORMATION, NOT TO COLLECT IT

A form is essential for recording the findings of the evaluation. It provides a convenient way to maintain past performance information and to make that information available when required for source selection purposes. A one- or two-page form that summarizes past performance information in a systematic way is easier for the source selection authority to use than a lengthy narrative assessment. In fact, it is the only practical way for the source selection authority

THE INITIAL PERFORMANCE ASSESSMENT

The initial performance assessment consists of collecting information on the contractor's performance, analyzing the data, and assigning a rating with a supporting rationale. This requires contacting those members of the acquisition team who are knowledgeable about the contractor's performance with respect to quality, timeliness, cost control, and business relations. The number of those contacts will vary depending on the size and complexity of the contract. For small contracts, it may mean contacting only one person, the technical officer who has been responsible for monitoring the contract for the customer. Larger and more complex contracts usually involve contacting more members of the acquisition team, such as program managers, item managers, field contract administrators, or auditors. For these, it may require contacting a different member for each of the assessment areas or several members for one assessment area or another. It may even require contacting end users of the products or services.

The contracting officer should use the same method of contacting the members of the acquisition team as he or she has been using for other contract administration activities. The contracting officer can do this directly or can delegate the responsibility to the authorized representative (COR, COTR). Which members the contracting officer or the authorized representative should contact is determined in accordance with agency procedures regarding contract administration.

For large or complex contracts, if an interim evaluation is anticipated, the scope of the contractor performance evaluation or evaluations should be incorporated into the contract administration plan. When it is necessary to initiate an evaluation of the contractor's performance, the contracting officer will know which member of the acquisition team to contact, and the members of the acquisition team will know what information they are to provide, and, if not directly to the contracting officer, through whom.

The contracting officer already knows much of the information needed to assess performance. In the course of administering the contract, the contracting officer has been making decisions or has been informed of decisions being made by the acquisition team. Thus, the contracting officer is knowledgeable regarding the contractor's performance, particularly with respect to quality, timeliness, and cost control. The contracting officer has direct knowledge of the contractor's performance regarding business relations based on their experience together executing the contract. When the time comes to prepare the evaluation, the contracting officer needs only to complement his or her knowledge of the contractor's performance by contacting specific members of the acquisition team.

Note, however, that although the contracting officer prepares the evaluation, the contracting officer relies on the technical office to assess the quality and timeliness of the product or service. It is the technical office that has the expertise needed to assess how well the contractor has performed in meeting the quality and timeliness requirements established by the customer. For this reason, the technical office assesses quality and timeliness for the contracting officer.

For cost control and business relations, because the contracting officer directly relates to the contractor regarding these two assessment areas (e.g., approval of payments, other business functions), the contracting officer makes the assessment. Where an authorized representative has had authority to approve payments, the authorized representative may assess this area for the contracting office or simply provide input to the contracting officer. Because business relations include customer satisfaction, the contracting officer would need to contract the requesting office, i.e., the customer.

The initial assessment requires analysis, rating, and a narrative summary for each of the assessment areas. This should not entail a review by team members, redrafting of sections, or clearance by different offices. The rating and the rationale for that rating are the judgment of the contracting officer.[6] The contracting officer has fulfilled his or her responsibility by obtaining input from the technical office and end users, as appropriate. Once the contractor has made the initial assessment, he or she sends it to the contractor for review.

BASIS FOR APPRAISING THE ASSESSMENT AREAS

The appraisal is made by comparing actual performance of the contractor against contractual performance requirements, which are found in various sections of the contract. Requirements regarding supplies or services are found in sections B and C of the contract schedule. Requirements for packaging, packing, preservation, and marking are found in section D. Inspection, acceptance, quality assurance, and reliability requirements are found in section E. Requirements for time, place, and method of delivery or performance are found in section F. Sections G, H, and I contain other requirements regarding administration of the contract.

The first thing that the contracting officer must do is identify the performance requirements and separate them out by assessment area—quality, timeliness, cost control, and business relations. There can be more than one performance standard for an assessment area, or there may be none. For example, there would be no assessment of cost control on fixed-price contracts.

Each of the performance requirements stated in the contract is specific, and each is modified by a performance standard that must be met. The contracting officer converts the performance requirements into questions to elicit information regarding whether the contractor's performance met the standard for the requirement. For example, if the performance requirement stipulates that the contractor is to deliver the product by the first of May, the question is simple: did the contractor deliver the product by the first of May? The contracting officer prepares questions for all the essential performance requirements stated or implied in the contract.

For each performance requirement, the contracting officer asks the member or members of the acquisition team who have had responsibility for the requirement for information on the contractor's compliance. The contracting officer then analyzes the information collected by assessment area and gives an initial rating and a rationale for the rating.

Rating Performance

The basis of the rating system for evaluating a contractor's performance is that the middle value on a five-point scale is equivalent to meeting the requirement or standards. On most contracts, the best that the contractor can expect to obtain is the middle value, or satisfactory performance. This is what the government requires, i.e., delivery of the product on time, according to specifications, and within cost. In evaluating the contract, the government wants to know if the contractor complied with the contractual requirements. That is all that the government needs to know and all that the contractor is expected to do.

If the contractor did not meet the requirements, an unsatisfactory rating is given. If the contractor did not fully meet the requirements, a marginal rating is given. If the contractor complied with the performance requirements for an assessment area, a satisfactory rating is given. A very good rating is given when the contractor's performance exceeded the performance requirements. An exceptional rating is given if the contractor is outstanding.

Obtaining a rating above satisfactory is not always possible. Rating a contractor above satisfactory recognizes performance above and beyond what was anticipated in the contract and resulted in a benefit to the government. Not every contract provides such opportunities. One circumstance that could warrant a higher rating would be when the contractor's initiative improved contract execution or the quality of the product or service. Another circumstance would be when the contractor's actions successfully resolved unintended or unanticipated problems. The more complex the contract, the more likely that this will occur. The simpler the contract, the less likely.

On the other hand, obtaining a rating below satisfactory is always possible. If the contractor's performance fell below the standard, the rating would be marginal. If the contractor failed, the rating would be unsatisfactory.

Satisfactory Is a Good Rating

A satisfactory rating on a contractor performance evaluation is a good rating. A satisfactory rating on an evaluation of offeror's past performance in source selection may not be good enough. These are two different kinds of evaluations. The evaluation of a contractor's performance relates to the performance standards for the requirements. The contractor is rated but not ranked. The evaluation of an offeror's past performance is in relation to the past performance of other offerors. In evaluating the offerors' past performance in source selection, the offerors are both rated and ranked.

Objectivity

If used correctly, the five-point scale, with the middle value being equivalent to meeting the requirement, contributes to the objectivity of the evaluation. The middle value serves as the benchmark, a point of reference from which other measurements can be made. By anchoring the ratings on the middle value, the five-point scale allows for two ratings above and below. Any rating higher or lower is in relation to meeting the standard, i.e., performing to the satisfaction of the customer.

The ratings reflect how well the contractor performed according to the standards for the requirements of an assessment area. The ratings are based on factual evidence. Giving a rating above satisfactory says that the contract not only meets the standards but also, in meeting the standards, that the contractor's action demonstrated very good or exceptional performance. One way to distinguish satisfactory performance from very good or exceptional is to consider the contractor's performance in dealing with problems and the solutions or remedial action taken. Another way would be to look at added benefits to the government that resulted because of the contractor's action. Not every contract will have problems nor will provide opportunities to add benefits, so a satisfactory rating is all that is expected of a contractor. However, a rating higher than satisfactory recognizes quality performance.

Incomplete Information

In those cases in which there are some but not sufficient grounds to give a contractor a higher rating, it is suggested that the score be biased downward when preparing the initial rating, i.e., before the contractor's review, and biased upward when making the final rating, i.e., after the contractor has responded. That is, if the contractor's performance appears to be between satisfactory and very good or between marginal and satisfactory, give the lower rating. Challenge the contractor to make the case for the higher rating. If there is still doubt after the response from the contractor, favor the contractor and give the higher rating.

If, after making a reasonable effort to obtain the information from other members of the team regarding the contractor's performance, there is insufficient information to determine that the contractor met the requirement, presume that the contractor did indeed meet the requirement and give a satisfactory rating. If there is no information, then indicate that the information was not available. The important consideration here is to expedite the process. This is the initial assessment, and the final assessment will not be made until the contractor has had the opportunity to respond.

Comments

Comments on the initial assessment are the government's perspective of the contractor's performance and are not final until the contractor has had a chance to review and to respond. Comments are supporting narrative rationales for the ratings. They should describe the action taken by the contractor that contributed to the success or failure in meeting the requirement.

Comments may be written so as to elicit a response from the contractor. Contractors are members of the acquisition team, and it is important to obtain their perspective. Every effort should be made to avoid a rebuttal by the contractor. If there are ongoing problems, try to resolve them before sending the evaluation to the contractor for review.[7] The contractor has a right to rebut the initial assessment, but that rebuttal should regard factual discrepancies and not merely differences of opinion or interpretations.

If a satisfactory rating is given, comments are optional. The rating speaks for itself—the contractor met the requirement. Comments are required to support a rating above or to explain a rating below satisfactory. Comments should address the requirement or standard as articulated in the contract and should be supported by facts and not personal opinions. This is particularly important when giving a rating below satisfactory. Deficiencies should be brought to the contractor's atten-

154 PAST PERFORMANCE HANDBOOK

tion before the evaluation takes place. If they were, the comment should reflect the responsiveness of the contractor in correcting that deficiency.

Although comments are optional when a satisfactory rating is given, there are occasions when comments should be given. Comments for a satisfactory rating on an interim evaluation can serve to motivate a contractor to optimum performance. Comments may be necessary for large or complex contracts. Comments on the final evaluation for a satisfactory rating are expected if the contractor has unsuccessfully rebutted the rating. (See Chapter 10.)

GUIDANCE FOR RATING THE FOUR ASSESSMENT AREAS

Ratings higher than satisfactory are not given for merely exceeding the performance standard. A very good rating for going over the standard or an exceptional rating for significantly exceeding the standard would be given only if it meant added value to the government. Ratings higher than meeting the performance standards are given in most instances to recognize superior performance in responding to problems that arise during the execution of the contract. These are not problems that are caused by the contractor but are unexpected. They require a solution and as such are a challenge to the contractor's technical ability. Because the solutions affect the quality of the product or service, ratings higher than satisfactory are usually confined to the quality assessment area. Only on rare circumstances should a higher rating be given in timeliness, cost control, and business relations. The following is guidance on applying these ratings by assessment area.

Quality of Product or Service

Quality of the product or service is an indicator of the technical ability of the contractor. The assessment is made by comparing the product or service delivered by the contractor to the specifications for the product or the performance standards for the service indicated in the contract. If the contractor met the specifications or performance standards, the rating would be satisfactory. For most contracts, a satisfactory rating is the best rating that can be expected.

A rating higher than satisfactory could be given if this were a performance-based service contract in which the performance standards were expressed in terms of an acceptable range. If the contractor met the low end of the range, the rating would be satisfactory. The rating would be very good if the contractor consistently met the high end of the range. An exceptional rating would not be given even if the contractor surpassed or always met the high end of the range.

A contractor's response to a problem can result in receiving a rating higher than satisfactory. The corrective action would have to have made an impact on the quality of the product or service. For example, without the contractor's technical expertise, specifications or performance standards would not have been met. Another example would be surpassing the performance standards to the benefit of the government because of the contractor's technical expertise. In the latter case, the rating could be very good or exceptional, depending on the resulting added value to the government.

A marginal rating would be given if some of the requirements were not met but were not sufficient to deny payment. An unsatisfactory rating would be given only if the contractor did not deliver the product or service, or the delivered product or service was of no value to the government.

Timeliness

Timeliness assesses the contractor's reliability. The assessment is made by comparing the contractor's adherence to requirements for time of delivery of product or service specified in Section F of the contract schedule. It is an objective assessment because it measures something factual. The two most common ratings would be satisfactory and unsatisfactory, as the contractor would either have met or missed the scheduled dates.

A contractor could meet the delivery dates and receive a marginal rating. An example would be if the contractor failed to adhere to other timeliness requirements, such as submitting reports on their due dates. Whether to give a marginal rating would depend on the adverse effect that the failure to adhere to other timeliness requirements had on the contract's ultimate objective. Giving a rating above satisfactory for timeliness is unlikely. However, it would be appropriate to do so where, but for decisive actions by the contractor, the schedule would not have been met.

Cost Control

Cost control assesses a contractor's financial management ability, which encompasses forecasting costs, controlling costs, submitting reasonably priced change proposals, and providing current, accurate, and complete billings. The evaluation involves the contractor's record of how accurately it estimated costs and how well it controlled the costs expended. This is the easiest assessment area to rate. If the contractor is doing better than projected, the rating is very good; if the contractor is not meeting projections, the rating is marginal. If the contractor is on target, the rating is satisfactory. An exceptional rating can be given, but only when the contractor's actions have resulted in added value for the government.

Business Relations

Business relations address the contractor's business management philosophy and practice, which includes the working relationship between the contractor and the government's acquisition team. The basis of the assessment is the administrative requirements implied or explicit in the contract. These could include:

- Reasonable and cooperative behavior

- Commitment of customer satisfaction

- Business-like concern for the interest of the customer

- Compliance with subcontracting plan goal for small disadvantaged business concerns (SDB),[8] monetary targets for SDB participation,[9] and notifications submitted under FAR 19.1204-4(b)

- Timeliness of problem identification and quality of corrective action

- Timely award and management of subcontractors

- Selecting, retaining, supporting, and replacing key personnel.

A marginal rating would be given to a contractor for failing in any one of these areas. If the contractor substantially met all the areas listed, the rating would be satisfactory. A very good rating could be given if the contractor met the standard in all the areas. An exceptional rating is not usually given for business relations.

TIME NEEDED TO PERFORM THE EVALUATION

The time needed to prepare the evaluation will depend on the size and complexity of the contract. Larger and more complex contracts will have more members on the acquisition team. The additional burden on the contracting officer, however, will be minimal if you follow the guidance provided. Performance evaluations require an appraisal of a contractor's performance in four assessment areas. The ratings are based on decisions already taken by the acquisition team. The additional work for the contracting officer is rating, writing a sup-

Post-Award: The Initial Evaluation of Contractor Performance **157**

porting narrative for the rating, and preparing the evaluation report. This is done once on contract completion and annually, at most, for contracts with a period of performance exceeding one year.

NOTES

[1] FAR 42.1503(a).

[2] FAR 42.302(b)(11).The contracting office may delegate authority for preparing the evaluation to a contract administration office but must do so in writing.

[3] FAR 1.102(c). "The acquisition team consists of all participants in government acquisition, including not only representatives of the technical, supply, and procurement communities, but also the customers they serve and the contractors who provide the products and services."

[4] FAR 36.201(a) and 36.604(a).Standard Form (SF) 1420 is used for construction contracts, and SF 1421 is used for A&E contracts.

[5] FAR 36.201(a)(3) and 36.604(a)(4).

[6] This guidance is consistent with DOD guidance, which states that the "performance assessments are the responsibility of the program/project/contracting team, considering customer's input; no one office or organization should independently determine a performance assessment." See Department of Defense, *A Guide to Collection and Use of Past Performance Information*, May 1999.

[7] DOD guidance encourages providing the contractor with a draft performance assessment report before the initial government assessment. This seems unnecessary, considering that the acquisition team has been communicating with the contractor during the period of contract execution concerning any issues that would be raised in the assessment report. See DOD, ibid.

[8] FAR 19.7.

[9] FAR 19.1202.

Chapter 10

Post-Award: Contractor Review and Response

by Joseph W. Beausoleil

Agency evaluations of contractor performance prepared under this subpart shall be provided to the contractor as soon as practicable after completion of the evaluation. Contractors shall be given a minimum of 30 days to submit comments, rebutting statements, or additional information.[1]

One of the unique features of contractor performance evaluation is that the contractor participates in the process. This participation is reactive. The government prepares the initial assessment, and the contractor is given an opportunity to review and respond to it before the final assessment is made.

CONTRACTOR'S INPUT

The contractor participates as a member of the acquisition team.[2] The contractor's input and that of the government are equally important. The contractor may provide a different perspective, add new information, or even rebut the government's initial assessment of performance. The final assessment is not made until the contractor has had an opportunity to respond and all disagreements between the contractor and the government have been resolved. The procedures related to contractor review, response, and resolution of differences are all aimed at achieving a fair and accurate evaluation of the contractor's performance.

Alerting the Contractor

The evaluation should not be a surprise to the contractor. Although not required, it is recommended that the contract schedule include a statement regarding the contractor performance evaluation, or evaluations, if the period of performance exceeds one year. The statement should alert the contractor that the evaluation will be conducted for the purpose of obtaining past performance information that may be used in future source selections. The statement may be included in section H of the contract schedule. At a minimum, the statement should contain the following:

> On completion of contract activities, the Government shall prepare an evaluation of contractor performance in accordance with FAR 42.15. (In addition, interim evaluations shall be conducted annually.) The contractor will have 30 days to review and respond to the evaluation(s) before final assessment is made. The evaluation(s) may be used for future source selection purposes.

Experience has shown that the knowledge that the evaluations will take place and that the information obtained may be used in future source selection decision is an incentive for the contractor to perform at optimal levels.

Contractor Should Understand the Process

In addition to being alerted about the evaluation, the contractor should understand the process. The more informed the contractor is about the process, the more efficient the response and the fewer chances there are for problems. The contractor should understand the basis on which initial assessment was made, including the scoring procedures, the purpose of the contractor's review and the response options, how disagreements are resolved, and the use that will be made of the evaluations.

Guidance for Contractors

It is recommended that every agency prepare a guide for use by contractors in reviewing the initial assessment. The guide need not be lengthy—one or two pages—and should include the following:

- **Basis on which the evaluation is made**—Emphasize that the evaluation assesses contractors' performance against the performance standards for the requirements stipulated in the contract with respect to the quality of the product or service, timeliness, cost control, and business relations.

- **The rating procedures**—Explain that there are five ratings—exceptional, very good, satisfactory, marginal, and unsatisfactory—and that a satisfactory rating is equivalent to meeting the performance standard for a requirement. Show that a rating above or below satisfactory is in relation to satisfactory performance. Describe what must be demonstrated to achieve a rating higher than satisfactory.

- **Contractor review and resolution of disagreements**—Explain that the contractor is given 30 days to review the initial evaluation and provide comments, rebutting statements, or additional information. Describe the process for resolving disagreements. Make sure that it is understood that if the contractor does not respond, the initial evaluation stands, and the contractor will not have a chance to comment later if the evaluation is used in future source selections.

- **Final ratings and evaluation reports**—Make clear that the final ratings are made only after the contractor has had an opportunity to provide its input to the evaluation. Reassure the contractor that a copy of the final report will be provided to the contractor as soon as it is finalized. Explain that the report will be maintained in a past performance information system and made available to other agencies for source selection purposes. Let the contractor know that the report will not be retained for more than three years in the past performance information system.

Alerting the contractor that the evaluation will be conducted and providing guidance to the contractor on reviewing and responding to the initial evaluation are good business practices. Taking these steps ensures fair treatment to all contractors, helps facilitate the process, and avoids unnecessary conflict.

Contacting the Contractor

The contracting official preparing the evaluation should be the one who forwards the evaluation to the contractor for review, using regular mail or fax. The evaluation should be sent in the name of the person who signed the contract for the contractor. If the agency has been dealing with a person other than the person who signed the contract, notifying that official may expedite the response. A cover letter to the contractor might contain the following:

> The Agency has prepared an initial assessment of performance for the subject contract. Your comments, rebutting statements, or additional information will be considered before making the final assessment. Please review the enclosed evaluation. If we do not hear from you in 30 days, the Agency's assessment will be considered final. These evaluations may be used to support future award decisions. You will receive a copy of the evaluation once it is finalized. More complete information regarding these evaluations can be obtained at the Agency's web site at www.agency.gov/contractor/evaluation/guide.

CONTRACTOR'S REVIEW

The purpose of the review is to complete the evaluation. Input has been provided by the technical and contracting offices, and, where appropriate, the end users. An initial rating and supporting statement have been made for each of

162   PAST PERFORMANCE HANDBOOK

the assessment areas. The contractor is now asked to review the initial assessment for accuracy, completeness, and fairness.

Review Process

The contractor's review of the evaluation should focus on the rating and the summary supporting narrative for the rating of each assessment area evaluated. This is the contractor's opportunity to improve the ratings if it can show that the government has reached its conclusion based on inaccurate, incomplete, or erroneous information. The contractor should review each rating by asking the following questions:

1. Did the agency assess the contractor's performance on all major requirements? If not, what was left out?

2. Did the agency interpret requirements in the same way as the contractor? If not, what are the differences?

3. Are the narrative statements supporting the ratings factually correct? If not, what should be corrected?

4. Do the narratives support the ratings, i.e., justify a rating higher than satisfactory or explain a rating lower than satisfactory?

5. Does the contractor agree with the ratings? If not, what evidence would support a higher rating?

How to Respond to the Agency

Based on the review, the contractor makes a decision as to whether a response to the agency is necessary. A response by the contractor adds to the integrity of the evaluation. The fact that the contractor has provided comments, rebutting statements, or additional information makes it a better evaluation. There are three situations in which a response is needed:

- **Correcting Factual Errors**—A factual error must be corrected by the contracting officer. The contractor would be expected to provide evidence to support its claim.

- **Providing Additional Information**—Additional information must be considered by the contracting officer but does not have to be incorporated into the evaluation. The exception would be when the additional information could affect the rating or the rationale for the rating. In this case the additional information would be presented as a rebuttal.

- **Rebutting the Government's Assessment**—If the contractor disagrees with the rating, it must convince the contracting officer that the agency's rating is incorrect. This may be done by providing information that was not taken into consideration in making the initial rating or showing that the initial rating was based on inaccurate or false information or on a misinterpretation of what transpired. If, after receiving the contractor's rebuttal, the contracting officer disagrees with the contractor, the disagreement must be resolved at a level above the contracting officer. (See Chapter 11.)

Contractors should feel free to discuss informally less than satisfactory ratings with agency personnel for clarification before responding in writing. The discussion could be with the contracting officer but preferably would be with a member of the acquisition team with whom the contractor has been working.

How Not to Respond

When the contractor does not understand the review process, the three most common reactions are: (1) the contractor responds by rebutting satisfactory ratings, (2) the contractor does not respond because the ratings were all above satisfactory, and (3) the contractor does not respond to low ratings because the contractor does not believe anything can be changed. Each of these reactions is misguided.

Satisfactory Ratings—If a contractor does not understand that a satisfactory rating is equivalent to meeting the standard and interprets it as average performance, it is normal for the contractor to be concerned. The fact that the contractor competed for and won the contract indicates that it was the most qualified of the offerors and definitely not an average performer. This mistaken understanding of a satisfactory rating usually ends in a lengthy rebuttal that adds nothing to the evaluation. Contractors must understand that a satisfactory rating on a performance evaluation is a good rating. It means that the contractor complied with contractual requirements for the assessment area. It does not mean that performance was average.

Inflated Ratings—The opposite reaction comes from the contractor who is given exceptional or very good ratings on all the assessment areas. The contractor is pleased and therefore does not respond. This is a mistake because such ratings could be inflated or the narrative might not support the higher ratings. Exceptional means out of the ordinary, or one of a kind. When it is given, the narrative must support the rating. If the narrative does not support an exceptional rating or a very good rating, these ratings will not be credited as such when used in source selection. The source selection authority makes its judgment based on the supporting narrative and not solely on an adjectival or numerical rating. The contractor should at least respond by offering language to support the higher ratings.

164 PAST PERFORMANCE HANDBOOK

Low Ratings—Some contractors accept the ratings as prepared by the agency. They either do not have the time to respond or do not believe that the evaluation will be changed. Doing nothing assumes that the agency has accurately and fairly assessed the contractor's performance. This may be a correct assumption in some cases, but by not responding, the contractor misses its only opportunity to respond.

Special Problems

Two common problems are: (1) responding to negative ratings that are the correct assessment of performance, and (2) responding when there is inconsistency between the ratings of contractor performance evaluations and other evaluations that were conducted during the same period of time.

Negative Rating—If a rating is negative but deserved, the best response is to accept responsibility for the failure and propose corrective action that will be taken to avoid failure in the future. This is especially critical if this is an interim evaluation, which will give the contractor the opportunity to prove itself on the subsequent evaluation. Trying to rebut negative ratings by offering excuses serves no purpose.

Inconsistent Evaluations—There should be consistency between the fee amount paid to contractors under award and incentive fee contracts and the contractor performance evaluation. When comparing the same performance areas, the general rule would be: (1) the higher fee amounts would be equivalent to a very good rating, (2) the lower fee amounts would be equivalent to a satisfactory rating, and (3) no fee payment above the minimum fee amount would be equivalent to a satisfactory rating or could be equivalent to a marginal rating, depending on the circumstances. Paying the highest fee amount does not automatically translate into an exceptional rating on a performance evaluation. It would be inconsistent, however, to give a negative rating if some fee payment were made. Contractors should rebut performance report ratings that do not closely parallel the fee determinations.[3]

NOTES

[1] FAR 42.1503(b).

[2] FAR 1.102(c). The acquisition team is defined as "all participants in government acquisition including not only representatives of the technical, supply, and procurement communities but also the customers they serve, and the contractors who provide the products and services."

[3] FAR 42.1500.

Chapter 11

Post-Award: Resolving Disagreements

by Joseph W. Beausoleil

Agencies shall provide for review at a level above the contracting officer to consider disagreements between the parties regarding the evaluation.[1]

The intent of the review is to resolve disagreements between the contracting officer and the contractor in an equitable and expeditious manner. Experience has shown that these reviews are seldom carried out expeditiously, and, more often than not, the contractor is not satisfied with the results. Part of the problem is in the interpretation of this directive. These three elements must be correctly interpreted: What constitutes a "level above the contracting officer"? How are "disagreements" defined? Who are the "parties" involved? The following definitions should be considered in preparing guidance regarding the agency review.

DEFINITIONS OF TERMS

Level above the Contracting Officer—This will differ depending on the contracting authority's organizational structure. "Level above the contracting officer" is used in various sections of the FAR. It can be the supervisor of the contracting officer or an official outside the contracting officer's supervisory chain. The question that must be asked is whether that official is capable of making an independent review.[2] The official designated to make a review of a protest should not have had previous personal involvement in the procurement.[3] Using this procedure as a precedent, the person designated could be in or outside the supervisory chain of the contracting officer, as long as the person did not have personal involvement in the evaluation. The contracting officer should not designate the official; this should be determined according to an established agency procedure.

Disagreements—For disagreements to be reviewed at a higher level, the contractor must submit a rebutting statement, and the contracting officer must reject the contractor's rebuttal. By submitting a rebutting statement, the contractor demonstrates that it disagrees with the agency's initial rating and argues for a change in the rating or ratings. By rejecting the contractor's rebuttal and not changing the rating or ratings, the contracting officer disagrees with the contractor. The higher-level review considers the opposing positions.

Not all disagreements are reviewed at a higher level; the only disagreements that are reviewed at a higher level regard the ratings. Disagreements regarding interpretation of facts that do not affect the ratings are not subject to higher review. A disagreement exists when the contractor refutes the agency's initial rating or ratings by presenting opposing arguments, and the contracting officer does not accept the contractor's arguments. Merely disagreeing with a rating without offering evidence or arguments to support a change in the rating is not a rebuttal.

Parties—The parties are the government and the contractor. The contracting officer, however, speaks for the government once the contractor responds to the initial assessment. The contracting officer is empowered to make the final assessment and does not have to obtain the concurrence of the acquisition team when he or she disagrees with the contractor. Going back to the members of the acquisition team after the contractor has responded is not necessary and only delays completing the evaluation.[4]

HOW TO AVOID AGENCY REVIEWS

When sending the initial assessment to the contractor, make sure that the contractor has access to agency guidance on responding to the initial assessment of performance. This is particularly important if this is the first time that the contractor has had the opportunity to be evaluated by your agency. The contractor may be familiar with performance evaluations of other agencies that may have procedures different from yours. The easiest way to do this is to advise the contractor when forwarding the evaluation. It is not necessary to include the guide; indicating how to access the guide is sufficient.

If any of the ratings are negative, make sure that there is backup documentation in the contract folder to support the agency's assessment. Never use the evaluation to advise the contractor for the first time that performance is unsatisfactory. Even when there is documentation, it may be useful to discuss this with the contractor before sending out the initial assessment. Personally contacting the contractor should prepare the contractor to accept the rating and could result in avoiding an unnecessary rebuttal. It is a good business practice and should be followed to the extent practicable.

If the contractor rebuts a rating, and the contracting officer does not agree with the contractor, an agency review is in order. Contacting the contractor at this point is not recommended. The contractor is given one opportunity to rebut the ratings. Further dialogue may be instructive to both parties but will not change the past performance of the contractor.

REQUESTING A REVIEW

The evaluation with the contractor response need not be sent to the agency official for review. The review is limited to the areas of disagreement—that is, those ratings where the contractor has responded with a rebuttal statement. All that is necessary to forward to the official making the review is the supporting statement for the ratings and the rebuttal from the contractor.

This material should be submitted in a way that facilitates the review process but does not burden the reviewing official. The suggested approach is to use a four-part action memorandum.

The first part would be a request for a review to resolve the disagreement between the contracting officer and the contractor. The second part would be the agency's supporting statement of the rating or ratings in contention. Using cut and paste, the supporting statement can easily be copied from the evaluation to part two of the memorandum. The third part would be the contractor's rebuttal, which would be attached to the memorandum and only referenced in this part of the memorandum. The fourth part would be a place for the reviewing official to indicate whether he or she concurs with the contracting officer. Concurrence or non-concurrence would be needed for each rating in contention. Space should be provided to allow for comments by the reviewing official.

The following is a sample of the suggested action memorandum.

To: Reviewing Official

From: Contracting Officer

Subj.:   Review of Disagreement between (Contractor's Name) and the Agency

Ref: Contract No.

Problem: The contractor has submitted a statement rebutting the Agency's initial evaluation of performance. The cognizant contracting officer does not agree with the contractor's rebuttal. In accordance with FAR 42.1503(b), "Agencies shall provide for review at a level above the contracting officer to consider disagreements between the parties regarding the evaluation." You are hereby requested to review this matter and render a decision. The Agency's rating and supporting statement are found below, followed by the contractor's rebuttal.

Agency's Rating: The following is a true and correct copy of the supporting statement(s) for the contested rating area or areas to which the contractor has responded. [Cut and paste statement from evaluation.]

Assessment Area: Timeliness   Rating: Satisfactory or 3

Timeliness: The contractor met the deadline for delivery of the product. The contractor did encounter some problems that caused delay in meeting production milestones. Timely identification of these problems and appropriate corrective actions minimized any adverse effects the delays would have had on timely delivery. The contract met the timeliness requirements and therefore is rated Satisfactory.

[Add other assessment areas and ratings, as necessary, and cut and paste appropriate supporting statements.]

Contractor's Rebuttal: The pertinent parts of the contractor's response in which the contractor did not agree with the Agency's evaluation are found in an attachment to this memorandum.

Reviewer's Decision: Please indicate your decision by initialing and dating in the appropriate area below. If you sustain the contracting officer, the rating and supporting statement stand. If you agree with the contractor, the rating and supporting statement will be changed accordingly.

I agree with the contractor with regard to the following assessment areas:

Assessment area(s): _____

Comment: _____

I agree with the contracting officer with regard to the following assessment areas:

Assessment area(s): _____

Comment: _____

Initials: _____ Date: _____

RESPONSIBILITY OF THE REVIEWER

The responsibility of the reviewing official is to consider the facts and decide whether he or she agrees with the contractor or the contracting officer. This decision should be in writing and should be issued within 15 days from receipt of a rebuttal statement.[5] Following the procedure explained above (i.e., using an action memorandum) simplifies and expedites the process. In most cases, there is no need for additional comments—a simple concurrence suffices.

DECISION IS FINAL

Based on the decision of the agency review, the contracting officer makes the final assessment of the contractor's performance.[6] Consulting with the acquisition team and further discussion with the contractor are not needed. There is no appeals process.

ADVISING CONTRACTOR OF DECISION

There is no need to acknowledge receipt of the contractor's response nor to advise the contractor that a higher-level review will take place when the contracting officer disagrees with the contractor's rebuttal. After the review, the contracting officer sends a copy of the evaluation report to the contractor at the same time that it is entered into the agency's past performance information system. The evaluation report should indicate that the agency review took place before the final assessment was made. The agency review document is filed with the contractor's rebuttal in the contract folder. The copy of the agency's review is not given to the contractor, nor is a copy attached to the evaluation report that is entered into the automated information system. If copies are needed in the future, they can be obtained from the contract file.

NOTES

[1] FAR 42.1503(b).

[2] Some would suggest that the reviewing official should have knowledge of the subject matter, as is the case with reviewing officials for evaluations of construction contracts [FAR 36.201(b)] or for architect/engineer contracts [FAR 36.604(b)]. This is a different kind of review. The construction and architect/engineer contract evaluations are reviewed for technical and professional accuracy. The review that is required here is to determine the merits of the opposing positions regarding a rating. The reviewing official acts as a judge and not as an expert in the matter.

[3] FAR 33.103(d)(4).

[4] The contracting officer should defer to the customer regarding the ratings of quality and timeliness but would be expected to make the decision regarding the ratings of cost control and business relations.

[5] Office of Federal Procurement Policy, *A Guide to Best Practices for Past Performance*, May 1995, p. 42.

[6] FAR 42.1503(b). "The ultimate conclusion on the performance evaluation is a decision of the contracting agency."

Chapter 12

Post-Award: Maintaining and Making Accessible Past Performance Information

by Joseph W. Beausoleil

Departments and agencies shall share past performance information with other departments and agencies when requested to support future award decisions.[1]

The purpose of conducting contractor performance evaluations is to provide information for use in source selection. All the effort in conducting contractor performance evaluations will be in vain if the information obtained is not used in making award decisions. This information must be maintained in such a way that it is accessible to source selection officials when reviewing the qualifications of offerors.

MAINTAINING PAST PERFORMANCE INFORMATION

The evaluation is retained in the contract file, which includes the evaluation report, the contractor's response, and the agency review, if a review was required to resolve disagreements between the contractor and the contracting officer. It does not include the working papers associated with conducting the evaluation, such as copies of e-mails to obtain input from the members of the government's acquisition team. These may be discarded once the evaluation is completed.

Treat As Source Selection Information

Because the evaluation may be used to support future award decisions, it should be identified as source selection information.[2] This can be accomplished by marking "Source Selection Material" on a cover sheet for the evaluation documents or on the folder in which the documents are filed. It is not necessary to mark each page of the evaluation at this time, but only when the evaluation is released to source selection officials.[3]

172 PAST PERFORMANCE HANDBOOK

Past Performance Information System

Only a copy of the evaluation report is retained in the past performance information system. It is not necessary to retain the contractor response or the agency review comments with the report. These are part of the evaluation but usually are not needed by source selection officials. The report contains relevant past performance information—the agency's rating and the rationale for the rating. This is all that the source selection official requires. The source selection official will not reevaluate the agency ratings by reviewing the related documentation but accepts the agency's interpretation. The evaluation report will indicate that the contractor was given the opportunity to review the evaluation and, if there were disagreements between the contracting officer and the contractor regarding the ratings, whether a review was made at a level above the contracting officer.

The past performance information system needs to be automated so that the reports can be transmitted to the system and accessed electronically. On completion of the evaluation, the contracting officer sends a copy of the evaluation report to the contractor.[4] At the same time, the contracting officer transmits an electronic copy of the evaluation report to the past performance information system.

Past performance information systems must have management and technical controls so that access is limited to authorized personnel.[5] This usually can be achieved by assigning user identification and passwords to acquisition officials who need to transmit or retrieve the evaluation reports.

SHARING PAST PERFORMANCE INFORMATION

Past performance information may be provided by interview or by sending the evaluation documents to the requesting official. Providing the information by interview is recommended when the requesting official only needs to verify specific information or to clarify a point or two. However, interviews are not recommended as a general practice because they have serious drawbacks. They take time for both the source selection official and the official or officials being interviewed. Furthermore, any negative findings from such an interview may require contacting the offeror. If the award is to be made without discussions, the offeror would have to be given an opportunity to respond to the negative past performance information.[6] If a competitive range is to be established, communications would have to be held with the offeror to address negative past performance information to which an offeror has not had an opportunity to respond.[7]

Sending the information to the source selection official is preferable. The evaluation and the comment documents may be sent, but this is not usually necessary. All that is necessary is relevant past performance information—the evaluation report. The evaluation report not only provides the ratings and supporting statements for each of the assessment areas, but also verifies that the contractor had the opportunity to respond to any negative findings. The report also would verify if it were necessary to have had an agency review at a level above the contracting officer.

Sending the evaluation report only, and not the contractor's response or agency review, does not imply that the two latter documents are not shared with other agencies. These documents would be shared with another agency in the event that, after making the evaluation report available to the requesting agency, questions arose that needed clarification. If the contracting officer could not resolve the issues by phone or by e-mail, the contracting officer would send the requested documents—contractor's response and agency review of disagreements—to the requesting agency.

Making these documents available, in addition to the evaluation report, would be the exception, not the rule. Copies of the documents requested would be made from the hard copy in the contract file, marked as source selection information, and sent to the requesting source selection official. The infrequency of requests for the contractor's response or for the agency review comments does not warrant maintaining these documents in the past performance information system. Only the evaluation reports with the ratings and supporting statements for the ratings need be maintained in an automated past performance information system.

EXPERIENCES IN MAINTAINING PAST PERFORMANCE INFORMATION

The U.S. Army Corps of Engineers (USACE) has managed two past performance information systems for over a decade. These systems, known as the Construction Contractor Appraisal Support System (CCASS) and the Architect-Engineer Contract Administration Support System (ACASS), maintain performance evaluation reports on construction and architect-engineer contracts, respectively. Originally established by USACE for its own use, all federal departments and agencies may use these systems as appropriate.[8] Although each system serves a specific clientele, their policies and procedures are similar.

Evaluation Reports on Construction Contracts

CCASS is an automated database of performance evaluations on construction contractors.[9] The evaluations are conducted in accordance with FAR 36.201, which requires the preparation of a report using a standard form (SF 1420). The reports are electronically transmitted to CCASS. The primary use of the contractor performance evaluations is to make the responsibility determination in awarding sealed bid contracts. Contractor performance evaluations are also used when past performance is an evaluation factor in the second phase of a two-phase design-build selection.[10] To retrieve the evaluation reports, the authorized user responds to a series of questions, and the results are transmitted to the requestor's computer.[11] The cost of using CCASS is based on a fee for service to cover operating and maintenance costs. No profit is made from the system. The performance reports are automatically purged from the system after six years from the date of the reviewing official signature.

Evaluation Reports on Architect-Engineer Contracts

ACASS is a database of selected information on architect-engineer firms. In addition to performance evaluations, ACASS tracks the amount of work an architect-engineer firm has been awarded by the Department of Defense and maintains qualifications and performance data of architect-engineer firms.[12] Performance evaluations are conducted in accordance with FAR 36.604, which requires the preparation of a report using a standard form (SF 1421). The reports are electronically transmitted to ACASS. Permission to access ACASS is granted to persons within any federal agency with authority to contract with architect-engineer firms. Like CCASS, the cost of using ACASS is based on a fee for service to cover operations and maintenance. No profit is made on the system, and the evaluation reports are automatically purged from the system after six years.

Lessons Learned

There are a number of lessons learned from the USACE experience. The evaluation report is entered into the past performance system. Other documentation used in preparing the evaluation report, including comments from the contractor, is maintained in the contract file. The system must be automated to make it possible for the data to be entered and retrieved electronically. Access can be controlled by providing a user identification and password to officials who use the system to enter or retrieve data.

Applying the Experience

The experience of USACE is applicable to other agency past performance systems except in one area: It is not necessary for an agency to set up separate past

Post-Award: Maintaining and Making Accessible Past Performance Information   **175**

performance information systems for each category of contracts that it administers. One past performance information system is sufficient for all other categories of contracts. USACE has two systems because the regulations governing the evaluation of construction contracts are different from the regulations governing architect-engineer contracts. Contracts other than construction and architect-engineer contracts are evaluated in accordance with the same regulations.[13]

There is no need for other agencies to maintain evaluation reports on construction and architect-engineer contracts since USACE already provides this service to all federal agencies through either CCASS or ACASS. For all other contracts, however, agencies must establish their own past performance information system, use another agency's past performance information system, or a combination of both.

Problems with Multiple Past Performance Information Systems

With the proliferation of past performance information systems—each agency establishing its own system—retrieving data from many systems can be a laborious process. The fewer the past performance information systems, the more efficient the process. This is because of the need to have a user identification and a password to gain access to each system. The user ID and password are required not just for the agency using the system but also for every contracting officer who enters data into the systems and for every source selection official who retrieves data from the system. This is not a problem when the contracts listed by the offeror are from one agency, but it becomes more difficult to retrieve the data when the contracts listed by the offerors are from different agencies. A user ID and password are required for each system where past performance information is maintained.

An example of the inefficiencies created by multiple systems would be a solicitation in which there were five proposals, each listing seven contracts that were similar to the requirements of the solicitation. This would require accessing 35 evaluation reports, which could come from one or from as many as 35 different past performance information systems. Even if it required only accessing five or six systems, it would mean obtaining a user ID and a password for that many systems for at least one source selection official. Every new solicitation would require obtaining a user ID and a password for different source selection officials.

The problem might be resolved by having one government-wide past performance information system. The technology exists to have such a system. The challenge is for all departments and agencies to agree on how such a system should be managed and supported.

Integration of Agency Past Performance Information Systems

DOD has taken the initiative in establishing a past performance report card retrieval system that addresses some of the issues. The system is the Past Performance Automated Information System (PPAIS), and it is designed to provide access to information about contractors and their performance that may be used by DOD acquisition personnel. PPAIS supports the retrieval of "report cards" collected across DOD.[14] It also allows any authorized DOD user to access a central database of "report card" information with one query to obtain access to records collected throughout DOD.[15]

On the civilian side of the federal government, which includes many departments and independent agencies, there is no comparable past performance information system. However, the National Institutes of Health (NIH) has taken a leadership role in providing this function. The NIH Contractor Performance System is a multiple agency, shared file system. Subscribers pay an annual fee based on the number of contracts that will be maintained for the department or agency. All authorized users have access to the completed evaluations of all subscribing agencies.[16]

Virtually Shared Information Network

Maintaining all performance reports in one government-wide past performance information system may not be practicable. However, recent advances in information technology make it possible for every agency to access past performance information collected by another without the need to merge all performance reports into one system. This could be accomplished by creating a virtually shared information network across agencies. Each agency would be responsible for maintaining its own past performance information system, but a virtual connection via lightweight directory access protocol (LDAP) could be used to allow users to access files within these information systems, regardless of the agency. The agency administrators would be in control of their information systems and could limit access through the use of access control lists (ACLs).

PROVISIONAL SOLUTION

Until there is a government-wide past performance system or until all agency systems are interoperable, there is a solution that could make evaluation reports that are maintained in many systems throughout the government accessible to one agency at the time of source selection—requesting that offerors submit the reports with their proposals. Contractors are now given copies of annual and completion evaluations.[17] Every evaluation report that is in a past performance information system is also in the possession of the contractor. It is easier to access the reports from the offeror than it is to have the source selection authority access the same reports from the various agency information systems where they might be contained.

Submitting Evaluation Reports with the Proposal

Source selection officials should not have to request copies of the evaluation reports from agency information systems. They should be made available when the offerors submit their proposals. In addition to listing contracts that are similar to the government requirement, offerors should include any evaluation reports that were completed on the listed contracts. This will save the source selection officials from having to access the same reports from the past performance information systems where the reports are maintained.

Providing the evaluation report when listing the contract is consistent with the opportunity afforded offerors to identify problems and corrective action taken on the listed contracts.[18] If there was a problem with the contract listed, and the contract was evaluated, the evaluation would have identified the problem and assessed the contractor corrective action taken. It would make no sense for the offeror to provide a new or different version of the problems and corrective action, as they would already have been documented in the evaluation report.

One could argue that the offeror could change the ratings, delete information, or doctor the evaluation report. The simple answer is to have the offeror certify that the evaluation report is a true copy of the evaluation report provided by the agency. It would be foolish not to be truthful, knowing that the source selection authority could verify the information because the original evaluation report could easily be accessed from the contract file or from the past performance information system where it was maintained.

Emphasis on Evaluating, Not on Collecting, Past Performance Information

Making the contractor responsible for submitting the evaluation reports will not do away with the need for past performance information systems. It will certainly obviate the need for the source selection official to access the reports in most instances. As mentioned, it may be necessary to access an evaluation report when the source selection authority suspects that the copy of an evaluation report submitted by the offeror appears to be altered. The past performance information systems also serve to access evaluation reports for contracts not listed by the offeror (for example, in the case in which the offeror did not list a contract because the evaluation report was negative).

Past performance information systems will be used primarily for maintaining the completed evaluation report. The need to access the reports will be substantially reduced. Making the contractor responsible for submitting the past performance information will allow the source selection officials to concentrate on evaluating past performance information rather than on collecting past performance information.

* * *

Past performance will be an effective non-cost source selection evaluation factor to the extent that past performance information is readily available.

NOTES

[1] FAR 42.1503(c).

[2] FAR 42.1503(b).

[3] FAR 3.104-5, Disclosure, protection, and marking of contractor bid or proposal information or source selection information.

[4] FAC 97-02 amended FAR 42.1503 in paragraph (b) by adding the following sentence at the end of the paragraph: "A copy of the annual or final past performance evaluation shall be provided to the contractor as soon as it is finalized."

[5] FAR 42.1503(d).

[6] FAR 15.306(a)(2).

[7] FAR 15.306(b)(1)(i).

[8] Office of Federal Procurement Policy, Policy Letter 92-5, December 30, 1992.

[9] USACE applies different thresholds for performance evaluations. While the FAR requires evaluations of construction contracts in excess of $500,000, or in excess of $10,000 if the contract was terminated for default, USACE requires evaluations of construction contracts of $100,000 or higher, $25,000 or higher if any element of performance is either unsatisfactory or outstanding, and $10,000 or higher if the contract is terminated for default. In addition, interim performance evaluations are prepared for contracts when a contractor's performance is generally unsatisfactory for a period of three months or longer.

[10] FAR 36.303-2.

[11] Federal agencies may request a user ID and password for access to CCASS by going to the website: http://www.nwp.usace.army.mil/ct/i/.

[12] FAR 36.603, Collecting data on and appraising firms' qualifications statements.

[13] FAR 42.15.

[14] The sources of data include the Department of Navy Contractor Performance Assessment Reporting Systems, the Army's Past Performance Information Management System, and the Defense Information Systems Agency's Past Performance Evaluation Tool.

[15] To gain access to the system, the acquisition official fills out an online request for a user ID and password. After obtaining a user ID and password, the acquisition official requests access to one of the component groups. Generally, the official would request access from the head of the component group affiliated with his or her command. Once access is granted, the official has

Post-Award: Maintaining and Making Accessible Past Performance Information **179**

access to all report cards in the system. The URL for PPAIS is: http://dodppais.navsea.navy.mil. See Department of Defense, *Past Performance Automated Information System, Past Performance Report Card Retrieval System, User's Guide*, 28 July 2000.

[16] Subscribing to the system are the Departments of Agriculture, Commerce, Energy, Health and Human Services, and Justice, the Environmental Protection Agency, the Federal Emergency Management Agency, the Nuclear Regulatory Commission, the U.S. Agency for International Development, the U.S. Coast Guard, and the U.S. Postal Service. See: National Institutes of Health, *Contractor Performance System, Fact Sheet*, modified 04/04/00.

[17] FAR 42.1503(b).

[18] FAR 15.305(a)(2)(ii).

Chapter 13

Legal Issues in Past Performance

by Thomas L. McGovern III and Timothy D. Palmer

Since promulgation of the federal regulations pertaining to past performance in 1995, agency practices for the evaluation of past performance have become more standardized and consistent. GAO, in particular, has fostered consistent practices among agencies by issuing numerous decisions that provide guidance as to how the regulations should work in practice. Still, because the evaluation of past performance is inherently subjective, no amount of guidance can completely eliminate questionable practices when it comes to evaluation of past performance. So, what legal rights can contractors invoke to ensure fair evaluation of their past performance?

While most of the legal challenges relating to an agency's use of past performance information involve the agency's evaluation of past performance information in the source selection process (FAR Part 15 negotiated procurements), there are actions that contractors can take during contract performance to enhance their competitive advantage in future procurements (FAR Part 42). The first part of this chapter addresses steps that a contractor can take during contract performance to improve the accuracy of an agency's evaluation of its performance and thereby avoid problems that might later damage its competitive position in the federal marketplace.

Once a contract is completed and the contemporaneous evaluations of past performance have been memorialized, the contractor's attention should turn to how those evaluations will be used in the context of future source selection decisions. Not surprisingly, a number of questions remain about how past performance should be weighed and scored in the context of a source selection process (notwithstanding the regulatory coverage in the FAR and OFPP's published guidance). At this stage, questions or disputes often are resolved through a formal bid protest filed either at GAO or the Court of Federal Claims. The resulting protest decision resolves the immediate protest ground on past performance. More importantly, however, these decisions, when considered as a body of law, fill in the "gaps" in the regulations and thereby serve both to inform federal contractors concerning their legal rights and to guide agency procurement officials' actions in connection with future procurements. Because of

182 PAST PERFORMANCE HANDBOOK

the importance of this collective body of protest decisions, the second part of this chapter is devoted to addressing protest decisions on key past performance issues.

HOW CONTRACTORS CAN USE PAST PERFORMANCE INFORMATION TO THEIR COMPETITIVE ADVANTAGE

Poor performance ratings can be nearly impossible to overcome and may seriously reduce business opportunities within the federal marketplace. Perhaps the most obvious way for contractors to avoid poor performance ratings is to perform well on their contracts. However, exemplary performance is not always possible or, for a host of reasons, not always recognized or acknowledged by agency evaluators. Thus, contractors should be vigilant and do everything possible to ensure an appropriate evaluation of contract performance.

Contractors can shape or influence the performance evaluation process and should take full advantage of every opportunity to do so to increase the likelihood that past performance information is accurate and is presented in the light most beneficial to the contractor.

As discussed below, contractors have four opportunities to provide input:

- *During and at the close of contract performance* by submitting comments on performance evaluations

- *During and at the close of contract performance* by requesting review by officials a level above the contracting officer when the contractor disagrees with the initial performance evaluation

- *During proposal preparation* by preparing proposals that address known problems head-on and by presenting performance records in the best possible light

- *During proposal evaluation* by participating actively in oral or written exchanges with the agency to ascertain and address each issue of potential concern to evaluators.

Submit Comments on Performance Evaluations

Agencies are required by FAR 42.1503(b) to allow contractors to review their performance evaluations and to give contractors at least 30 days to submit comments and rebuttals. Like the evaluations themselves, any comments and rebutting statements made in response to the contractor's review of an evaluation will, for the three years after contract completion, be part of the evaluation file used for future source selection decisions.

Because the evaluation file will form the basis for future source selections, contractors should treat it as critical to their future success in winning contracts and devote as much time and resources toward ensuring its accuracy as is necessary. Contractors should assume that the 30-day period will be their only chance to comment on performance evaluations, and thus should make the most of the opportunity. Any aspect of an evaluation report that could be perceived as negative or marginal should be addressed in as much detail as possible, within any space constraints imposed by the agency. In addition, if possible, documentation should be provided to bolster the credibility of the contractor's position.

Performance evaluations cover such areas as quality of performance, cost control, timeliness, and business relations (including customer satisfaction). Optimally, every score below "excellent" or "good" in these areas should be explained. Detailed explanations should address such factors as:

1. The government's role in contributing to any perceived performance problems

2. The excusable nature of the problem—how the problem was beyond the contractor's control

3. Efforts the contractor undertook at the time to address the issue

4. Corrective actions taken to prevent future occurrences of the problems

5. The uncharacteristic nature of the problem in light of the contractor's overall performance record.

Obtain Review at a Level above the Contracting Officer

In instances where the parties cannot come to terms and the contractor disagrees with how potentially damaging information is characterized, the contractor should be sure to take advantage of the provisions in FAR Part 42 requiring review of the evaluation at a level above the contracting officer. The contractor should prepare its case as thoroughly as possible and explain why performance problems either were beyond its control or how they have been corrected and will not be repeated. Again, documentary support may be crucial for supporting the contractor's position and should be provided if available or reasonably attainable.

Prepare Proposals to Present Past Performance in the Best Light Possible

In addition to the performance evaluations available to procuring agencies, agencies will rely to varying extents on offerors' proposals as a primary source of PPI. It follows that contractors should carefully consider the contracts and references they choose to identify in their proposals as "relevant." It should be assumed that procuring agencies will contact all such references and use them as a primary source of information. Contractors should also assume that relevant PPI will come to light, even if not discussed in their proposals.

In the event a contractor has a poor performance record on a particular contract effort, it should closely examine all aspects of that contract to determine how best to distinguish it from the effort being solicited. In this way, inclusion of the problematic effort in the proposal as a relevant contract may be avoided. Factors such as (1) technical similarities, (2) dollar amount, (3) age, (4) contract type (fixed price or cost type), (5) performance period, and (6) nature of customer may each be used as distinguishing factors. If the contract cannot in good faith be distinguished and must be included in the proposal as a relevant contract, the circumstances surrounding any performance problems should be thoroughly explained if the opportunity is presented. The issues addressed above—the government's role in contributing to the problems, the excusable nature of the problems, and the contractor's corrective action to prevent future occurrences—should be emphasized. Bad experiences should be cast as "lessons learned," and assurances should be given to the evaluator that, because of changes implemented, there will be no similar problems in the future.

Use Discussions to Enhance Your Position

FAR 15.306(b) requires agencies to allow offerors to address adverse PPI to which they have not had an opportunity to respond, if the PPI is the determining factor preventing them from being placed within the competitive range or if their inclusion or exclusion from the competitive range is uncertain. Such PPI, of course, normally will not include evaluation reports prepared under FAR Part 42 and PPI the offeror has presented in its proposal. The provision is generally meant to address PPI the agency has obtained from third-party sources that may be unknown to the offeror. Once such PPI is raised with the offeror, the offeror should marshal its resources to research the circumstances that gave rise to the adverse PPI and to provide strong responses, if possible, that address the issues summarized above.

While disagreements on a personal level may, and often do, lead to poor references on a contract performance level, contractors should bear in mind that, under FAR 15.306(e)(4), government personnel involved in the procure-

Legal Issues in Past Performance **185**

ment are forbidden to disclose the names of the individuals providing reference information about an offeror's past performance. Thus, the substance of the information is the only material to which contractors are entitled during discussions. This fact may serve to hinder a contractor's understanding of, and explanation for, why it received a poor past performance reference from what was otherwise presumed to be a friendly reference.

CHALLENGING AGENCY PAST PERFORMANCE EVALUATIONS

Protests of an alleged improper agency evaluation of past performance are extremely commonplace, despite the fact that protesters face an uphill battle in trying to convince GAO that impropriety exists. GAO's general rule is that it "will examine an agency's past performance evaluation only to ensure that it was reasonable and consistent with the stated evaluation criteria and applicable statutes and regulations, since determining the relative merit of an offeror's past performance is primarily a matter within the contracting agency's discretion." (*OSI Collection Servs.*, Inc., B-286597, 2001 CPD ¶ 18.)

Scope of the PPI Review—Relevancy and Currency

A significant body of GAO case law addresses the issue of what past performance an agency may, must, or must not consider in its evaluation. GAO has summarized its rulings on this issue as follows:

> [A]n agency has discretion to determine the scope of the vendors' performance history to be considered, provided that it evaluates all submissions on the same basis and consistent with the solicitation. An agency properly may base its evaluation on contracts it believes are most relevant to the solicitation; it has discretion to consider information other than that provided by the vendors, and need not consider all references a vendor submits. [(Power Connector, Inc., B-286875.2, 2001 CPD ¶ 39 (internal citations omitted).]

In *Power Connector, Inc.,* the agency, Federal Prison Industries, Inc., issued a solicitation for glove leather. In evaluating the protester's past performance, the agency declined to consider two contracts for communications components because it viewed them as too dissimilar to the instant procurement to be relevant. GAO agreed that this decision was reasonable and well within agency discretion. The protester also complained that the agency had treated it disparately, as the agency had considered a dissimilar contract performed by another offeror, for fiberboard, when evaluating that offeror's past performance. GAO found that the agency had acted properly in the evaluation because the offeror had had no similar contracts the agency could consider. Further, although the

186 PAST PERFORMANCE HANDBOOK

offeror had received a "good" rating for its past performance, the contracting officer had identified the offeror as an unacceptable performance risk because it had no experience in contracts similar to the procurement.

Agencies are not required to contact all references an offeror identifies in performing a past performance evaluation. Because there is no statutory or regulatory requirement that all references be contacted, GAO has held that an agency may choose to contact only those that it believes are relevant to the instant procurement. (*Quality Elevator Co.*, B-271899, 96-2 CPD ¶ 89.) In one case involving an Air Force design/build project, for example, GAO found the agency had acted reasonably when it deemed relevant only two of 15 projects identified by the offeror because the two projects were the only design/build projects the offeror had performed for the government. (*Black & Veatch Special Projects Corp.*, B-279492.2, 98-1 CPD ¶ 173.) In fact, GAO has even found it proper for an agency to contact only one of many identified references, based on the agency's determination of relevance. (*Neil R. Gross & Co.*, B-275066, 97-1 CPD ¶ 30; *HLC Indus., Inc.*, B-274374, 96-2 CPD ¶ 214.)

Similarly, an agency may ignore an entire class of references when evaluating past performance. In *Lynwood Machine & Eng'g, Inc.* (B-285696, 2001 CPD ¶ 113), for example, the protester complained that the agency had failed to contact any of its commercial references. GAO found that the agency had reasonably regarded the protester's government contracts to be more relevant to the instant procurement than its commercial contracts and thus had acted properly. Interestingly, the agency had made telephone calls to the protester's largest commercial customer but its calls were not returned. GAO found that the agency properly proceeded with its evaluations without that customer's reference, as an agency is "only required to make a reasonable effort to contact a reference."

GAO has even accepted an agency evaluation in which the agency purposefully excluded the past performance of all key personnel as irrelevant. (*Olympus Bldg. Servs., Inc.*, B-282887, 99-2 CPD ¶ 49.) GAO found reasonable the agency's contention that, because it was contracting with the corporate entity and not the individuals, the corporate entity's PPI was more indicative of future performance.

In addition to considering whether a referenced project is relevant to the instant procurement based on the *similarity* of the subject matter of the two projects, agencies may also consider whether the *size or scope* of the projects makes them comparable for past performance purposes. (*Northeast MEP Servs., Inc.*, B-285963.5, 2001 CPD ¶ 28.) Indeed, an agency may even downgrade an offeror's past performance evaluation where its references provided high marks, if the size or scope of the highly regarded performance nonetheless is incomparable to the instant procurement's size or scope. (*Walsh Distrib., Inc.*, B-281904, 99-1 CPD ¶ 92.)

Although offerors are generally required to provide a certain number of past performance references in their proposals, this does not mean that the agency is restricted to those references in evaluating an offeror's past performance. Indeed, an agency may seek PPI from any source, regardless of whether or not the offeror identifies the source as a reference (*TEAM Support Servs., Inc.*, B-279379.2, 98-1 CPD ¶ 167), so long as the source has specific knowledge of the contract performed by the offeror. (*Black & Veatch Special Projects Corp.*, B-279492.2, 98-1 CPD ¶ 173.)

Agencies are not, however, given complete discretion to determine what PPI they will consider and what they will ignore. For example, protesters have successfully argued that agency evaluators who had personal knowledge of relevant past performance acted unreasonably by failing to take it into consideration in proposal evaluation. (*GTS Duratek, Inc.*, B-280511.2, 98-2 CPD ¶ 130; *International Business Systs., Inc.*, B-275554, 97-1 CPD ¶ 114.)

In *GTS Duratek*, the protester was the incumbent on a contract considered so similar to the instant solicitation that it was used as the basis for the government's cost estimate. Additionally, the contracting officer's representative for the protester's contract was a member of the Technical Evaluation Board for the instant solicitation. The agency defended its failure to consider the contract in its past performance evaluation by contending that the protester's failure to complete a Contractor Past Performance Data Sheet for the contract had prevented the agency from sending out a past performance survey. Under the circumstances, however, GAO found that "the agency could not reasonably ignore personally known information" about the protester's prior experience "merely because the firm did not submit a Contractor Past Performance Data Sheet for that contract." *See also SCIENTECH, Inc.*, B-277805.2, 98-1 CPD ¶ 33 (protest sustained where agency failed to consider another contract with same agency for same services).

The rule that evaluators must use such personal knowledge may also cut against the offeror, of course. In *Omega World Travel, Inc.* (B-271262.2, 96-2 CPD ¶ 44), for instance, GAO held that agency evaluators acted reasonably when they downgraded a proposal based on their personal knowledge of complaints about the offeror's performance on other contracts.

The currency of PPI may also affect an agency's scope of review during an evaluation of past performance. As outlined above, FAR Part 42 directs that PPI "shall not be retained to provide source selection information for longer than three years after completion of contract performance." [FAR 42.1503(e).] This restriction, however, pertains only to agencies' administration of their past performance information systems; it does not affect an agency's authority to include PPI older than three years in its source selection determinations. Indeed, Part 15, which governs the procedures for negotiated source selections, con-

188 PAST PERFORMANCE HANDBOOK

tains no such restriction on the age of PPI. As a result, agencies commonly request PPI from contracts completed more than three years prior to the instant solicitation.

It is important to bear in mind, however, that agencies will often adjust the value of PPI according to the age of the prior contract to which it relates. GAO has approved of such weighting of PPI, stating, not surprisingly, that agencies may give more weight to PPI relating to recent contracts than they give to that relating to older contracts. (*Chemical Demilitarization Assocs.*, B-277700, 98-1 CPD ¶ 171.)

Challenging the Accuracy of PPI

Ensuring that exceptional contract performance is reported accurately may be as important to future business as ensuring the exceptional performance itself. GAO generally does not look kindly upon protester challenges to the accuracy of PPI that has been relied upon in a source selection. Thus, contractors are advised, in the first instance, to seek out opportunities to review, and correct if necessary, their PPI to which agencies may have access. The second line of defense against inaccurate PPI is to challenge its use after the fact, which is usually much more difficult, as the following case law suggests.

Agencies are generally required to consider PPI of an exculpatory nature if it tends to counter negative past performance ratings; however, there is no requirement that agencies seek out such information. Rather, offerors are obligated to provide the agency with their most current PPI, even if the agency could otherwise gain access to the PPI. In one case, for example, the protester argued that the agency's past performance evaluation was flawed because the agency failed to update its files to reflect a recent Armed Services Board of Contract Appeals decision that cast doubt upon the accuracy of an earlier negative past performance evaluation. The protester had not brought the decision to the attention of the agency prior to the PPI evaluation. GAO dismissed the protest, holding that there exists no legal obligation on the part of agencies to search for PPI not already on hand. (*Cessna Aircraft Co.*, B-261953.5, 96-1 CPD ¶ 132.)

Contractors have also had little success in challenging the use and accuracy of government-maintained past performance databases, such as contractor performance assessment reports (CPARs) and the mechanization of contract administration system (MOCAS). In one case, the protester contended that the agency's use of MOCAS data was flawed because the system overstated the protester's delinquency rate and that of its proposed subcontractor. The agency countered that it used the MOCAS data only to determine annual performance trends and not for reviewing performance on individual contracts. GAO agreed that where the data were only "used to identify current trends in overall performance in the most general terms," the protester's concerns of inaccuracy were unfounded. (*Lockheed Aircraft Service Co.*, B-255305, 94-1 CPD ¶ 205.)

In *Engineered Air Systs., Inc.* (B-283011, 99-2 CPD ¶ 63), the agency had relied on a computer-generated CPAR that admittedly contained a typographical error. The incorrect CPAR stated that the author "definitely *would not* award" to the protester again, while the correct hard copy of the document stated that the author "definitely *would* award" to the protester again. The protester argued that the agency had relied heavily on the incorrect CPAR, as it was repeatedly cited in the evaluation record, and thus the past performance evaluation was fatally flawed. GAO disagreed, accepting the agency's contention that it did not "rely solely" on the inaccurate CPAR in assessing the protester's past performance and finding that other evidence in the record supported the protester's past performance rating.

Time and again, GAO decisions show that protesters bear a heavy evidentiary burden when challenging past performance evaluations. In *Dragon Services, Inc.* (B-255354, 94-1 CPD ¶ 151), for example, the protester lost an Army contract for hospital nutritional care services because of a higher risk assessment derived from its past performance history. The Army's assessment was based in part on disputed information from another Army facility. The protester offered excuses, interpretations, and documentation that GAO admitted tended to place the past performance problems in a light more favorable to the protester. However, GAO still found that the protester failed to meet its burden of showing that the disputed PPI was inaccurate. It then reiterated its general rule that "an agency's evaluation of past performance may be based upon the procuring agency's reasonable perception of inadequate prior performance, even where the contractor disputes the agency's interpretation of the facts." In other words, as in other areas of bid protests, a contractor's mere disagreement with the agency on an evaluation issue will usually get the contractor nowhere—hard evidence must be provided showing that the agency's position is unreasonable.

In another case, the protester provided evidence to support its challenge to the accuracy of PPI accumulated for the agency by Dun & Bradstreet (D&B). (*OSI Collection Servs.*, B-286597, 2001 CPD ¶ 18.) The protester argued that one negative assessment it had received from a reference was suspect, and provided a statement from an individual who purported to be the only person at the reference authorized to provide such information. The individual stated that she did not recall being contacted by D&B, and if she had been, she would have provided a favorable assessment of the protester. GAO pointed out that D&B is an independent and impartial data-gathering service often used by agencies to evaluate past performance. It also pointed out that the negative assessment was consistent with at least one other reference in the protester's D&B past performance evaluation, and the agency had no information that would have alerted it to the purported inaccuracy.

190   PAST PERFORMANCE HANDBOOK

GAO found that, under these circumstances, the "agency had no reason to question the accuracy of the D&B past performance evaluation, and, thus, no duty to independently verify the references. It was entitled to rely upon this information as a component of its past performance evaluation."

However, there are limits to an agency's discretion to rely on or interpret the PPI before it. In *OneSource Energy Servs., Inc.* (B-283445, 2000 CPD ¶ 109), the agency had found the protester's past performance to be "marginal" during proposal evaluations, largely based upon purported comments from a customer's technical specialist on a previous contract. At a hearing held by GAO, however, the technical specialist testified that he did not recall making certain statements the agency attributed to him, that the agency misinterpreted other statements, and that other statements in the agency's evaluation record were inaccurate or mischaracterized. GAO sustained the protest.

Exchanges Regarding Past Performance

After submission of proposals, exchanges between offerors and agencies regarding past performance vary depending upon the stage of the source selection. As noted previously, exchanges may come in the form of "clarifications," "communications," or "discussions," each of which is treated distinctly by the FAR and GAO.

If the agency intends to make award without discussions, GAO has held that the contracting officer has "broad discretion" to decide whether to address an offeror's past performance history by seeking a "clarification." (*A.G. Cullen Constr., Inc.*, B-284049.2, 2000 CPD ¶ 45.) If the clarification would involve adverse PPI upon which the offeror has not had a chance to comment, the offeror must be given "an opportunity to respond where there clearly is a reason to question the validity of the past performance information, for example, where there are obvious inconsistencies between a reference's narrative comments and the actual ratings the reference gives the offeror." (*A.G. Cullen Constr.*) Conversely, if the contracting officer has no reason to question the validity of PPI, "he or she can reasonably rely on the information furnished without seeking to verify it or permitting the protester an opportunity to rebut it." (*Lynwood Machine & Eng'g, Inc.*, B-285696, 2001 CPD ¶ 113.)

Agencies must have "communications" with certain offerors if a competitive range is to be established. [FAR 15.306(b).] With respect to past performance, communications must be held with offerors whose PPI is the determining factor preventing them from being in the competitive range. In one of the few cases addressing this issue, GAO conducted a review of the agency's report, found nothing in that record showing that the protester's PPI was the reason it failed to make the competitive range, and thus denied the protest. (*The Community Partnership LLC*, B-286844, 2001 CPD ¶ 38.)

If a competitive range is established, the contracting officer must discuss with each offeror any "significant weaknesses, deficiencies, and other aspects of its proposal," including past performance, that could be altered or explained so as to enhance materially the proposal's potential for award. Problems of past performance that fall under one or more of these descriptions must be discussed.

In determining whether an agency considered particular items of PPI "significant weaknesses" or "deficiencies," GAO usually just refers to the agency evaluation report. (*Digital Systems Group, Inc.*, B-286931, 2001 CPD ¶ 50.) In *Digital Systems Group*, GAO denied a protest after it noted that while the report had identified the disputed PPI problems as "weaknesses," the evaluators considered them neither "significant weaknesses" nor "deficiencies." Conversely, in *CRAssociates, Inc.* (B-282705.2, 2000 CPD ¶ 63), GAO sustained a protest where the agency's report did not even discuss, much less downplay, the significance of PPI problems. GAO stated, "[w]hile these negative evaluations were not specifically relied upon in the [source selection board's] tradeoff, we cannot conclude that they did not have an impact on [the protester's] overall rating."

Agencies may not expend any effort to conduct discussions on past performance problems if they believe such discussions are unlikely to alter the evaluation result. In *Maytag Aircraft Corp.* (B-287589, 2001 CPD ¶ 121), the protester contended that the agency had failed during discussions to raise past performance issues that the agency considered to be weaknesses. The contracting officer explained that because the problems had been well-documented by the protester and the agency, and because two of the pertinent references were also evaluators on the source selection committee, she had determined that additional discussions of the problems would not have changed the facts known to the evaluators. GAO agreed.

As with other protest grounds, it is not enough just to show that the agency did not hold proper discussions. The protester must also show that it was *prejudiced* by the agency's failure—that "but for the agency's actions, it would have had a substantial chance of receiving the award." (*NAHB Research Center, Inc.*, B-278876, 98-1 CPD ¶ 150.) GAO has stated the threshold for prejudice as follows: "[A] reasonable possibility of prejudice is a sufficient basis for sustaining the protest . . . . In other words, we will deny a protest only where it is clear from the record that the protester was not prejudiced." (*Daun-Ray Casuals, Inc.* B-255217, 94-2 CPD ¶ 42.)

Even when the agency errs in evaluating past performance, GAO has found that protesters are not prejudiced by erroneous negative comments if the record indicates that other significant negative comments were made about the protester's past performance. (*Lynwood Machine & Eng'g, Inc.*, B-285696, 2001 CPD ¶ 113.) In another case, GAO held that the protester was not prejudiced by a disputed past performance evaluation because it "would not have been able to improve its past performance rating of neutral, which was based on its lack of experience in manufacturing the same or similar items, through discussions (presumably if the protester had such experience, it would have mentioned it in its initial proposal) . . . ." (*Charleston Marine Containers, Inc.* B- 283,393, 99-2 CPD P 84.)

Contractors should also keep in mind that to win over the agency during discussions they may need to show not only that they adequately addressed past performance problems in a past contract, but also that they have taken action to minimize occurrence of the same problems in future contracts. In *Engineered Air Systs., Inc.* (B-283011, 99-2 CPD ¶ 63), the protester argued that the agency had not conducted meaningful discussions on the protester's past performance problems. GAO noted that the protester had responded to the adverse PPI at the time it was being compiled and had opportunity during discussions to respond to negative information received by the agency through customer feedback. GAO then stated that, "[w]hile [the protester] provided responses that indicated that appropriate corrective action was taken, we do not find it unreasonable for the agency to conclude that [the protester] had not demonstrated that certain systemic problems had been corrected."

Evaluation Consistent with the Solicitation Factors

An agency's evaluation of proposals must be "reasonable and consistent with the stated evaluation criteria" set forth in the solicitation. (*W R Systs., Ltd.*, B-287477, 2001 CPD ¶ 118.) At times, this may simply be a matter of interpreting the terms of the solicitation. In *Lynwood Machine & Eng'g, Inc.* (B-285696, 2001 CPD ¶ 113), for example, the protester argued that the agency had acted improperly when it evaluated PPI from projects completed more than two years before, while the solicitation had instructed offerors to provide references for projects completed *within* the past two years. GAO denied the protest, holding that "[a]lthough the RFQ requested references for projects completed within the last 2 years, it did not indicate that the evaluation of past performance would be based exclusively on such projects. . . . Accordingly, we do not think that it was inconsistent with the terms of the solicitation for the agency to have considered projects completed more than 2 years previously in evaluating Lynwood's past performance."

Sometimes it is not clear under which particular evaluation criterion PPI will be evaluated. GAO has held that agencies generally may consider an element of one evaluation criterion under one or more other evaluation criteria, as long as the "element is relevant and reasonably related to each criterion under which it is considered" and the practice does not "exaggerate the stated importance of any one evaluation criterion." (*RAMCOR Servs. Group, Inc.*, B-276633, 98-1 CPD ¶ 121.) This approach was approved by GAO in *OSI Collection Servs., Inc.* (B-286597.3, 2001 CPD ¶ 18), where the protester complained that the practice resulted in "double-counting" of periodic performance reports prepared by the agency during previous contract performance. The agency had considered the reports in evaluating the protester's past performance, and then again when evaluating the past performance of the protester's key personnel. GAO found this approach reasonable, stating that "[i]t is obvious that the contributions made by key personnel to a firm's [performance reports] are relevant to the [agency's] consideration of their past performance."

Another case illustrates the latitude GAO will give an agency to interpret the meaning of its own solicitation. In *USS Defense Systems, Inc.*(B-260702.2, 95-2 CPD ¶ 22), the protesters contended that the agency had violated a solicitation provision stating that the agency would evaluate the offerors' performance during the past three years on contracts for "the same or similar work." The awardee received 18 points out of a possible 20 for past performance, while the protesters received scores of 18 and 19. The protesters each had significant experience performing the identical type of overseas guard services called for by the solicitation; they argued that the awardee should not have received essentially the same past performance rating as theirs because the awardee had "no previous experience/past performance in providing guard and security services and only limited experience in providing these services at federal facilities." The agency countered that the solicitation allowed it to credit the awardee for having "provided comparable services for a presidential library and for several private entities." GAO agreed with the agency:

> Since the RFP did not require an offeror to have specific experience/past performance in providing guard and security services at overseas embassies and at federal facilities, we believe the agency's assessment that [awardee] has provided comparable guard and security services for a presidential library and for private entities was reasonable in light of the RFP requirement that an offeror's experience/past performance be for "the same or similar work."

Similarly, GAO sustained a protest where the agency assigned the same past performance rating to the awardee and the protester despite the agency's knowledge that the protester was the only offeror that had actual experience with the relevant equipment under contracts that were the same size and scope called for by the solicitation. (*NavCom Defense Electronics, Inc.*, B-276163, 97-1 CPD ¶ 189.)

GAO will also uphold awards resulting from an agency's reasonable efforts to deal with unexpected problems arising from the agency's intended approach for evaluating PPI. In *NAHB Research Center, Inc.* (B-278876, 98-1 CPD ¶ 150), a solicitation for multiple ID/IQ contracts provided that five references would be used for the past performance evaluation; however, for several of the offerors, fewer than five references responded to the agency's queries. More than five of the protester's references responded. As a result, the agency evaluated five of the protester's references at random, but for awardees with fewer than five references responding, it evaluated all responding references. The protester contended that the agency had failed to abide by the evaluation approach set out because it had used different numbers of references for different offerors.

GAO found this approach proper, holding that the agency's approach did not result in competitive prejudice to the protester because there was no indication that knowledge of the approach would have caused the protester to change its proposal to its advantage. GAO also noted that the agency had not relaxed the solicitation's requirements (offerors were still required to submit seven references), and did not eliminate the randomness inherent in the selection of evaluated references (which references responded, GAO reasoned, was random).

Finally, there must be an adequate record of the agency's source selection decision for GAO to ensure that solicitation requirements were followed. (*Ogden Support Services, Inc.*, B-270012.2, 96-1 CPD ¶ 77.) GAO has sustained a number of protests on the basis of inadequate support on the record for the agency's decision. In *Si-Nor, Inc.* (B-282064, 2000 CPD ¶ 159), the agency awarded to a higher-priced offeror with outstanding past performance instead of to the protester's lower-priced/satisfactory past performance offer, in a solicitation where price was weighted twice as important as past performance. GAO found it "significant that the agency had failed to document its reasoning for this outcome. In the absence of an adequate record, GAO could not determine whether the agency's evaluation followed the solicitation criteria, and it thus sustained the protest.

Reasonableness of Evaluation Methodology

Obviously, the evaluation methodology used to evaluate past performance must be rational, and GAO has sustained protests where it was not. In *American Development Corp.* (B-251876.4, 93-2 CPD ¶ 49), the Army gathered PPI on offerors from other agencies that had contracted with the offerors in the past. Under the Army's evaluation methodology, offerors received points simply for the *number* of "relevant" contracts they performed. The protester argued that the evaluation methodology irrationally assigned the awardee points for having performed a "relevant" contract, whether or not the awardee's performance on the contract was good. GAO sustained the protest, finding the Army's methodology irrational: "In effect, the methodology chosen rewarded offerors which had held at least one contract relevant to the work to be performed under the RFP without consideration of the quality of the work performed under the contract."

Similarly, in *Green Valley Transp., Inc.* (B-285283, 2000 CPD ¶ 133), the protester argued that the agency had conducted an improper past performance evaluation under a solicitation for freight transportation services. The agency had required offerors to submit copies of corrective measures taken by them in response to disciplinary actions and had collected various performance data on the offerors from the distribution center involved in past shipments. The agency then summarized the negative performance actions received by each offeror and determined that the protester's high number of such negative actions caused it to fail the requirements for the subfactor.

The protester contended that this methodology was unreasonable in that it failed to take into account the volume of shipments the offerors had moved while getting the negative performance actions. GAO held: "In our view, it was unreasonable for [the agency] to compare the absolute number of negative performance actions an offeror received, without considering that number in the context of the number of shipments the offeror had made over the relevant period." The protest was sustained.

Another issue involves how agencies should treat a neutral rating when making a "best value" determination. This question typically arises where the low-priced offeror is given a neutral past performance rating and is competing against an offeror with a successful past performance record. GAO has found that agencies have discretion to trade off price for past performance (and vice versa) in such situations, as long as the tradeoff is rational and consistent with the stated evaluation criteria. (*International Bus. Systs., Inc.* B-275554, 97-1 CPD ¶ 114.)

Thus, GAO has approved awards where the agency reasonably determined that the higher-priced offeror with a successful past performance record would provide a better value to the government than the lower-priced offeror with no past performance record. (*Engineering & Computation, Inc.*, B-275180.2, 97-1 CPD ¶ 47.) Conversely, GAO has approved awards where the agency reasonably determined that the lower-priced offeror with no past performance record would provide the better value to the government than the higher-priced offeror with a successful past performance record. (*Hughes Georgia, Inc.*, B-272526, 96-2 CPD ¶ 151.)

The agency must still ensure that its best value determination accords with FAR requirements not to penalize an offeror with no relevant past performance. In *National Aerospace Group, Inc.* (B-281958, 99-1 CPD ¶ 82), the protester challenged an award to a higher-priced offeror that was based on the agency's determination that the higher offer represented the "best value" to the government. The award went to the higher offeror because its higher Automated Best Value Model (ABVM) score purportedly "represented a lesser risk of nonperformance" than the protester's neutral ABVM score. The contracting officer had offered no other rationale for her award decision. GAO sustained the protest because the contracting officer's decision "was tantamount to rejecting [the protester's] quotation based on its lack of past performance history."

196 PAST PERFORMANCE HANDBOOK

A protester, however, cannot withhold relevant PPI to force the agency to assign a neutral PPI rating. In considering such a case, GAO stated:

> *Although FAR 15.305(a)(2)(iv) requires an agency to assign a neutral rating where past performance information is not "available," here, the protester's proposal represented that its proposed subcontractors are engaged in projects that would illustrate their performance capability. The information thus was available, but MDA chose not to present the information in its proposal, in direct contravention of the terms of the RFP. In our view, an offeror cannot simply choose to withhold past performance information—and thereby obtain a neutral rating—where the solicitation expressly requires that the information be furnished, and where the information is readily available to the offeror.*

Offeror's History of Claims/Disputes

Generally speaking, agencies may not downgrade an offeror's past performance based solely on the offeror's history of contract claims submitted against the government. (*Nova Group, Inc.,* B-282947, 99-2 CPD ¶ 56.) In that case, the agency requested claims history from each offeror and downgraded the protester's past performance because it had filed nine claims over the previous 15 years. The agency contended the claims raised questions regarding the protester's "cooperation/responsiveness with regards to customer satisfaction."

GAO fell short of holding that evaluating claims history under the past performance factor was always unreasonable but did hold that the evaluation was unreasonable under the instant circumstances. GAO found that, unless there existed evidence of an abuse of the contract dispute process, agencies should not downgrade past performance ratings based solely on claims filed. GAO went on to find the agency's action unreasonable because the protester had prevailed on eight of the claims, with the final claim still pending, and because the protester had received no substandard past performance ratings on its prior contracts.

A different result obtained in *TEAM Support Servs., Inc.* (B-279379.2, 98-1 CPD ¶ 167), where the incumbent contractor's past performance rating was lowered because the contracting officer, who was project officer on the previous contract and sole evaluator of the instant solicitation, stated that the protester's management was "uncooperative" in resolving disputes arising out of a government shutdown. GAO denied the protest and stated that the contracting officer's determination was reasonable, as it had more to do with the protester's working relationship with the agency.

Offeror's Status As Incumbent

Even if its performance record is exceptional, an incumbent contractor should not assume its past performance will be evaluated favorably merely because of its incumbency. In *Management Technical Services* (B-251612, 93-1 CPD ¶ 432), the incumbent protested the Air Force's award to another offeror. GAO found that the protester's proposal was "minimal" with regard to a pre-performance plan and description of past experience required by the solicitation. The protester apparently had believed it could rely on the agency's knowledge of its performance as incumbent to satisfy these requirements. GAO denied the protest, stating:

> *A procuring agency's technical evaluation of a proposal is dependent upon the information furnished in the proposal. There is no legal basis for an agency to favor an offeror with presumptions on the basis of the offeror's prior performance; on the contrary, all offerors must demonstrate their capabilities in their proposals.*

Accordingly, incumbents should not assume that their status as incumbents relieves them of the obligation to submit detailed PPI.

Additionally, an incumbent should not expect "extra credit" because of its incumbency, even if the agency has consistently been pleased with its performance. In *Modern Technologies Corp.* (B-278695, 98-1 CPD ¶ 81), the incumbent contractor protested award to another offeror and argued that it should have received higher ratings in a number of areas because of its incumbency. The protester argued, for example, that it should have received a higher rating for "subcontractor management" because it did not need as many subcontractors due to its past experience on the contract. Indeed, the protester went so far as to claim that it should have received a higher rating than any other offeror for "performance risk" because it should have been given "extra credit" for its incumbent experience.

GAO remarked: "In essence, [the protester] argues that its incumbency—or the lack of incumbency of other offerors—should have affected every facet of the evaluation. . . . In our view, [the protester] asks too much of its status as an incumbent contractor." As for performance risk, GAO noted that the protester had received the highest rating, but this did not foreclose the possibility of other offerors being rated highly in the same area. GAO found that "there was nothing unreasonable about the agency's conclusion that other offerors had relevant past experience, even if the experience was not in performing this very contract for the Air Force. Nor is there a requirement that an incumbent be given extra credit for its status as an incumbent."

Use of PPI of Subcontractors, Affiliates, and Key Personnel

An agency's past performance "evaluation *should* take into account past performance information regarding predecessor companies, key personnel who have relevant experience, or subcontractors that will perform major or critical aspects of the requirement when such information is relevant to the instant acquisition." [FAR 15.305(a)(2)(iii) (emphasis added).] Notwithstanding this rule, GAO has held in several cases that an agency is free to weigh the relevancy of the performance history of such parties when evaluating an offeror's proposal. Indeed, not surprisingly, GAO has found the provision permissive, in that agencies may exclude such parties' PPI altogether from an offeror's evaluation. (*Olympus Bldg. Servs., Inc.*, B-282887, 99-2 CPD ¶ 49.)

If an agency evaluation does focus on a third party's PPI, such as PPI for a proposed subcontractor, it may help improve the past performance rating of the offeror. In *Hago-Cantu Joint Venture* (B-279637.2, 98-2 CPD ¶ 99), the Army rated the awardee's past performance "acceptable" in a food service contract procurement, even though the awardee had no experience at all in food service. The protester, who had food service experience and had also received an "acceptable" rating, objected to the Army's reliance on the awardee's subcontractor's past performance for the awardee's evaluation, because the prime contractor was required to perform 50 percent of the contract.

GAO found that the Army had recognized the offeror's lack of experience as a weakness but had balanced this weakness with the proposed subcontractor's strong past performance record, resulting in the "acceptable" rating. GAO held that the Army's method "reasonably reflected a blend of the experience of both the prime and subcontractor." Similarly, with respect to evaluations of joint ventures, GAO has held that agencies may "appropriately consider the experience of the joint venture's individual team members and at the same time consider the lack of experience of the joint venture itself." (*ITT Federal Servs. Int'l Corp.*, B-283307, 99-2 CPD ¶ 76.)

While offerors may help their past performance by choosing an exceptional subcontractor, this tactic can only get the offeror so far. Agencies are free to determine the relevance of a proposed subcontractor's past performance, segregate the proposed subcontractor's past performance from that of the offeror, and rate the offeror's proposal based on a comparison of the prime contractor and subcontractor levels of effort. (*Oceanometrics, Inc.*, B-278647.2, 98-1 CPD ¶ 159.) An agency also may simply choose not to credit an offeror with the past performance of its subcontractor, especially if the subcontractor's effort on the contract will be minimal. (*Acepex Management Corp.*, B-279135.5, 98-2 CPD ¶ 128.)

Allowing offerors to use the past performance of their subcontractors can result in somewhat unusual situations. For example, in *Battelle Memorial Insti-*

tute (B-278673, 98-1 CPD ¶ 107), the awardee received credit for a previous contract under which the critical work was performed by its then-subcontractor. That subcontractor teamed with the protester for the instant procurement, and the protester argued that the awardee should not have received credit for work that had actually been done by its subcontractor. GAO rejected that argument, pointing out that the protester was "essentially arguing that the only entity that may properly list a prior contract for purposes of a past performance evaluation is the concern which actually performed the work relevant to that covered in the solicitation." GAO also stated that because the contract called for directing subcontractors, it was reasonable for the agency to include the earlier contract in the awardee's past performance evaluation.

Using similar logic, GAO has also found it reasonable for an agency to downgrade a protester's past performance rating where the protester derived its experience from work as a subcontractor or joint venture participant, rather than as a prime contractor. (*Acepex Management Corp.*, B-279135.5, 98-2 CPD ¶ 128.) This result was based on the inherent differences between performing as prime contractor and performing as subcontractor.

The general rule is that a prime contractor will be held responsible for the performance of its subcontractors. Thus, agencies may downgrade an offeror's proposal because of problems its subcontractor experienced on a prior contract, even if the offeror had little or nothing to do with the problems aside from being prime contractor. For instance, in *Federal Environmental Services* (B-260289, 95-1 CPD ¶ 261), the protester claimed that its past performance had been improperly evaluated under a procurement for hazardous waste removal and disposal services, based primarily on the protester's performance on an earlier contract with the same agency. Under that contract, the protester had delivered hazardous waste to its subcontractor, which then improperly disposed of the waste. The protester argued that the agency's past performance evaluation improperly punished it for the misdeeds of its subcontractor and claimed that it had done everything possible to control the subcontractor.

GAO denied the protest, finding reasonable the agency's conclusion that the matter indicated problems with the protester's earlier performance: "A prime contractor is responsible for the performance of its subcontractors . . . . In view of the seriousness of the subcontractor's misconduct here—a fact not in dispute—the agency had a reasonable basis to conclude that [the protester] had not properly monitored and supervised its subcontractor."

There are some exceptions, however, to the general rule that an offeror will be held responsible for a subcontractor's performance. For example, in *Crown Clothing Corporation* (B-277505, 97-2 CPD ¶ 127), the protester argued that the agency should have downgraded the awardee, who had been the protester's prime contractor under a previous contract, for defective goods delivered under that contract. The agency instead downgraded the protester because its past performance review indicated that the protester had actually produced the defective goods for the awardee. GAO found the agency's downgrade reasonable, holding that "a protester will not be heard to challenge the past performance of a competing offeror as a prime contractor based on its deficient performance as that competing offeror's subcontractor."

Because a prospective subcontractor's past performance may be considered along with the offeror's when determining a past performance rating, agencies must allow an offeror the opportunity to respond to unfavorable evaluations concerning its prospective subcontractor's past performance, at least under circumstances where the offeror would be allowed to respond to its own PPI (such as where the subcontractor's PPI could be explained to materially enhance the potential for award). In *Alliant Techsystems, Inc.* (B-260215.4, 95-2 CPD ¶ 79), the agency downgraded the protester's past performance evaluation because of problems with its major subcontractor's past performance but did not raise the issue with the offeror during discussions. The agency claimed that the protester was aware of and could have addressed its subcontractor's past performance history during negotiations but did not. GAO rejected the agency's reasoning and sustained the protest:

> [Protester's] knowledge that [subcontractor] had performance problems under the prior contract does not abrogate the agency's obligation to inform [protester] of its serious concerns regarding [subcontractor's] involvement in the [contractor's] "team." In this respect, an offeror could reasonably expect during discussions to be apprised of evaluated deficiencies in its subcontractors' past performance that significantly impact the offeror's evaluation standing.

GAO's holding in *Alliant Techsystems* makes practical sense, as offerors may switch prospective subcontractors if necessary to eliminate an agency's past performance concerns.

The FAR states that agencies should consider in their past performance evaluation "key personnel who have relevant experience." GAO has allowed agencies following this regulation practically to base an offeror's entire past performance rating upon the experience of a single individual. In *SDS International* (B- 285822, 2000 CPD ¶ 167), the protester contended that it was unreasonable for the awardee, a recently formed firm with no prior experience, to receive a high rating on past performance. GAO disagreed, however, finding that the background and role of the awardee's vice president, summarized in the awardee's proposal, were sufficient to warrant the high rating: "Based on [the awardee's] vice president's extensive, unique, recent, and relevant experience, and in view of the degree of his involvement in managing this effort, we conclude that the SSET reasonably assigned the firm a high rating under the past performance evaluation subfactor."

Agencies generally have discretion as to whether to evaluate an offeror's affiliates for past performance purposes. The affiliates must, however, have some role in the procurement or the offeror's management structure.

In *ST Aerospace Engines Pte. Ltd*. (B-275725, 97-1 CPD ¶ 161), the protester had been downgraded because of the poor past performance of its affiliated companies. Because there was no indication that the affiliates would be involved in contract performance, however, GAO found the evaluation of their past performance with that of the protester to be unreasonable. GAO set out the following standard for determining whether one company's performance should be attributed to its affiliates: "the agency must consider not simply whether the two companies are affiliated, but the nature and extent of the relationship between the two—in particular, whether the workforce, management, facilities, or other resources of one may affect contract performance by the other." *See also Universal Bldg. Maint., Inc.*, B-282456, 99-2 CPD ¶ 32 (finding agency had improperly given awardee added past performance credit for affiliate without evaluating relationship between companies).

CONCLUSION

The initiative to formalize the use of past performance represented a significant step in the evolution of federal procurement toward commercial practices. If followed by government procuring agencies, the past performance regulations should result in a source selection decision that is better, more efficient, and fairer for both the government and for reputable contractors. The attainment of this goal, however, requires that agencies and contractors work together to ensure that current and accurate PPI is used appropriately in all procurement evaluations.

Government personnel must abide closely to the letter and intent of the regulations and their interpretation by GAO. At least as important, contractors must take an informed and proactive role in the collection and evaluation of PPI. Contractors must target the several avenues discussed to provide accurate and up-to-date supplementary information on PPI to which agencies may have access. Contractors must also have some familiarity with the past performance evaluation case law developed by GAO to recognize and then seek a remedy in the event that a concerted agency-contractor approach to past performance proves unworkable in a given situation.

Appendix A

BEST PRACTICES
for

COLLECTING AND USING CURRENT AND PAST PERFORMANCE INFORMATION

Office of Federal Procurement Policy
Office of Management and Budget
Executive Office of the President

MAY 2000

TABLE OF CONTENTS

FOREWORD

CHAPTER 1. INTRODUCTION 1

Statutory and Regulatory Basis 1

Working with Contractors 2

Recording Current Contract Performance Information 3

Using Past Performance as a Source Selection Factor 4

Concerns Expressed by Contracting Officers 5

Orders under Multiple Award Contracts and Multiple
Award Schedule Contracts 6

Simplified Acquisitions... 7

**CHAPTER 2. EVALUATING AND RECORDING CURRENT
PERFORMANCE** 9

Contractor Performance Systems 9

Automated Systems 9

Contractor Performance Report Forms 10

Who Assesses Contractor Performance 10

Frequency of Assessments 11

Assessment Areas 11

End User Feedback 12

Performance Ratings 12

Subcontractors, and Teaming, and Joint Venture Partners 13

206   PAST PERFORMANCE HANDBOOK

Contractor Response and Agency Review 14

Release of Contractor Assessment 15

Planning for Good Contractor Performance 15

CHAPTER 3. USING CURRENT AND PAST PERFORMANCE AS A SOURCE SELECTION FACTOR **19**

Planning for Using Past Performance Information 20

Drafting Sections L and M of the Solicitation 21

Section L, Instructions to Offerors 22

Section M, Evaluation Criteria 24

Evaluating Past Performance 25

Conducting Discussions 29

APPENDIX I—SAMPLE CONTRACTOR PERFORMANCE REPORT AND INSTRUCTIONS **31**

APPENDIX II—DOD PERFORMANCE ASSESSMENT ELEMENTS FOR LARGE SYSTEMS **35**

APPENDIX III—PERFORMANCE RATING GUIDELINES **37**

APPENDIX IV—SAMPLE QUESTIONS AND IDEAS FOR TELEPHONE INTERVIEWS AND QUESTIONNAIRES **40**

APPENDIX V—AUTOMATED PAST PERFORMANCE INFORMATION SYSTEMS **42**

FOREWORD

Since the passage of the Federal Acquisition Streamlining Act of 1994, all Federal Departments and Agencies have initiated procedures to record contractor performance on in-process contracts and to use past contractor performance information in source selection. We have learned from the experience of agencies and contractors that recording contractor current performance information periodically during contract performance and discussing the results with contractors is a powerful motivator for contractors to maintain high quality performance or improve inadequate performance before the next reporting cycle. Current performance assessment is a basic "best practice" for good contract administration, and is one of the most important tools available for ensuring good contractor performance.

Current performance assessments when completed become past performance information for use in future source selections. Completion of these assessments improves the amount and quality of performance information available to source selection teams. The use of past performance as a major evaluation factor in the contract award process is instrumental in making "best value" selections. It enables agencies to better predict the quality of, and customer satisfaction with, future work.

The techniques and practices used to implement the current and past performance initiatives that are discussed in this document are not mandatory regulatory guidance. They should be viewed as useful examples of techniques for recording and using contractor performance to better assess contracts and to enhance the source selection process.

I wish to thank the agency procurement and program officials and representatives from the private sector who shared their experiences. I am particularly thankful for the participation of those working level acquisition officials who prove every day that these "best practices" actually work to improve contractor performance. In addition, special thanks go to the interagency team that developed the initial recommendations for this edition: Joseph Beausoleil - U.S. Agency for International Development; John Corso - Department of Veterans Affairs; Linda Davis - Defense Logistics Agency; Marilyn Goldstein - Department of Education; Helen Hurcombe - Social Security Administration; and Richard Leotta - Department of Energy. Melissa Rider - Defense Acquisition Regulation Directorate, was instrumental in preparing this edition.

Copies of this guidebook are available on line at www.arnet.gov. For hard copies or if you have questions, comments or suggestions contact David Muzio, phone 202-395-6805, fax 202-395-5105, email dmuzio@omb.eop.gov or Yvette Garner, phone 202-395-7187, email ygarner@omb.eop.gov.

Deidre A. Lee
Administrator
Office of Federal Procurement Policy

CHAPTER 1
INTRODUCTION

The Federal Government is in a continuous process to reinvent itself, with a goal of becoming a government that works better and costs less. The Government is the largest acquisition organization in the world with expenditures of about $200 Billion a year for commercial goods and services. This is one third of the Federal discretionary budget of about $600 Billion. How well the Government's acquisition teams administer in-process contracts and discuss with contractors their current performance, determines to a great extent how well agencies can achieve their missions and provide value to the taxpayers. By increasing attention to contractor performance on in-process contracts and ensuring past performance data is readily available for source selection teams, agencies are reaping two benefits: (1) better current performance because of the active dialog between the contractor and the government; and (2) better ability to select high quality contractors for new contracts, because contractors know the assessments will be used in future award decisions.

Statutory and Regulatory Basis

The 1994 Federal Acquisition Streamlining Act (FASA), signaled a "sea change" in Federal acquisition. FASA was signed into law by the President on October 13, 1994 (P.L. 103-355). In FASA, Congress acknowledged that it is appropriate and relevant for the Government to consider a contractor's past performance in evaluating whether that contractor should receive future work. Section 1091 of FASA states:

> Past contract performance of an offeror is one of the relevant factors that a contracting official of an executive agency should consider in awarding a contract.

> It is appropriate for a contracting official to consider past contract performance of an offeror as an indicator of the likelihood that the offeror will successfully perform a contract to be awarded by that official.

FASA requires the Administrator of the Office of Federal Procurement Policy (OFPP) to "establish policies and procedures that encourage the consideration of the offerors' past performance in the selection of contractors." Specifically, it requires that the Administrator establish:

> Standards for evaluating past performance with respect to cost (when appropriate), schedule, compliance with technical or functional speci-

fications, and other relevant performance factors that facilitate consistent and fair evaluation by all executive agencies.

Policies for the collection and maintenance of information on past contract performance that, to the maximum extent practicable, facilitate automated collection, maintenance, and dissemination of information and provide for ease of collection, maintenance, and dissemination of information by other methods, as necessary.

Policies for ensuring that offerors are afforded an opportunity to submit relevant information on past contract performance, including performance under contracts entered into by the executive agency concerned, by other agencies, State and local governments, and by commercial customers, and that such information is considered.

The period for which past performance information may be maintained.

FASA also states that an offeror for which there is no information on past contract performance or with respect to which information on past contract performance is not available, may not be evaluated favorably or unfavorably on the factor of past contract performance.

These policies and procedures are contained in the Federal Acquisition Regulation (FAR) Parts 9, 12, 13, 15, 36 and 42. FAR PART 36 provides specific procedures, dollar thresholds, and forms for evaluation of A&E and construction contracts; however, Contracting Officers are still encouraged to evaluate past performance on these contracts if they exceed $100,000. This "Best Practices" adds further background and assistance in implementing the FAR provisions.

Working With Contractors

In meetings with OFPP, contractors of all sizes and many industry associations have emphasized the power of past performance as a tool for motivating contractors to make their best efforts. However, they have raised concerns that many assessments are not being done, or are being done inconsistently. Contractors seek an above-board, timely evaluation process. They want frank discussions early in the process so they have an opportunity to improve performance, if necessary, before final assessments are given. They want to be advised of any negative comments being entered into official reports and given ample opportunity for a rebuttal. They fear inflated assessments as much as poor assessments because inflated assessments help poor contractors and hurt good contractors. This document addresses inflated assessments in Chapter 2, "Performance Ratings," where the rating scale for full contract compliance has been adjusted from 4 to 3 to reduce rating creep.

2

Appendix A   **211**

Communication is critical. Commercial companies have come to recognize that two-way communication is vital to a productive relationship with their suppliers. On-going open discussion with the contractor about the Government's requirements and how the contractor can best meet them, can greatly improve the quality of deliverables under Government contracts. The better the contractor performance evaluation, the more competitive the contractor will be for future work. We go into further detail on this process in Chapter 2.

Recording Current Contract Performance Information

The key to the long-term success of this important initiative is for each agency to assess and maintain a record of contractors' performance on procurement actions exceeding $100,000[1]. Each agency is encouraged to adopt a current performance information system that will systematically record contractor performance in the following areas:

Quality of performance—as defined in contract standards;

Cost performance—how close to cost estimates;

Schedule performance—timeliness of completion of interim and final milestones.

Business relations—history of professional behavior and overall business-like concern for the interests of the customer, including timely completion of all administrative requirements and customer satisfaction.

FAR Subpart 42.15, *Contractor Performance Information* aims to ensure a clear and concise record of a contractor's performance on every contract, task order or other contractual document exceeding $100,000, based on a discussion with the contractor about recent performance. These assessment records are to be readily available for use on source selections anywhere in the Government. The record can be maintained in the contract file, in a separate manual file, or, preferably an automated database. Agencies should make the performance assessment process a seamless part of the normal contract administration process. Systems in place that meet or exceed FAR Part 42 requirements do not need to be changed. Reports prepared by award fee boards, from earned value

---

[1]Although agencies are not required to evaluate performance for contracts awarded under Subpart 8.6, Acquisition from Federal Prison Industries, Inc., and Subpart 8.7, Acquisition from Nonprofit Agencies from Employing People Who Blind or Severely Disabled (See FAR 42.1502(b)), Contracting Officers are still encouraged to be cognizant of contractors' performance, and record and discuss that performance as a matter of good contract administration practices.

3

212 PAST PERFORMANCE HANDBOOK

management system reports, or other similar contract administration records, may be used as the past performance record. Separate reports are not required. The additional work needed to make these reports formal performance reports is to include contractor discussion and comments on the evaluation, and file it for source selection use.

A few tips: <u>Keep</u> the record simple. <u>Focus</u> on information that answers the following question: "Would I do business with this contractor again?" Augment any numerical or adjectival scores with supporting rationale. This allows other Contracting Officers to understand the rationale for the overall rating. Remember that other Contracting Officers may need to consider a contractor's rebuttal and they need to know the story behind your scores. We go into further detail on contractor performance evaluations in Chapter 2.

We expect that the Government-wide contract performance assessment process will evolve to where assessments are consistently performed on time on all appropriate contractual instruments electronically. When this happens, solicitations will need only to ask offerors to provide a list of past Government contracts that they have performed that were similar to the potential contract. The source selection teams will be able to electronically access the various agency contractor information systems and download the required information. This streamlined process of obtaining Government references will provide much, if not all, of the information necessary to evaluate the offeror's past performance. Source selection boards will not need to conduct extensive interviews with the contract administration team, or conduct other investigations to verify an offeror's past performance. Because contractors will have been offered the opportunity to comment on the ratings as they were prepared, further comment in the proposal or during discussions, if held, will be streamlined.

However, until all agencies adopt an automated system connected to other Federal Government systems, the Contracting Officer and evaluation team will still need to occasionally use questionnaires and conduct interviews to obtain necessary information. Because contractors may submit references from state and local governments and private sector contracts, the use of questionnaires and telephone calls to gather information will always be necessary, but on a limited scale compared to today.

Using Past Performance as a Source Selection Factor

Commercial firms rely on information about a contractor's current and past performance as a major criterion for selecting a high quality supplier. It is not surprising that use of performance information as an evaluation factor was identified by Congress as a method for Federal acquisition streamlining. Too often in the past, the Government relied heavily upon detailed technical and man-

Appendix A **213**

agement proposals and contractor experience to compare the relative strengths and weaknesses of offers. This practice often allowed offerors that could write outstanding proposals, but had less than stellar performance, to "win" contracts—even when other competing offerors had significantly better performance records and, therefore, offered a higher probability of meeting the requirements of the contract. Emphasizing past performance in source selection, helps ensure that the Government will contract with firms likely to meet performance expectations.

OFPP encourages agencies to make contractors' performance records an essential consideration in the award of all negotiated acquisitions. When the Government demands high quality service as a requirement for future business opportunities similar to the private sector, competition will produce higher quality service by contractors. We go into further detail on the source selection process in Chapter 3.

Concerns Expressed by Contracting Officers

1) *Past performance and quality certifications are not perfect predictors.*

Nothing is a perfect predictor. However, many Contracting Officers successfully use past performance information and quality certifications as source selection factors and have found that the resulting contractor performance is of a higher quality than in the past. Also, most large private sector purchasers consider past performance. Whenever relevant, Contracting Officers should use these sources of information to buy best expected value.

2) *Past performance and quality certifications do not always apply.*

No predictors are universally useful, but they should be used in the majority of cases where they do apply. For example, on purchases made once a generation, past performance history does not provide the same probability of predictability of future performance as it would on repetitive purchases. When it does not make sense to include past performance information, Contracting Officers may waive it (FAR 15.304(c)(3)(iii).

3) *Past performance is not always a discriminator in source selections.*

Achieving a state where all potential contractors offer the same risk free, high quality service, and only cost plays in the source selection decision, is the ultimate goal. That is not likely anytime soon. If we did not assess and record contractor performance during the contract and then use that information in source selections, we would lose a significant motivator for contractors to perform all contracts at a high level. Past performance information improves your chances

214 PAST PERFORMANCE HANDBOOK

that all the technical and cost information provided is a reliable predictor of future performance. Those who receives offers only from firms with exceptional past performance, such that it not a discriminator, are fortunate.

4) Giving a contractor a poor evaluation can lead to legal action against the Government raters.

Problems with poor performance can lead to frustrations for both the contractor and Government. Early identification of concerns and open lines of communication (e.g., including the preparation of interim reports) can lead to constructive dialogue that can help to improve performance on the instant contract and avoid adversarial feelings that might otherwise develop if potential misunderstandings are ignored until late into contract performance.

While straightforward dialogue should lessen the likelihood of legal action against a government rater, suits may occasionally arise. If agency officials are acting within the scope of their employment (e.g., preparing an unbiased assessment in accordance with FAR Part 42.15), the Federal Torts Claims Act will protect such officials from personal liability for common law torts. In those instances, if an agency official were sued, upon certification by the Attorney General, the official would be dismissed from the lawsuit and the United States would be substituted as the defendant.

If a claim is filed by the contractor on the past performance ratings, the contract file and assessment record should be updated. This information should be provided to source selection teams along with the other contractor performance records. The offeror should also include in the proposal a discussion on claims filed. The source selection team should evaluate the data provided and use appropriately.

Orders under Multiple Award Contracts and Multiple Award Schedule Contracts

Multiple award task and delivery order contracts (MACs) and the multiple award schedules (MAS) have become increasingly popular procurement vehicles for satisfying agency needs. Both vehicles enable agencies to apply competitive pressures efficiently in placing orders after considering a small number of capable contractors, thus allowing customers to take advantage of advances in technology and changes in agency priorities in an opportune manner. Ensuring meaningful consideration of contractor performance prior to placement of an order under either of these vehicles is just as important—and can be just as effective in making a best value decision—as consideration of past performance in the award of the underlying vehicle itself. FAR 8.404(b) (addressing order placement under MAS) and FAR 16.505 (covering order placement under MACs) both address the consideration of past performance at the order level.

Appendix A **215**

The basic practices discussed in this document, relating both to the evaluation of contractor performance and its consideration in source selection, are applicable to the administration and placement of orders under MACs and MAS contracts. However, it is reasonable to assume with respect to orders—as would be assumed for any contractual actions—that these techniques will be tailored to the nature and complexity of the work being performed. The key is to ensure that the ultimate approach taken results in effective consideration of the four fundamental elements of past performance: (1) quality of performance, (2) cost performance, (3) schedule performance, and (4) business relations.

Given that there may be numerous assessments under one contract, the source selection evaluator should use a trend analysis to determine the risks of successful performance on future task orders and multiple award contracts.

Agencies have successfully applied general concepts and best practices described in this document to the placement and administration of orders. With respect to MACs, for instance, agencies are, among other things:

- Using past performance as an initial screen to determine which awardees will receive further consideration for a task or delivery order.

- Conducting interim evaluations and conducting customer satisfaction surveys.

- Holding meetings with contractors experiencing performance and quality problems.

- Collecting past performance information in a database for use in the issuance of future orders.

The division of responsibilities between agencies <u>using</u> MACs (customers), and agencies <u>issuing</u> them (servicers) may vary. However, it is important that each party have a clear understanding of its role in assessing and recording contractors performance—especially when the customer and servicer are from different agencies. This includes use of MAS contracts as well. As a general matter, the customer agency maintains current and past performance records on their particular contractors for future task or delivery order awards, as well as, provides feedback to the servicing agency. The servicing agency should use this information from users for purposes of future source selections on MACs and MAS.

Simplified Acquisitions

This guide focuses on purchases above the simplified acquisition threshold (SAT). However, Contracting Officers may consider past performance in pur-

216 PAST PERFORMANCE HANDBOOK

chases under the SAT, including purchases conducted electronically (see FAR 13.106-1(a)(2)). Contracting Officers may use whatever information is available to the buying office about an offeror's past performance or is available in the agency or other available database when making an award decision. The Contracting Officer need not prepare a formal evaluation plan, conduct discussions, or score offers. However, the Contracting Officer should give the contractor an opportunity to discuss any negative performance. Simplified documentation procedures can be used to support the final action taken. For example, a note can be inserted in the file stating instances of late deliveries or poor quality on prior awards. Upon request by the unsuccessful offeror, the Contracting Officer should explain the award rationale. The procuring activity should ideally establish a simple, but consistent, system for applying past performance in simplified acquisitions that rewards contractors that provide timely, high quality products and services.

Appendix A **217**

CHAPTER 2
EVALUATING AND RECORDING
CURRENT PERFORMANCE

Contractor Performance Systems

The key to an efficient and effective Government-wide contractor performance system is the establishment, by each agency to the maximum extent practicable, of an automated mechanism to record and disseminate this information. Agency systems need to be easy to use and part of normal contract administration duties of the program office and the Contracting Officer. The performance evaluations should flow directly from agency contract administration procedures. Where Performance-Based Service Contracts are used, the Quality Assurance Surveillance Plan should include the formal performance evaluation as an element of the plan. Agencies using Earned Value Management Systems to monitor contract performance may use the information directly from the system reports as the basis for the performance evaluation. Agencies may also use award fee determinations as the basis for the evaluations. In all cases, performance evaluations must be consistent with the results of these determinations. Ideally, agency systems should have the capability to connect to other Government systems. Agencies that do not have automated systems should retain their information in a manual system where the data can be readily available to source selection teams. The initial recording of the information may be done by the program manager or Contracting Officer according to agency procedures, but should reflect the acquisition team's assessment of the contractor's performance. The final report that will be used for dissemination to source selection boards and provided to the contractor should be signed by the Contracting Officer.

Automated Systems

FASA espouses a preference for automated systems. Currently, the National Institutes of Health (NIH) has a comprehensive automated system that is available to all agencies for a minimal fee. At the time this document was published there were 14 organizations that were subscribers to the NIH system. The Department of Defense (DOD) also has a number of automated systems. Points of contact for the DOD and NIH systems can be found in Appendix V. Where agencies have systems in use that meet the requirements of FAR 42.15, they may be continued at the discretion of the agencies. Over time, we expect most Federal agency systems to be able to interface with each other to provide Contracting Officers an easy, quick way to access contractor performance information. Agency systems will need to migrate toward a uniform Government-wide format for recording contractor performance information to make this possible.

9

218   PAST PERFORMANCE HANDBOOK

Agencies should investigate other systems periodically to determine the feasibility and cost effectiveness of joining together to create a uniform system.

Contractor Performance Report Forms

A sample Contractor Performance Report form is provided in Appendix I. This form is not the only way to comply with FAR Subpart 42.15, Contractor Performance Information. Agencies may use another format if it would permit more cost-effective evaluation of contractor performance. The DOD has developed a more comprehensive format for recording information on major system acquisitions. (See Appendix II.) The content and format of performance evaluations may be established in accordance with agency procedures and should be tailored to the size, and complexity of the contractual requirements. However, all rating systems should track four basic assessment elements—**cost, schedule, technical performance** (quality of product or service) and **business relations including customer satisfaction**, and use five basic ratings—**exceptional (5), very good (4), satisfactory (3), marginal (2), and unsatisfactory (1)**—as discussed below. This enhances interagency sharing of past performance information.

Construction and architect-engineer (A&E) contract assessment elements and ratings are established under FAR Part 36. However, some agencies, (DOD and NIH) have developed formats other than the forms 1420 and 1421 prescribed in Part 36. Agency forms may be used if they record the same or more information as the FAR forms. The U.S. Army Corps of Engineers operates two automated centralized databases to collect performance information on construction and A&E contracts. These databases are open to all agencies, if the agency adopt the DOD forms. The NIH automated system also contains an A&E/construction module acceptable for use.

For classified contracts, the same past performance policy and guidance are applicable. Recording information on these type contracts needs to address "how well" the contractor performed, and not on "what" the contractor did.

Who Assesses Contractor Performance

The Contracting Officer and program office (e.g., Contracting Officer's Technical Representative (COTR), the Contracting Officer's Representative (COR) and Quality Assurance Evaluator (QAE) or whatever term is used by the agency for the technical person monitoring the contract, are jointly responsible for assessing contractor performance. The person responsible for preparing the initial assessment must consider inputs from the program manager, end user, the Contracting Officer, and other parties affected by the item or service.

10

Appendix A **219**

Frequency of Assessments

A final assessment must be prepared for contract actions (i.e., contracts, task & delivery orders) exceeding $100,000 upon completion of the contract or order. In addition, interim assessments should be prepared as specified by the agencies to provide current information for discussion purposes and for source selection purposes. We strongly emphasize interim assessments as part of good contract management. If the performance period exceeds 18 months, then the Contracting Officer should conduct interim assessments at least every 12 months.

Interim assessments provide essential feedback to contractors on their performance. They provide Contracting Officers an opportunity to give contractors performing well a "pat on the back" and encouragement to keep up the good work. Interim assessments give contractors experiencing problems the opportunity to correct problems before they jeopardize contract completion. They also provide current performance information on comparable contracts to source selection teams. Most Agency's contract administration practices dictate that interim assessments be prepared at least every twelve months for contracts. However, it is recommended they be prepared and discussed with contractors at least every six months, sometimes more often depending on contractor performance problems. An honest discussion of the contractor's performance is important. Contractors know past performance assessments directly affect their ability to compete for future contracts and will normally take actions necessary to improve their rating. The contractor should always know how the agency rates its performance—no surprises! Likewise, during your discussions, you should ask the contractor if there are areas that the Government could improve its performance, such as in partnerships, contributions to achieving mission success, etc. The key to the process is communication!

Assessment Areas

The sample Contractor Performance Report form sets out four assessment areas to rate the contractor's performance—**Quality, Timeliness, Cost Control**, and **Business Relations.**

For three of the areas—**Quality, Timeliness and Cost Control**, the ratings should reflect how well (how close) the contractor complied with the specific contract performance requirements for each area. The ratings should be concise, but provide supporting rationale that address questions about the performance that would be asked by a source selection team. Here are a few examples of appropriate rationale:

> The software met all contract performance requirements for ease of use and output. The speed and accuracy of the financial system package exceeded expectations.

220   PAST PERFORMANCE HANDBOOK

The contractor met all contract milestones for system development and field installation. Some internal contractor management milestones were missed, but timely identification of problems and corrective actions kept the program on schedule.

The contractor's cost management was excellent and resulted in a 2 percent under-run from target cost. The contractor submitted a value engineering change proposal that resulted in a price decrease of 10 percent.

The fourth assessment area, **Business Relations,** assesses the working relationship between the contractor and contract administration team, and some of the other requirements of the contract not directly related to cost, schedule and performance such as:

- user satisfaction

- subcontract management including achievement of small/small disadvantaged and women-owned business participation goals, and incentive fees earned on exceeding subcontracting goals

- integration and coordination of all activity needed to execute the contract, change proposal submissions, and the contractor's history of professional behavior with all parties.

End User Feedback

When assessing feedback from end-users, remember that they may be unfamiliar with the contract requirements. Remind end-users that their feedback should relate directly to the cost, schedule, and technical performance requirements explicitly expressed in the contract and an assessment of the business relations. The Contracting officer should evaluate the end user comments to determine if the contractor reasonably tried to meet their demands within the contract requirements. Only rate the contractor on work that is within the contract requirements. If end-users are dissatisfied with the work as specified in the contract requirements, an assessment of the work requirements may need to be undertaken.

Performance Ratings

Each rating area may be assigned one of five ratings as listed below. The ratings given by the government should reflect how well the contractor met the cost, schedule and performance requirements of the contract and the business relationship. (See Appendix III for rating summaries.) Contractors are not expected to be perfect in their execution to reach contract requirements. A critical aspect of the assessment rating system described below is the second sentence of each rating that recognizes the contractor's resourcefulness in overcoming challenges that arise in the context of contract performance. The government is looking for overall results, not problem free management of the contract. If references are using a different scale that does not easily correlate to the source selection team's rating scale, then the source selection team must make a correlation between the two scales. If necessary, contact the reference for more information on definitions used for its rating scale.

Exceptional (5). Performance meets contract requirements and <u>significantly exceeds</u> contract requirements to the Government's benefit. For example, the contractor implemented innovative or business process reengineering techniques, which resulted in added value to the Government. The contractual performance of the element or sub-element being assessed was accomplished with few minor problems for which corrective actions taken by the contractor were highly effective.

Very Good (4). Performance meets contractual requirements and <u>exceeds some</u> to the Government's benefit. The contractual performance of the element or sub-element being assessed was accomplished with some minor problems for which corrective actions taken by the contractor were effective.

Satisfactory (3). Performance <u>meets</u> contractual requirements. The contractual performance of the element or sub-element contains some minor problems for which proposed corrective actions taken by the contractor appear satisfactory, or completed corrective actions were satisfactory.

Marginal (2). Performance <u>does not meet some</u> contractual requirements. The contractual performance of the element or sub-element being assessed reflects a serious problem for which the contractor has submitted minimal corrective actions, if any. The contractor's proposed actions appear only marginally effective or were not fully implemented.

Unsatisfactory (1). Performance <u>does not meet</u> contractual requirements and <u>recovery is not likely</u> in a timely or cost effective manner. The contractual performance of the element or sub-element contains serious problem(s) for which the contractor's corrective actions appear or were ineffective.

Subcontractors, Teaming, and Joint Venture Partners

It is important to maintain a record, on the contractor performance report form, of the major subcontractors and any team or joint venture partners on the contract. This is a listing of the firms participating, the work they are responsible for (if segregable for team or joint venture partners), and the key personnel. As the Government only has privity of contract with the prime contractor, subcontractors teams and joint venture partners should not be given a separate rating. Comments on the performance of these firms will be reflected in the ratings for the prime. Listing these firms allows them to cite the contract for past performance purposes in proposals for future work either as prime contractors or as subcontractors or other partners. Source selection teams may review the assessment to determine the ratings given for the work for which these firms were responsible. Because the past performance rating given by the source selection team would not have been discussed with these firms, Contracting Officers must ensure the contractor has an opportunity to comment on the rating before including it in the source selection process. This process will reduce the number of firms that do not have a relevant past performance history in the source selection.

Contractor Response and Agency Review

While the ultimate conclusion on the performance assessment is a decision of the contracting agency, the FAR provides for contractor comment. Upon completion of the initial assessment by the program and contracting office, the assessment should be signed by the program office person most familiar with the contractor's performance and initialed by the Contracting Officer. The Contracting Officer should sign the final assessments. As soon as practicable after the form is signed, and ordinarily within a day, it should be sent to the contractor for comments. The required turnaround time for contractor response may not be less than thirty days (see FAR 42.1503(b)), but in most cases, 30 days should be a sufficient response time. Contracting Officers may extend the response period as warranted. If the contractor fails to provide a response by the established deadline, the Contracting Officer should call the contractor and initiate discussions on the performance and request a written reply. If all attempts fail, then the Government's comments can stand alone.

If the contractor submits a rebuttal for any or all of the ratings and an agreement on the ratings cannot be reached by the contractor, the Contracting Officer and lead assessor, the contractor may seek review at least one level above the Contracting Officer, as prescribed by the agency (see FAR 42.1503(b)). In the event the contractor and Contracting Officer do not agree on the performance rating(s), the Contracting Officer and lead assessor should make every effort to discuss with the contractor the details of the performance assessment and the contractor's response. In these cases, such effort should require a face-to-fact meeting between the parties. The contractor's statement and agency review must be attached to the performance report and must be provided to source selection officials requesting a reference check.

Appendix A **223**

When the Government has completed its review of the contractor's comments, but in no case later than the insertion of the assessment into an automated PPI System or other agency system, the Contracting Officer must send a copy of the completed assessment to the contractor.

The completed assessments, including any contractor response or rebuttal, and agency reviews above the Contracting Officer, should be filed in the contract file, in a separate file, or automated database where they can be readily accessible by contracting office personnel. Automated databases should be accessible by source selection teams in other agencies through use of a secure system. Interim assessments should be retained for the duration of the contract and included with the final assessment in the file. The interim assessment allows source selection teams to analyze performance trends during the contract.

Assessments may not be retained to provide source selection information for longer than three years after completion of contract performance[2]. The assessment storage system used should provide individual contractor access to only that contractor's assessments.

Release of Contractor Assessment

Since contractor assessments may be used to support future award decisions, FAR 42.1503(b) require that they be marked "Source Selection Information." FAR 42.1503(b) further states that the completed evaluation "shall not be released to other than Government personnel needing the information for source selection purposes and the contractor whose performance is being evaluated during the period the information may be used to provide source selection information." The rationale for handling information in this manner is stated in the FAR itself: disclosure could (i) cause harm to the commercial interest of the Government, (ii) cause harm to the competitive position of the contractor being evaluated, and (iii) impede the efficiency of government operations[3].

Planning For Good Contractor Performance

The Government acquisition team (program office, contracting, and end user) must work closely with the contractor to obtain our goal of satisfying the customer in terms of cost, quality, and timeliness of the delivered product or service.

---

[2]"After contract completion" means the date (month) when work is complete (all contract line items have been delivered), not at contract closeout. For contracts with warranties, the performance period is not complete until the end of the warranty period.

[3]Questions regarding the release of contractor evaluations under the Freedom of Information Act may be referred to the Office of Information and Privacy, U.S. Department of Justice (202) 514-3642.

224 Past Performance Handbook

The Contracting Officer should communicate often with the contractor, starting with a good post award conference. This part of the process ensures that everyone has the same vision of successful performance. Members of the Government acquisition team (Procuring Contracting Officer (PCO), Administrative Contracting Officer (ACO), program manager, Contracting Officer Technical Representative (COTR), Contracting Officer's Representative (COR), Quality Assurance Evaluator (QAE), legal, and contractor counterparts) should get together in one room. All should read the contract and clearly establish the Government's expectations. Everyone should understand how past performance information will be recorded. The Government acquisition team should agree on how often the Lead Evaluator/Contracting Officer and the contractor will discuss contract performance.

Status meetings should be planned at least quarterly on large contracts. The focus should be on the contractor's performance against cost, schedule, and performance goals. The team should discuss the contractor's performance deficiencies, corrective actions, areas where the contractor is meeting Government expectations, and any Government deficiencies. This process applies to smaller contracts as well, adjusting the meeting frequency to match the relative complexity of the contract requirement. Contracting Officers are also encouraged to have an open door policy that allows contractors to voluntarily discuss performance problems as they arise. These meetings should be a complete discussion on the contractor's performance, both good and bad, and the Government's compliance with contract requirements.

The Naval Undersea Warfare Center has seen the effects of this Best Practice in the reactions of contractor and government employees in administration of current contracts. The greatest benefit is the improvement in communication both between the Government and the contractor and within the Government. Contractor managers are initiating discussion of performance expectations and achievements with Government personnel. Officials of the smaller and medium sized companies in industries with intense competition are especially concerned about Past Performance rating information which will affect future contract awards. Often they do not consider a "Satisfactory" rating acceptable and expect their contract managers to achieve "Very Good" or "Exceptional" ratings. A secondary benefit is the improvement of internal Government communication as contract specialists and technical/program managers discuss problems and successes in contract administration in the effort to establish appropriate annual Past Performance ratings.

Remember—the goal is excellent contract performance that provides products or services at the best value for the taxpayer's dollar! This goal can't be achieved unless the acquisition team does some homework:

- Track and document contract performance closely

- Read and understand the contractor's cost, schedule and performance reporting data

- Know how well the contractor is meeting its other contract requirements such as socio-economic goals

- Know if the Government contributed to performance problems

- Actively work to eliminate Government roadblocks to excellent performance

- Document the discussions (They need not go in the "formal" past performance information system, but the contracting officer must be able to track the steps the contractor and the Government take to improve contract performance).

- Recognize successful efforts to improve performance

Appendix A **227**

CHAPTER 3
USING CURRENT AND PAST PERFORMANCE
AS A SOURCE SELECTION FACTOR

The Government has always considered a contractor's performance record during the acquisition process. However, agencies traditionally have considered it as an aspect of contractor responsibility. A prospective contractor must have a satisfactory performance record in order to do business with the Government (see FAR 9.104-1(c)). This helps ensure that taxpayer dollars are not wasted on contracts with nonresponsible contractors. Past performance can and should be used to do more than just help the Government decide whether a contractor is capable of performing. The Government must also compare the past track records of competing offerors to help identify which one offers the best relative value in order to get the best deal for the taxpayer. Using past performance as an evaluation factor to rank an otherwise responsible contractor for award of a contract is not, therefore, part of the responsibility determination. Evaluation factor rankings are not subject to the Small Business Administration's Certificate of Competency (COC) ratings.

It is important to distinguish **comparative** past performance evaluations used in the tradeoff process from **pass/fail** performance evaluations.

Pre-award surveys and pass/fail evaluations in the low price technically acceptable process help you determine whether an offeror is responsible. Responsibility is a broad concept that addresses whether an offeror has the **capability** to perform a particular contract based upon an analysis of many areas including financial resources, operational controls, technical skills, quality assurances, compliance with Government laws, and past performance. These surveys and evaluations provide a "yes/no," "pass/fail," or "go/no-go" answer to the questions, "**Can** the offeror do the work?" to help you determine whether the offeror is responsible.

Referral to the SBA may be necessary if a small business is eliminated from the competitive range solely on the basis of past performance. SBA referral is not required as long as the use of past performance information requires a **comparative** assessment with other evaluation factors and not as a pass or fail decision. The comparative assessment of past performance information is **separate** from a responsibility determination required by the FAR.

On the other hand, a comparative past performance evaluation conducted using the tradeoff process seeks to identify the **degree of risk** associated with each competing offeror. In short, the valuation describes the degree of confidence the Government has in the offeror's likelihood of success.

19

228 PAST PERFORMANCE HANDBOOK

Emphasis in this chapter is placed on using current and past performance information primarily available from Government-wide and Agency-wide databases, to help expedite and streamline the evaluation process. If such information is not readily available from these databases, then seek to gather it from other government entities and private sector sources. In using past performance as a source selection factor, there are primarily three key points which should be conveyed in the solicitation (Sections L and M), and are discussed in more detail later in this chapter:

(1) Contractors should list in the proposal 5 to 10 specific contracts (not more than 3 years old) and a list of contact names and addresses for each of the references requested in the solicitation;

(2) Contractors should be encouraged to discuss any negative performance issues and corrective actions taken; and

(3) Government must include the method of evaluating the information and its relevancy, and the relative rank or applicable weight assigned to current and past performance.

Planning For Using Past Performance Information

The Government must evaluate past performance in all competitively negotiated acquisitions expected to exceed $100,000 [see FAR 15.304(c)(3) (ii)], unless otherwise documented by the Contracting Officer why past performance is not an appropriate evaluation factor pursuant to FAR 15.304(c)(3) (iii).

Past performance evaluations become distinct discriminators when a best value award is made. Tradeoffs among cost or price, and non-cost factors and subfactors permit the Government to accept other than the lowest-priced, technically acceptable offer. In accordance with FAR 15.304(c)(1) & (2), price or cost, and quality shall be addressed in every source selection. Quality may be evaluated through past performance. The Contracting Officer has the full flexibility to award on these two factors alone when determined appropriate and consistent with the FAR.

The acquisition team should take advantage of synergy between past performance and other critical evaluation factors. For example, the management plan could be replaced by a past performance evaluation that focuses on management effectiveness. This will help streamline the source selection process by selecting only a few critical evaluation factors; focusing on offerors' ability to carry through as promised; emphasizing experience and past performance; and eliminating the need for a proliferation of management and quality plans where the past performance evaluations will suffice.

20

The acquisition team should determine the relative rank or weight to place on past performance during the acquisition planning phase, and the type or kind of past performance that could be considered similar or relevant to the pending procurement. It could use market research or the source selection team's previous experience on similar acquisitions to determine whether the evaluation of past performance should be a critical factor in the procurement (i.e., a high ranking or heavily weighted factor). For instance, the source selection team may know that all contractors under the most recent (5 to 10) contracts for similar requirements had excellent performance or market research may reveal that prospective offerors have very similar records of successful past performance. There may be procurements where past performance is not a meaningful discriminator among prospective offerors, and therefore, should be a relatively less important source selection factor in those cases.

Agency officials may assign any weight or relative importance to past performance compared to any other evaluation factor, and have broad discretion regarding the source and type of past performance information to be included in the evaluation. However, it is recommended that the weight assigned to past performance be at least 25 percent of the total evaluation; or, equal to the other non-cost evaluation factors to ensure significant consideration is given to past performance. A very low weighting (5-10%) may reduce the overall perception of how important good contract performance is as an element of the source selection process.

It is good to involve industry early to help identify and resolve concerns regarding the approach to assessing past performance information (see FAR 15.201) before releasing the final solicitation. Early communications could consist of meetings with prospective offerors via presolicitation conferences or sending out requests for information, draft solicitations, or advertising in trade publications. These are all useful market research tools for obtaining preliminary information from industry, or familiarizing the source selection team with the nuances of a particular business or industry, that will ultimately help the team develop an evaluation plan and Sections L and M of the solicitation.

Drafting Sections L and M of the Solicitation

The key to successful use of past performance—and with any other evaluation factor—in the source selection process is the establishment of a clear relationship between the statement of work (SOW), Section L (instructions to offerors) and Section M (evaluation criteria). The factors chosen for evaluation must track back to the requirements in the SOW. They should be reasonable, logical, and coherent.

230 PAST PERFORMANCE HANDBOOK

Accordingly, Section L and Section M should be clear with respect to what past performance information the Government will evaluate and how it will be ranked or weighted. Past performance information that is not important to the current acquisition should not be included.

Section L, Instructions to Offerors

Consider the following when developing proposal submission requirements. See FAR 15.305(a)(2):

1. Tailor the requirements to reflect the complexity of the procurement, and the relative importance of past performance and any of its subfactors to that procurement.

2. Ask offerors for a list of references for on-going contracts or contracts completed not more than 3 years ago that demonstrates performance relevant to the solicitation performance requirements. Keep the number of references requested to as few as possible to give an accurate reflection of past performance. We recommend 5 to 10 references as the norm, with more than 15 to be a seldom occurrence. FAR 42.1503(e) states that past performance information shall not be retained to provide source selection information for longer than 3 years after completion of the contract. For contracts where there are lots of actions and many contractors provide the products or services, a shorter period may be appropriate. It is best to request the most recent references, many times this would mean limiting references to 1 or 2 years back.

3. Limit the contractor's ability to "cherry pick" only the best references. All relevant contracts performed during the identified period, or the last "X" relevant contracts performed by the entity within the identified period should be sought. The goal is to get a true picture of the contractor's overall, recent performance record.

4. Provide potential offerors the opportunity to provide information on problems encountered on the identified contracts. Limit this section to the discussion of problems and corrective actions taken. It is not necessary or efficient to burden the process by asking that the contractor prepare a description of its past performance history. The references will inform the source selection team of the contractor experience and performance.

5. Inform potential offerors that past performance information on work for State and local governments, private sector clients, and subcontracts that

Appendix A   **231**

is similar to the Government requirement will be evaluated equally with similar Federal contracts. This will help ensure that firms new to the Federal process are given a fair opportunity to compete.

6. Remind potential offerors that they may submit information on key personnel, major subcontractors, work performed as part of a team or joint venture, and other previous reincarnation of its current organization. This will allow most firms without prime contract history to provide past performance information. This will reduce the cases of neutral past performance ratings.

7. Past performance information is proprietary source selection information. Therefore, Section L should explain that the Government will only discuss past performance information directly with the prospective prime or sub-contractor that is being reviewed. If there is a problem with the proposed subcontractor's past performance, the prime can be notified of a problem, but no details, may be discussed without the subcontractor's permission.

8. Rely on existing documentation from Federal systems or other systems to the maximum possible extent. This will expedite and streamline the source evaluation process significantly. If adequate documentation is not readily available (Government evaluations not completed, State and Local governments and private sector references), then a brief survey with follow up calls, or phone interviews should be used to verify past performance. It is strongly recommended that the survey be no longer than 1-2 pages and prior contact be made with the cognizant officials before sending out the survey. Experience shows that long surveys are not returned timely (if returned at all), which slows down the evaluation process. If a survey is to be used include a copy in the solicitation. You could use the same format in Appendix 1 for the survey.

9. It is important to ask for at least two references on each non-Federal reference. In addition to ensuring that all aspects of the contractor's performance will be discussed, it also ensures that anonymity of the references can be maintained. There is considerable concern that there will be a tendency for inflated rating from references if the name of the person providing the rating is revealed to the offeror.

10. Section L should include a statement that the Government may use past performance information obtained from other than the sources identified by the offeror and that the information obtained will be used for both the responsibility determination and the best value decision.

232   PAST PERFORMANCE HANDBOOK

11. Where large, multi-function firms are likely to submit a proposal, ask for references only on work done by the segment of the firm (division, group, unit), not the firm in general.

12. If the source selection team expects a large volume of proposals, the solicitation may request early submission of the past performance volume with the rest of the proposal to follow at a later date. This practice allows more time to conduct a thorough review of the past performance information.

13. Do not ask the offeror to obtain replies from listed references and submit them to the Contracting Officer by a certain date. Obtaining the past performance information from the listed references is a Government source Selection Team's responsibility, not an offeror's responsibility.

Section M, Evaluation Criteria

Section M of the solicitation contains the evaluation factors and subfactors, and their relative importance (with weights if appropriate). This section is very important to offerors, and should be clear and consistent with the instructions provided in Section L. The Government should describe the approach for evaluating past performance in this section, including offerors with no relevant performance history. Consider the following when drafting the past performance evaluation factor:

1. Use Past Performance as A Distinct Factor

The past performance factor should be distinct and identifiable in order to reduce the chances of its impact being lost within other factors and to ease the evaluation process. However, if integrating past performance with other non-cost/price factors provides a more meaningful picture, each agency should use its own discretion. The key is to not dilute the importance or impact of past performance when determining the best value contractor.

2. Choose Past Performance Subfactors Wisely

Tailor the subfactors to match the requirement and to capture the key performance criteria in the statement of work. Carefully consider whether subfactors add value to the overall assessment, warrant the additional time to evaluate and enhance the discrimination among the competing proposals.

a. Quality of Product or Service—The offeror will be evaluated on compliance with previous contract requirements, accuracy of reports, and technical excellence to include Quality awards/certificates.

Appendix A **233**

b. Timeliness of Performance—The offeror will be evaluated on meeting milestones, reliability, responsiveness to technical direction, deliverables completed on-time, adherence to contract schedules including contract administration.

c. Cost Control—The offeror will be evaluated on the ability to perform within or below budget, use of cost efficiencies, relationship of negotiated costs to actuals, submission of reasonably priced change proposals, and providing current, accurate, and complete billing timely.

d. Business Relations—The offeror will be evaluated on the ability to provide effective management, meet subcontractor and SDB goals, cooperative and proactive behavior with the technical representative(s) and Contracting Officer, flexibility, responsiveness to inquires, problem resolution and customer satisfaction. The offeror will be evaluated on satisfaction of the technical monitors with the overall performance, and final product and services. Evaluation of past performance will be based on consideration of all relevant facts and circumstances. It will include a determination of the offeror's commitment to customer satisfaction and will include conclusions of informed judgment. However, the basis for the conclusions of judgment should be substantially documented.

3. Subcontractor, and Teaming, and Joint Venture Partner's Past Performance

For the purpose of evaluation of past performance information, offerors shall be defined as business arrangements and relationships such as joint ventures, teaming partners, and major subcontractors. Each firm in the business arrangement will be evaluated on its performance under existing and prior contracts for similar products or services.

Evaluating Past Performance

The source selection team should validate the prospective offeror's past contract information as part of the overall evaluation process and then assign a performance risk rating. The final past performance rating may be reflected in a color, a number, adjective rating, or some other means, depending on the agency policy for indicating the relative ranking of the offerors. Performance risk assessments should consider the number and severity of problems, the demonstrated effectiveness of corrective actions taken (not just planned or promised), and the overall work record. Instances of good or poor performance should be noted and related to the solicitation requirement. If problems were identified on a prior contract, the role the Government may have played in that result should be taken into account. The evaluation team should look for indications of excellent or exceptional performance in the areas most critical to the requirement.

234   PAST PERFORMANCE HANDBOOK

The source selection team first evaluates how well a prospective offeror performed, and then rates the relevancy of that performance. Generally, the final evaluated rating is used along with other rated evaluation factors in a comparative assessment to determine which offeror is the most highly rated and most likely to be awarded the contract. An effective evaluation of past performance allows the Contracting Officer to focus on contractors with sound performance records that are among the most highly rated.

A significant achievement, problem, or lack of relevant data in any aspect of the requirement can become an important consideration in the source selection process. A negative finding may result in an overall high performance risk rating, depending upon the significance placed on that aspect of the requirement by the source selection team. Relate the ratings to the solicitation requirements and provide rationale that identifies the strength or weakness. Determine if the Government may have contributed to a weakness, and, if so, to what extent.

A past performance rating is not a precise mechanical process, therefore, a supporting rationale for the final rating needs to be included in the contract file. The documentation need not be voluminous. The assessment should include rationale for the conclusions reached. As long as that rationale is reasonable, i.e., based on analysis, verification, or corroboration of the past performance information, and is evaluated against the evaluation factors stated in the solicitation, it will withstand scrutiny by the courts.

The source selection team should commit reasonable efforts to obtain information from all references. Failure of timely responses from Federal agencies should be pursued to a level necessary to obtain a response. The source selection team should be cautious not to downgrade or penalize offerors for the judicious use of the contract claims process.

For large complex contracts, it may be best for an agency to establish a separate past performance evaluation team, especially if the agency anticipates receiving a large number of proposals. Include contracting and program office representatives on the team. Maximum effectiveness occurs when the evaluator's background matches that of the reference. This allows the Government to obtain a more complete picture of the offeror's performance.

Upon completion of the reference check, the source selection team should review trends to determine the risks of successful performance on the contract. When checking private-sector references, the source selection team should consider the potential of any conflict of interests between the offeror and the reference.

Appendix A **235**

> Naval Facilities Engineering Command's Southwest Division in San Diego used past performance information as an important part of its procurement for a two-phase design-build contract to obtain a fixed price, total effort in design, engineering and construction of a 10,240 square foot youth Center at Point Mugu, California. As part of the Phase I Past Performance criteria, contractors were evaluated through the use of surveys, on adherence to schedule commitment to customer satisfaction, change order history, and commitment to safety. This evaluation resulted in the selection of three firms to submit design/construction proposals for Phase II of the acquisition process. Performance is still in process; however, interim assessment of the contractor selected indicate that the quality of design was very good, there were very few changes except those desired by the customer, and the completion date is on target.

Consider the following while evaluating proposals:

1. Rely on existing evaluations to the maximum extent possible

Utilize National Institutes of Health (NIH), DOD, or other agency wide databases to abstract pertinent information in conducting the past performance review. Information on agency wide databases and points of contacts may be found in Appendix V. If, information is not available via the databases, use brief surveys or phone interviews with the cognizant Contracting Officers to gather the required information. Sample questions and ideas for telephone interviews and questionnaires can be found in Appendix IV.

2. Recency and Relevancy

Past performance information must be relevant and recent regarding an offeror's actions under previously awarded contracts. Similar or relevant past performance efforts could be defined by the size, scope, complexity, and contract type.

Each prospective offeror has the responsibility to provide references that are relevant to the new work and must explain the relevance of its past performance information submitted, particularly when it may not be easily apparent. For instance, in the case of a newly formed business entity or in contractor teaming arrangements where the company is relying mostly on the past performance and experience of its key personnel, partners on the team, or on a major subcontractor(s), the proposal must clearly explain "whose" past performance, and "how" that past performance is relevant to the procurement.

Giving prospective offerors opportunities to submit non-similar past contract performance information, although it may not be given much weight or

236 PAST PERFORMANCE HANDBOOK

may be rated a higher risk will, in the long run, enhance the integrity and fairness of Government acquisitions, and increase the competitive base.

3. Lack of Past Performance

Given the number of mergers and acquisitions in today's American business environment, potential offerors may not have existed under their current name for very long. This creates an interesting wrinkle in the source selection process. Agencies must recognize this dynamic world marketplace and accommodate new prospective offerors by being more flexible in their procurement rules and practices.

The past performance of the offeror's resources is a good indicator of future performance for new companies entering the marketplace that lack relevant experience, or mergers of previously established companies. If the key management personnel, subcontractors, or other resources, have experience on contracts similar to the pending requirement for another contractor; state and local government contracts; private contracts; or was a major subcontractor; then the source selection team can perform the appropriate evaluation and risk assessment. This reduces the chance of needing to "neither reward nor penalize" an offeror with no other relevant past performance information.

If the contractor is truly a new entity and none of the company principals ever performed relevant work for others, the company is considered to have no past performance. Special rules apply in this situation. Section 1091(b)(2) of FASA states that "in the case of an offeror with respect to which there is no information on past contract performance or with respect to which information on past contract performance is not available, the offeror may not be evaluated favorably or unfavorably on the factor of past contract performance." This requirement is implemented at FAR Part 15.305(a)(2)(iv): "In the case of an offeror without a record of relevant past performance or for whom information on past performance is not available, the offeror may not be evaluated favorably or unfavorably on past performance." We expect this will happen very rarely.

There are various methods that may be used to evaluate a competitive offeror with no past performance history and it is at the discretion of the agency to determine the most appropriate method on a case-by-case basis. Remember that the evaluation method selected must be clearly stated in the solicitation.

4. Evaluating Subcontractors, and Teaming, and Joint Venture Partners

Treat subcontractor, and teaming, and joint venture partners past performance information the same as any prime contractor past performance information. Past performance information cannot be disclosed to anyone other than Government personnel with a "need-to-know" without the firm's consent. The

Appendix A **237**

Government must obtain the consent of the separate entities before disclosing it's past performance information to the prime during discussions. The consent may be provided as part of the prime's proposal. This approach lets the Government discuss any negative or unfavorable past performance information on a proposed firm with the prime offeror and greatly facilitates the conduct of meaningful discussions. It also gives the prime contractors an opportunity to mitigate the impact to their evaluated standing by enabling them to find out more about the other firm's past performance problems, or to even replace the proposed firm with another firm having a better past performance.

> REMINDER: You can only evaluate what you <u>told</u> the contractor you would evaluate. Therefore, be very clear in the solicitation!!

> Superintendent of Shipbuilding (SUPSHIP) Portsmouth saved $10.9 million during the first two years of administration of its first Best Value Source Selection for an Indefinite Quantity contract to obtain Chemical Holding Transfer (CHT) Systems services over past sole source or separate contracts for similar services. The criteria for source selection were Past Performance and Technical Capability considered to be equal importance and both combined as more important than price. Since the Navy CPARS was not extensively operational at that time, they required contractors to list similar contracts and then interviewed the listed Points of Contact. Wide advertisement resulted in more proposals than they were previously aware of and expanded price competition. The eventual awardee was a contractor who had been performing similar services in cleaning drinking water for municipalities but had never before considered Navy ships as potential clients. This contract was so successful for the Navy that its use is being extended to the U.S. Coast Guard.

Conducting Discussions

The offeror must be provided an opportunity to address adverse past performance information obtained from references on which the offeror has not had a previous opportunity to comment, if that information makes a difference in the Government's decision to include the offeror in or exclude the offeror from the competitive range. Any past performance deficiency or significant weakness must be discussed with offerors within the competitive range during discussions. This allows the offeror a fair opportunity to rebut any negative information that may not be due solely to the poor performance of the contractor, or that may not have been adequately resolved since the date of the information provided. For example, budget and funding reductions may not always equate to a corresponding reduction in scope of work, and the contractor's performance may be negatively impacted. There may be times when excessive Government–driven requirement changes and last minute changes may also negatively impact the contractor's performance.

238   PAST PERFORMANCE HANDBOOK

Section M must describe where in the evaluation process past performance will be used to rank offerors. Some agencies evaluate past performance on all offerors and rank them to determine the competitive range. Others consider past performance only on the firms in the competitive range when the mission suitability is paramount. If this is the case, then Section L should clearly state the Government's intent.

In the interest of fairness, also consider allowing offerors to rebut all negative past performance information or clarify relevance of past performance information even when discussions are not anticipated. This type of exchange is a clarification (see FAR 15.306(a)). The Government may still award without discussion following clarifications.

Appendix A **239**

APPENDIX I
SAMPLE CONTRACTOR PERFORMANCE REPORT

CONTRACTOR PERFORMANCE REPORT	
[ ] Final or [ ] Interim – Period Report: From___/___/___ To___/___/___	
1. Contractor Name and Address:	2. Contract Number: Task Order Number:
	3. Value: $
	4. Award Date: Completion Date:
5. Type of Contract:(Check all that apply)-[ ]FP [ ]FP-EPA [ ]CPFF – Completion [ ]CPFF-Term [ ]CPIF [ ]CPAF [ ]ID/IQ [ ]BOA [ ]Requirements [ ]Labor Hour [ ]T&M [ ]CR [ ]Other	
6. Description of Requirement:	
7. Ratings. After commenting, score, in column on the right, using 1 for unsatisfactory, 2 for marginal, 3 for satisfactory, 4 for very good, and 5 for exceptional.	
Quality – Comments	
Cost Control – Comments	
Timeliness – Comments	
Business Relations – Comments	
Total Score (sum of scores from each area)	
Mean Score (sum of scores divided by number of areas evaluated):	
8. Subcontractors and Teaming and Joint Venture Partners List major subcontractors, team, joint venture partners, by name with brief description of Work and names of key personnel. A. B. C.	

240 PAST PERFORMANCE HANDBOOK

9. List Key Personnel of Prime Contractor	
Name/Title	Employment Dates
Comments:	
Name/Title	Employment Dates
Comments:	
Name/Title	Employment Dates
Comments:	

10. Would you select the firm again? Yes _____ No _____
    Is/Was the contractor committed to customer satisfaction? Yes _____ No _____

11. Assessing Officers Name/Org. ID	Signature:	Phone/Fax Number:
Date Sent to Contractor:		CO's Initials:

12. Contractor's Review. Were comments, rebuttals, or additional information provided?
    [ ] No   [ ] Yes. Please attach comments.

13. Returned by (type name):	Signature
Phone/Fax/Internet Address	Date

14. Agency Review. Were contractor comments reviewed at a level above the Contracting Officer?
    [ ] No [ ] Yes. Please attach comments. Number of pages

15. Final Ratings. Re-assess the Block 7 ratings based on contractor comments and agency review.
Validate or revise as appropriate.

Quality	Cost Control	Timeliness	Business Relation

Mean Score (Add the ratings above and divide by the number of areas rated)	0.00

16. CO's Name	Signature
Phone/Fax/Internet Address	Date

Release of Information: This Contractor Performance Report may be used to support future award decisions, and will be treated as <u>source selection information</u> in accordance with FAR 3.104-4(k)(1)(x) and 42.1503(b). The completed report shall not be released to other than Government personnel and the contractor whose performance is being evaluated during the period the information is being used to provide source selection information.

32

Appendix A **241**

APPENDIX I (Continued)
SAMPLE CONTRACTOR PERFORMANCE REPORT INSTRUCTIONS

Block 1: Contractor Name and Address. Identify the specific division being evaluated if there is more than one.

Block 2: Contract number/task order number being evaluated.

Block 3: Contract value, including options.

Block 4: Contract award date and (anticipated) contract completion date.

Block 5: Type of Contract: Check all that apply.

Block 6: Provide a brief description of the work being done under the contract and identify the key performance indicators.

Block 7: Indicate rating in far right column. In the comment area, provide rationale for the rating. Indicate the contract requirements that were exceeded or were not met by the contractor and by how much.

Block 8: Identify major Subcontractors, and Team Partners, and their work responsibilities. List the key personnel employed during the rating period that played a major role in the performance rating. Do not list key personnel not employed long enough to affect performance. In some cases, more than one individual may have served in a key position. List persons that had an affect on the ratings.

Block 9: Identify prime contractor key personnel. See Block 8 above for instructions.

Block 10: Explain why you would or would not select the contractor for this contract again.

Block 11: Provide information indicated.

Blocks 12–13: The contractor may provide comments but must sign block 13 to indicate it has reviewed the rating.

Block 14: If the contractor and Contracting Officer are unable to agree on a final rating, the contractor may seek review at a level above the Contracting Officer, as required. Provide information indicated.

242 PAST PERFORMANCE HANDBOOK

Block 15: Adjust the ratings assigned in block 7, if appropriate, based on any comments, rebuttals, or additional information provided by the contractor and, if necessary, by agency review. Calculate a mean score.

Block 16: The Contracting Officer's signature indicates concurrence with the initial and final ratings.

Appendix A   **243**

APPENDIX II
DOD PERFORMANCE ASSESSMENT ELEMENTS
FOR LARGE SYSTEMS ACQUISITIONS

For Large System Acquisition, DOD uses an expanded set of review elements as follows:

TECHNICAL (QUALITY OF PRODUCT). This element is comprised of an overall rating and six sub-elements. Activity critical to successfully complying with contract requirements must be assessed within one or more of these sub-elements. The overall rating at the element level is the Program Manager's integrated assessment as to what most accurately depicts the contractor's technical performance or progress toward meeting requirements. It is not a predetermined roll-up of the sub-elements assessments.

Product Performance—Assess the achieved product performance relative to performance parameters required by the contract.

Systems Engineering—Assess the contractor's effort to transform operational needs and requirements into an integrated system design solution.

Software Engineering—Assess the contractor's success in meeting contract requirements for software development, modification, or maintenance. Results from Software Capability Evaluations (SCEs) (using the Software Engineering Institute (SEI's) Capability Maturity Model (CMM) as a means of measurement), Software Development Capability Evaluations (SDCEs), or similar software assessments may be used a source of information to support this evaluation.

Logistic Support/Sustainment—Assess the success of the contractor's performance in accomplishing logistics planning.

Product Assurance—Assess how successfully the contractor meets program quality objectives, e.g., producibility, reliability, maintainability, inspectability, testability, and system safety, and controls the overall manufacturing process.

Other Technical Performance—Assess all the other technical activity critical to successful contract performance. Identify any additional assessment aspects that are unique to the contract or that cannot be captured in another sub-element.

SCHEDULE—Assess the timeliness of the contractor against the completion of the contract, task orders, milestones, delivery schedules, administrative requirements, etc.

244 PAST PERFORMANCE HANDBOOK

COST CONTROL—Assess the contractor's effectiveness in forecasting, managing, and controlling contract cost. For fixed price contracts this assesses whether contractor met original cost estimated or needed to negotiate cost changes to meet program requirements.

MANAGEMENT—This element is comprised of an overall rating and three sub-elements. Activity critical to successfully executing the contract must be assessed within one or more of these sub-elements. This overall rating at the element level is the Program Manager's integrated assessment as to what most accurately depicts the contractor's performance in managing the contracted effort. It is not a predetermined roll-up of the sub-element assessments.

Management Responsiveness—Assess the timeliness, completeness and quality of problem identification, corrective action plans, proposal submittals (especially responses to change orders, engineering change proposals, or other undefinitized contract actions), the contractor's history of reasonable and co-operative behavior, effective business relations, and customer satisfaction.

Subcontract Management—Assess the contractor's success with timely award and management of subcontracts, including whether the contractor met small/small disadvantaged and women-owned business participation goals.

Program Management and Other Management—Assess the extent to which the contractor discharges its responsibility for integration and coordination of all activity needed to execute the contract; identifies and applies resources required to meet schedule requirements; assigns responsibility for tasks/actions required by contract; communicates appropriate information to affected program elements in a timely manner. Assess the contractor's risk management practices, especially the ability to identify risks and formulate and implement risk mitigation plans. If applicable, identify and assess any other areas that are unique to the contract, or that cannot be captured elsewhere under the Management element.

Appendix A **245**

APPENDIX III
PERFORMANCE RATING GUIDELINES

These are suggested guidelines for assigning ratings on a contractor's compliance with the contract performance, cost, and schedule goals as specified in the Statement of Work. The guidelines for Business Relations are meant to be separate ratings for the areas mentioned. All the areas do not need to fit the rating to give the rating for the category. Ensure that this assessment is consistent with any other Agency assessments (i.e., award fee assessments).

Technical Performance (Quality of Product/Service)

Exceptional
- Met all performance requirements/Exceeded 20 % or more
- Minor problems/Highly effective corrective actions/Improved performance/quality results

Very Good
- Met all performance requirements/Exceeded 5% or more
- Minor problems/Effective corrective actions

Satisfactory
- Met all performance requirements
- Minor problems/Satisfactory corrective actions

Marginal
- Some performance requirements not met
- Performance reflects serious problem/Ineffective corrective actions

Unsatisfactory
- Most performance requirements are not met
- Recovery not likely

Cost Control

Exceptional
- Significant reductions while meeting all contract requirements
- Use of value engineering or other innovative management techniques
- Quickly resolved cost issues/Effective corrective actions facilitated cost reductions

246 Past Performance Handbook

Very Good
- Reduction in overall cost/price while meeting all contract requirements
- Use of value engineering or other innovative management techniques
- Quickly resolved cost/price issues/Effective corrective actions to facilitate overall cost/price reductions

Satisfactory
- Met overall cost/price estimates while meeting all contract requirements

Marginal
- Do not meet cost/price estimates
- Inadequate corrective action plans/No innovative techniques to bring overall expenditures within limits

Unsatisfactory
- Significant cost overruns
- Not likely to recovery cost control

Schedule (Timeliness)

Exceptional
- Significantly exceeded delivery requirements (All on-time with many early deliveries to the Government's benefit)
- Quickly resolved delivery issues/Highly effective corrective actions

Very Good
- On-Time deliveries/Some early deliveries to the Government's benefit
- Quickly resolved delivery issues/Effective corrective actions

Satisfactory
- On-time deliveries
- Minor problems/Did not effect delivery schedule

Marginal
- Some late deliveries
- No corrective actions

Unsatisfactory
- Many late deliveries
- Negative cost impact/Loss of capability for Government
- Ineffective corrective actions/Not likely to recover

Appendix A **247**

Business Relations

Exceptional
- Highly professional/Responsive/Proactive
- Significantly exceeded expectations
- High user satisfaction
- Significantly exceeded SB/SDB subcontractor goals
- Minor changes implemented without cost impact/Limited change proposals/Timely definitization of change proposals

Very Good
- Professional/Responsive
- Exceeded expectations
- User satisfaction
- Exceeded subcontractor goals
- Limited change proposals/Timely definitization of change proposals

Satisfactory
- Professional/Reasonably responsive
- Met expectations
- Adequate user satisfaction
- Met subcontractor goals
- Reasonable change proposals/Reasonable definitization cycle

Marginal
- Less Professionalism and Responsiveness
- Low user satisfaction/No attempts to improve relations
- Unsuccessful in meeting subcontractor goals
- Unnecessary change proposals/Untimely definitization of change proposals

Unsatisfactory
- Delinquent responses/Lack of cooperative spirit
- Unsatisfied user/Unable to improve relations
- Significantly under subcontractor goals
- Excessive unnecessary change proposals to correct poor management
- Significantly untimely definitization of change proposals

APPENDIX IV
SAMPLE QUESTIONS AND IDEAS FOR TELEPHONE INTERVIEWS AND QUESTIONNAIRES

- Confirm the following data from the offeror's proposal:
  - –Contract number
  - –Contractor's name and address
  - –Type of contract
  - –Complexity of work
  - –Description and location of work (e.g., types of tasks, products, services)
  - –Contract dollar value
  - –Date of award
  - –Contract completion date (including extensions)
  - –Type and Extent of Subcontracting

- Verify any past performance data to which you may have access

- If the award amount or delivery schedule changed, find out why.

- Ask what role the reference played (e.g., COR, contract specialist, ACO, etc.) and for how long.

- If a problem surfaced ask what the Government and contractor did to fix it.

- Ask for a description of the types of personnel (skill and expertise) the contractor used and the overall quality of the contractor's team. Did the company appear to use personnel with the appropriate skills and expertise?

- Ask how the contractor performed considering technical performance or quality of the product or service; schedule; cost control (if applicable); business relations; and management.

- Ask whether the contractor was cooperative in resolving issues.

- Inquire whether there were any particularly significant risks involved in performance of the effort.

- Ask if the company appeared to apply sufficient resources (personnel and facilities) to the effort.

Appendix A **249**

- If the company used subcontractors, ask: What was the relationship between the prime and subcontractors? How well did the prime manage the subcontractors? Did the subcontractors perform the bulk of the effort or just add depth on particular technical areas? Why were the subcontractors chosen to work on specific technical areas, what were those areas and why were they accomplished by the subcontractors rather than the prime?

- If a problem is uncovered that the reference is unfamiliar with, ask for another individual who might have the information.

- Ask if this firm has performed other past efforts with the reference's agency.

- Ask about the company's strong points or what the reference liked best.

- Inquire whether the reference has any reservations about recommending a future contract award to this company.

Inquire whether the reference knows of anyone else who might have past performance information on the offeror.

APPENDIX V
AUTOMATED PAST PERFORMANCE
INFORMATION SYSTEMS

Agency	System Nomenclature	Point of Contact	Phone Number
NIH	Contractor Performance System	Ms. Jo Ann Wingard	301-496-1783
Army	Past Performance Information Management System (PPIMS)	Barbara Mather/ functional Terry Thacker/ technical	703-681-9158 540-731-3459
	Architect-Engineer Contract Administration Support System (ACASS)	Donna Smigel	202-761-0336
	Construction Contractor Appraisal Support System (CCASS)	Marilyn Nedell	503-808-4590
Navy	Product Data Reporting and Evaluation Program (PDREP)	John Deforge Paul Couture	603-431-9460 x450 603-431-9460 x480
	Department of the Navy Contractor Performance Assessment Reporting System (CPARS)	Wendell Smith Paul Couture	603-431-9460 x451 603-431-9460 x480
Air Force	CPARS	Ms. Lois Todd Roger Hanson	937-257-4657 or DSN 787-4657 937-257-6057 or DSN 787-6057
Defense Logistics Agency	Automated Best Value System (ABVS)	Melody Readrdon	703-767-1362
Defense Information Systems Agency (DISA)	Contractor Past Performance Evaluation Toolkit	Mary Jenkins Nathan Maenie	703-681-/DSN 761 703-681-1673 DSN 761

Appendix B

DEPARTMENT OF DEFENSE

A GUIDE TO
Collection and Use of
PAST PERFORMANCE INFORMATION

A product of the DoD Past Performance IPT
DUSD(AR)
May 1999

Appendix B **253**

TABLE OF CONTENTS

Foreword ii

Acknowledgments iii

Top Ten List iv

Introduction
PPI Objectives 1
Business Sectors 2

Obtaining Past Performance Information
PPI Collection Approaches 3
Performance Assessment Reports 3
Administrative Information 6
Team Assessment Inputs 7
Performance Ratings 8
Contractor Review and Comment on PPI 8
Handling of PPI 9
Automation of PPI 9
Orders Issued Under Contracts or Ordering Agreements 9

Use of Past Performance Information in Source Selection
Role of Past Performance in Source Selection 11
Planning the Past Performance Evaluation 13
The Past Performance Evaluation Process 19

Appendices

A: Definitions, References, & GAO Cases 26
B: Business Sectors 29
C: PPI Evaluation and Report Thresholds 34
D: Performance Assessment Elements 35
E: Construction & Architect-Engineering 38
F: Performance Rating Level 40
G: Collection of PPI During Source Selection 41
H: Automated PPI Systems 47

i

254 PAST PERFORMANCE HANDBOOK

FOREWORD

This guide is designed to articulate the key techniques and practices for the use and collection of past performance information. Consistent with the spirit of acquisition reform, it provides guidance to encourage the use of innovative techniques in acquiring the best value goods and services. Its purpose is to provide you with a practical reference tool regarding DoD past performance policy.

This guide is designed for use by the entire acquisition workforce in both government and industry to promote the goal of achieving "best value". It explains best practices for the use of past performance information during source selection, ongoing performance, and during collection of the information. The guide was a joint team effort of members from the Past Performance Integrated Product Team, and the FAR 15 rewrite team. I commend the rewrite and IPT teams for a job well done, and want to thank those members of industry for their comments on the guide as well.

I encourage you to read and use this guide in your efforts to obtain the best value for the Department of Defense and the American taxpayer.

Stan Soloway
Deputy Under Secretary of Defense
(Acquisition Reform)

Appendix B **255**

ACKNOWLEDGMENTS

The DoD Past Performance Integrated Product Team (IPT) was created by the Under Secretary of Defense (Acquisition and Technology) in February 1997 to develop a uniform methodology for the collection and use of DoD Past Performance Information (PPI). In November 1997, the Under Secretary of Defense (Acquisition and Technology) established a new policy by memorandum for the collection of PPI. This guide updates and supercedes that policy memorandum.

Additionally, contracting by negotiation, FAR Part 15, establishes one framework for our business relationship with industry and is critical to obtaining best value goods and services. In 1996, Dr. Steven Kelman, the Administrator of the Office of Federal Procurement Policy and the Department of Defense began a major effort to reform the rules governing source selection procedures for the federal and defense sectors. The new FAR 15 rule, which also includes the policy for the use of past performance information, was effective January 1, 1998.

These teams were comprised of representatives from the Office of the Under Secretary of Defense (Acquisition & Technology), the Departments of the Army, Navy, and Air Force, the Defense Logistics Agency, the Office of Federal Procurement Policy and members of the Federal Sector for the FAR 15 rewrite. The teams, in coordination with the Defense Acquisition University, the Federal Acquisition Institute and industry, are now working to provide training to our workforce. This guide, produced by the DoD Past Performance IPT, is designed to provide additional guidance for both collection and use of past performance.

This guide does not supercede nor take precedence over more restrictive Agency procedures. Electronic versions of this guide are available on the Acquisition Reform Homepage at http://www.acq.osd.mil. If you have further questions about this subject, you are encouraged to submit questions to the Defense Acquisition Deskbook "Ask a Professor" program at: http://www.deskbook.osd.mil.

PAST PERFORMANCE TOP TEN LIST

1. FAR and DFARS rules apply to all PPI, however and whenever collected. This includes ensuring that contractors have the opportunity to comment on adverse PPI on report cards as well as other PPI gathered under less formal collection methods. (Page 1)

2. PPI is "For Official Use Only" and should be so marked. (Page 2)

3. The performance assessment process begins with solicitation evaluation factors, and continues through contract performance assessments of award fee and past performance. Normally, the form and content of this assessment continuum should be consistent throughout the contract performance period to ensure successful performance. (Page 2)

4. The narrative is the most critical aspect of PPI assessments. (Page 4)

5. Performance assessments are the responsibility of the program/project/contracting team, considering the customer's input ; no one office or organization should independently determine a performance assessment. (Page 5)

6. Performance assessments should be developed throughout the period of contract performance, and not held to the end of the performance period. (Page 6)

7. Use and evaluation of PPI for a specific acquisition should be tailored to fit the needs of each acquisition and clearly articulated in the solicitation. (Page 7)

8. Source selection officials should use the most relevant, recent PPI available in making the source selection decisions. They must consider updated information provided by the contractor regarding relevant PPI. (Page 9)

9. Personnel collecting PPI for use in a particular source selection should consider whether the data received comes from reputable and reliable sources. (Page 13)

10. The Government should share all relevant PPI with contractors as part of the past performance evaluation during the source selection process, and must share adverse PPI on which contractors have not had the opportunity to comment. (Page 13)

THE KEYS TO EFFECTIVE PPI ARE FAIRNESS, OPENNESS, AND A COMITMENT TO USING THE INFORMATION AS A TOOL TO IMPROVE PERFORMANCE.

INTRODUCTION

Confidence in a prospective contractor's ability to perform satisfactorily is an important factor in making a best value source selection decision. One method of gaining this confidence is the evaluation of a prospective contractor's performance on recently completed or ongoing contracts for the same or similar goods or services. Past Performance Information (PPI) motivates contractors to improve their performance because of the potential use of that information in future source selections. It is equally useful as a means of communication, providing feedback and additional performance incentives for ongoing contracts. Excellent past performance also indicates a heightened probability of delivery of high quality products, which are on time and within cost. Definitions of terms and references used in this guide are set forth in Appendix A.

PPI OBJECTIVES

PPI objectives provide a consistent evaluation methodology to identify and describe the performance of the wide array of DoD contractors and suppliers, including foreign companies, educational and non-profit institutions, and other federal agencies.

PPI may be used with other criteria to:

- enhance market research

- help establish the competitive range and make award decisions

- provide a basis for discussing progress with contractors during contract performance

- help decide whether to exercise contract options

- help decide between different vendors on multiple award contracts when awarding delivery orders

- aid the development of acquisition strategies

- recognize good performers.

PPI is also essential to ensure enhanced performance on existing contracts, and is not just for future source selections.

BUSINESS SECTORS

To enable the effective sharing of PPI between government buying activities, a reasonable degree of uniformity in assessments of contractor performance is essential. This consistency should be applied to report card (annual) assessments as well as to award fee evaluations or to other PPI collection methods.

> FAR AND DFAR rules apply to all PPI, however and whenever collected. This includes ensuring that contractors have the opportunity to comment on adverse PPI on report cards as well as other PPI gathered under less formal collection methods.

DoD policy is to collect PPI for report cards using a consistent management approach across the designated business sectors categorized as key or unique. This approach includes tailored dollar thresholds, consistent elements used to assess contractors, or other government agencies, and consistent ratings applied to those elements. DoD's six business sectors are defined in Appendix B.

Source selection authorities must be given maximum latitude to focus on those specific areas of contractor performance that will provide the best predictors for successful performance for each specific acquisition.

Appendix B **259**

OBTAINING PAST PERFORMANCE INFORMATION

DoD has established common assessment elements within individual business sectors, and ratings to standardize the methodology used to rate contractor performance under Defense contracts. Government buying activities should share PPI among themselves, while ensuring it is managed as source selection information. PPI collection should be efficient, but effective.

PPI is "For Official Use Only" and should be so marked.

PPI COLLECTION APPROACHES

PPI can be obtained through a number of methods including:

- Government assessments, or report cards

- Published commercial evaluations

- References submitted by the Contractor

- Surveys or questionnaires, verbal or written, conducted by Government personnel

PPI from a variety of sources should be considered including:

- Government contracts

- State, local or foreign governments

- Commercial companies

- Information regarding predecessor companies, key personnel and subcontractors

PERFORMANCE ASSESSMENT REPORTS

Performance Assessment Reports, or report cards, may be written during contract performance and shall be written after the end of the performance period. Report cards are prepared by either the Program or Requirements Manager or Contracting Officer according to agency procedures and should reflect a team assessment of contract performance. This guidance does not apply to

260 PAST PERFORMANCE HANDBOOK

procedures used by agencies in determining fees under award or incentive fee contracts. However, the fee amount paid to contractors should be an indicator of the contractor's performance and the past performance evaluation should complement the award fee determinations. In short, our goal is to ensure that all performance assessments, award fee determinations, incentive allocations or any other performance measures be evaluated consistently throughout the contract performance.

> The performance assessment process begins with solicitation evaluation factors, and continues through contract performance assessments of award fee and past performance. Normally, this assessment continuum should be consistent as to form and content throughout the contract performance period to ensure successful performance.

Contractor assessments should not be written by support service contractors. Integrity in this assessment process is essential. Contractors must be given the opportunity to comment on their own assessment reports at the time they are written, and those comments shall be maintained as part of the government record.

Collection Thresholds

The mandatory DoD collection thresholds by business-sector are set forth in Appendix C. Buying activities may choose to collect and use performance assessments for contracts under these thresholds.

Performance Assessment Elements

The mandatory DoD assessment elements for the DoD Business Sectors are set forth in Appendix D. There are a minimum of six assessment criteria required for systems assessments.

Construction and Architect-Engineering sector assessment elements and ratings are established under FAR Part 36 (See Appendix E).

For the Science and Technology sector, no dollar threshold has been established nor is there a requirement to maintain an automated database. Collection of PPI for the Science and Technology Sector shall be limited to relevant information as determined by the Source Selection team, and shall be collected at the time of the particular acquisition. Requests for PPI shall be tailored to each procurement during the source selection process with emphasis placed on the expertise of key personnel. As always, contractors shall be given the opportunity to comment on any adverse reports.

4

Appendix B   **261**

Annual Performance Assessment Reports

Annual performance assessment reports must be completed for contracts with performance periods exceeding one year and according to the thresholds articulated above. These assessments will be made as close as practicable to each anniversary of the effective date of the contract. However, the agencies will determine the specific dates.

Initial Draft Performance Assessment Reports

Use of draft performance assessment reports provided to the contractor, prior to initial government assessment, are encouraged. They are to be used to improve information flow and to encourage dialog between the parties.

Final Assessment Reports

Final assessment reports will be prepared upon contract performance completion. For contracts with performance periods exceeding one year, final reports will address only the last period of performance. They will not be used to summarize or "roll up" the contractor's performance under the entire contract. In short, each annual report together with the final assessment report will comprise a total picture of the contract performance. The expectation is that source selection evaluation teams will determine an overall performance assessment based on these performance snapshots. Contractor comments on each of these reports shall be maintained as a permanent part of the record.

Addendum Assessment Reports

Addendum assessment reports may be made at buying activities' discretion to record contractors' performance relative to contract close-out and other administrative requirements (e.g., final indirect cost proposals, technical data, etc.) No annual assessment for the period of time between contract performance completion and contract close-out are required, regardless of whether an addendum assessment is prepared. Again, any adverse reports shall be provided to the contractor for comment, and those comments shall be part of the official records.

Narrative Rationales

Supporting narrative rationales for any performance ratings assigned are mandatory in DoD to enable the user to establish that performance under a

262   PAST PERFORMANCE HANDBOOK

previous contract will be relevant to a future contract. The narratives are critical to any PPI assessment, and necessary to establish that the ratings are credible and justifiable. These rationales need not be lengthy; but, if there were performance successes or problems, they should include a description of the problems or successes experienced, an assessment of whether the problems were caused by the contractor, or the government, or other factors, and how well the contractor worked with the Government to resolve the problems (including problems with subcontractors, or "partners" in joint venture or teaming arrangements).

The narrative is the most critical aspect of PPI assessments.

Retention of Performance Assessment Reports

Performance assessment reports shall not be retained longer than three years after completion of the contract performance (except for Construction and Architect-Engineering which are to be retained for six). The performance period is not complete until the end of the warranty period. The completion of the contract, not the age of the annual contract reports, determines the retention period for those reports. Data, older than three years, may be available on long-term contracts. While such data may be meaningful in developing performance trends in certain source selections, its use should be limited to circumstances in which more current, equally relevant data is not available. In any event, the existence of such data does not relieve Source Selection Authorities (SSAs) of the responsibility to use current PPI.

Independent Government Review

Agencies shall provide for an independent review of performance evaluations at a level above the contracting officer or assessing official, as determined by the head of agency, to consider disagreements between the parties regarding the evaluation. The ultimate conclusion on the performance evaluation is a decision of the government.

ADMINISTRATIVE INFORMATION

Each PPI assessment will include, as appropriate:

- the contractor's name

- the facility address and telephone number

Appendix B **263**

- the Commercial and Government Entity (CAGE) code and Data Universal Numbering System (DUNS) number

- the business sector and sub-sector

- the contract number, initial value, award date, and completion date

- the type of contract, and whether it resulted from competition

- a description of the requirement, including the Federal Supply Class and Service Code, if available

- a list of the key subcontractors and tasks performed for Systems, Services and Information Technology sector contracts

- the period of performance being assessed

- a statement that the assessment is a organizational code, final, annual, or addendum report

- the evaluator's name, organization code, telephone number, and dated signature

- the Contractor's comments

- the resolution of contractor comments, if any

TEAM ASSESSMENT INPUTS

DoD buying activities should ensure that their PPI assessment procedures provide for input as appropriate, from:

- program management offices

- end users

- contracting offices

- item managers

- Defense Contract Management Command (DCMC) contract administration offices

- Defense Contract Audit Agency (DCAA) field audit offices

264   PAST PERFORMANCE HANDBOOK

DCMC will notify buying activities whenever they identify deficiencies or problems in contractors' technical and management systems (e.g., quality control, engineering and systems management, purchasing, accounting, billing, and estimating) that they believe will present risks to satisfactory contract performance.

> Performance assessments are the responsibility of the program/ project/contracting team, considering customer's input; no one office or organization should independently determine a performance assessment.

Feedback to contractors regarding ongoing performance should be developed through discussions, spot-checks or reviews on a regular basis.

PERFORMANCE RATINGS

The DoD Components have agreed that there are five mandatory performance rating levels for use in evaluating all performance elements in periodic assessments of contractor performance. The only exception to those mandatory ratings would be for the Construction and Architect-Engineering contracts. These ratings, provided in Appendix F, are mandatory for use by the Science and Technology business sector as well. A fundamental principle for rating is that contractors shall not be assessed below a rating of satisfactory for not performing beyond the requirements of the contract. When rating contractors, performance 'beyond the requirements of the contract' refers to the quality level of the performed work not the scope. A performance assessment may not be used to elicit performance of tasks, or to reflect a failure to perform tasks that are not required by contract.

CONTRACTOR REVIEW AND COMMENT ON PPI.

Contractors shall be allowed to review and comment on any past performance assessments and shall be provided copies of performance assessments as soon as practicable after they have been prepared. Contractors then have 30 days to submit comments, rebutting information, or other information for the buying activity's consideration before the assessments are made final. Any disagreements between the DoD lead assessor and contractor must then be reviewed at a level above the assessor. The original assessment, the contractor's comments, and the reviewer's independent assessment of those comments will be retained together on file. As soon as the government has completed its review of the contractor's comments, but in no case later than the insertion of the assessment into a PPI automated system, DoD buying activities will send a copy of the completed assessment to the contractor. These procedures provide

Appendix B **265**

an opportunity to establish a fair record of a contractor's performance, and thereby ensure that PPI will be a reliable indicator of future performance.

> Performance assessments should be developed throughout the period of contract performance, and not held to the end of the performance period.

HANDLING OF PPI

All PPI evaluations and assessments may be used to support future award decisions, and should therefore be marked "For Official Use Only—to be used for deliberative source selection purposes within the Executive Branch and for source selection and other deliberative purposes within DoD." The completed evaluation shall not be released to other than Government personnel and the contractor whose performance is being evaluated.

Contractor Access to PPI

Contractors must be given copies of all annual, final or addendum PPI assessments. Contractors should also be given copies of surveys, and responses to reference checks as soon as they are completed to ensure they are aware of information being evaluated by the government. Only negative information must be shared with contractors, however, PPI should not be a mystery to the contractor.

AUTOMATED PPI SYSTEMS

Appendix H provides information regarding existing DoD automated systems containing PPI. Departments and agencies shall share past performance information with other departments and agencies when requested to support future award decisions. One means to achieve efficiently this objective is to automate the access to existing PPI. DoD is developing an automated PPI retrieval system to access PPI data from a central Web-based location.

ORDERS ISSUED UNDER CONTRACTS OR ORDERING AGREEMENTS

For orders placed against contracts or ordering agreements (e.g., provisioned items orders, task orders, orders under indefinite-delivery or indefinite-quantity type contracts), DoD buying activities should decide whether to assess contractors' performance on an order-by-order or "total" contract/agreement ba-

266 PAST PERFORMANCE HANDBOOK

sis. This will depend on which approach they believe will produce more useful past performance information. In either case, the assessment procedures to be followed should be specified in the basic contract or agreement, particularly when other buying activities may also place orders against those instruments. The goal of periodic assessments shall be to incentivize higher performance levels on the contract involved.

Appendix B **267**

USE OF PAST PERFORMANCE INFORMATION IN SOURCE SELECTION EVALUATIONS

Source selection authorities should be given maximum latitude to focus on those specific areas of contractor performance that will provide the best predictors for successful performance of a specific acquisition.

Use and evaluation of PPI for a specific acquisition should be tailored to fit the needs of each acquisition and clearly articulated in the solicitation.

ROLE OF PAST PERFORMANCE IN SOURCE SELECTION

Decision to Use PPI in Source Selections

Past performance shall be included as an evaluation factor in competitively negotiated acquisitions unless the contracting officer determines that it is inappropriate and documents the rationale. Appendix C sets forth the mandatory thresholds for collection and use of PPI in source selections. Use of PPI is encouraged in source selections below that threshold when the source selection team considers it to be appropriate for the acquisition.

Past Performance versus Experience

There is an important distinction between a contractor's experience and its past performance. Experience reflects *whether* contractors have performed similar work before. Past performance, on the other hand, describes *how well* contractors performed the work. In other words, how well did they execute what was promised in the proposal. Both of these areas are considered when making a responsibility determination. Either past performance or experience can be considered as source selection factors or subfactors, where they can either stand alone or be considered under performance risk.

Make certain that you clearly define the terms experience and past performance in the solicitation. This will help you avoid the potential for double counting by asking for the same information under both factors. It is proper, however, to distinguish company experience from personnel experience and evaluate both.

268 PAST PERFORMANCE HANDBOOK

Proposal Risk versus Performance Risk

It is important to differentiate between risk types when DoD buying activities choose to evaluate different types of risk in each proposal. The two types of risk typically evaluated in a source selection are proposal risk and performance risk. These two types of risk are defined in Appendix A.

Past Performance versus Responsibility Determinations

It is important to distinguish **comparative** past performance evaluations used in the tradeoff process from **pass/fail** performance evaluations.

Pre-award surveys and pass/fail evaluations in the low price technically acceptable process help you determine whether an offeror is responsible. Responsibility is a broad concept that addresses whether an offeror has the *capability* to perform a particular contract based upon an analysis of many areas including financial resources, operational controls, technical skills, quality assurance, and past performance. These surveys and evaluations provide a "yes/no," "pass/fail," or "go/no-go" answer to the question, *"Can* the offeror do the work?" to help you determine whether the offeror is responsible.

Referral to the Small Business Administration may be necessary if a small business is eliminated from the competitive range solely on the basis of past performance. SBA referral is not required as long as the use of past performance information requires a **comparative** assessment with other evaluation factors and not as a pass or fail decision. The comparative assessment of past performance information is **separate** from a responsibility determination required by the Federal Acquisition Regulations.

Unlike a pass/fail responsibility determination, a comparative past performance evaluation conducted using the tradeoff process is a very specific endeavor that seeks to identify the *degree of risk* associated with each competing offeror. Rather than asking whether an offeror *can* do the work, you should ask, *will* it do that work successfully? In short, the evaluation describes the degree of confidence the government has in the offeror's likelihood of success. If properly conducted, the comparative past performance evaluation and the responsibility determination will complement each other and provide you with a more complete picture of an offeror than either one could by itself.

Lowest Price Technically Acceptable (LPTA) Strategies

The criteria by which past performance will be evaluated should be articulated in the solicitation. If a 'pass/fail' scoring scheme is to be used, a failing

Appendix B **269**

score may be equivalent to a non-responsibility determination. The source selection team should seek guidance from legal counsel to ensure the evaluation of past performance on a 'pass/fail' basis is applied appropriately.

Source selection teams may want to consider choosing a strategy where technical proposals are evaluated on a pass/fail basis and the final source selection decision is based on a tradeoff between past performance and price, or a Performance Price Trade Off (PPT). PPT permits tradeoffs between price and the past performance evaluation of technically acceptable proposals. This technique may be applied in acquisitions, which include an evaluation for technical acceptability, as well as negotiated acquisitions for which price and past performance are the only discriminators.

Defacto Debarment

The General Accounting Office has determined that as long as there is no indication that the procuring agency intends to automatically exclude the offeror from future procurements, there is no defacto debarment.

PLANNING THE PAST PERFORMANCE EVALUATION

Forming an Evaluation Group

In complex acquisitions it may be necessary to establish a formal group to specifically evaluate past performance. In smaller dollar value acquisitions that do not involve complex requirements, the evaluation may be accomplished with only one or two people. This evaluation group may operate separately from the proposal evaluation team or may operate as a separate subgroup of that team.

The following discussion will focus on the structure, composition and evaluation process of a formal evaluation group, but bear in mind that while the functions of informal evaluations are basically the same, they should be less complicated.

Objectives of the Evaluation Group

The evaluation group is responsible for conducting the past performance evaluation to determine the degree of risk involved in accepting each offeror's proposal. This analysis results in a performance risk assessment. The evaluation group documents these performance risk assessments and identifies strengths and weakness in each offeror's past performance focusing on those areas of performance most relevant to the source selection. A plan for evaluat-

270   PAST PERFORMANCE HANDBOOK

ing past performance should be developed early in the process and made a part of the source selection plan.

Evaluation Group Membership and Training

The membership and structure of your evaluation group should be tailored to each acquisition. Ideally, the membership should be reasonably diverse representing different disciplines.

The heart of the performance risk assessment is the information gathering process. Through questionnaires, telephone interviews, and site visits, and by tapping existing data sources, the group can obtain a detailed and useful picture of an offeror's past performance. It is absolutely critical that group members have the ability to conduct meaningful telephone interviews, assimilate data, exercise sound judgment, arrive at conclusions that make common sense, and communicate those conclusions effectively both orally and in writing.

The best practice is to limit the size of the group to as small a number as is realistic for the specific circumstances of the acquisition. A group of at least two members of different functional disciplines enhances opportunities for dialogue, brainstorming, and in-depth fact finding.

What Factors or Subfactors Should Be Used?

The past performance factors and subfactors, if any, should be designed to evaluate the key performance requirements of the solicitation. At a minimum, the solicitation should request the offeror's record for on time delivery, technical quality and cost control.

PPI Relevancy

Source selection officials have broad discretion to determine which PPI to consider relevant for an individual procurement. Relevancy is a threshold question when considering past performance, not a separate element of past performance. Relevancy, as defined in Appendix A, should not be described as a subfactor. Irrelevant past performance shall not form the basis of a performance risk evaluation. PPI with applicable, but limited relevance may be used for evaluation but should be given less weight.

The source selection team may consider data available from any sources, but should attempt to obtain information from references cited by offerors in their proposals. Upon receipt of proposals, the team will determine which of the

14

Appendix B **271**

offeror's past contract efforts relate closely to the solicitation requirements. The evaluation group should screen the information provided for each of the referenced contracts to make an initial determination of its relevance to the current requirement. However, the source selection authority may assign his/her own relevancy rating in making the source selection decision, which may differ from that of the performance risk assessment group.

> Source selection officials should use the most relevant, recent PPI available in making the source selection decisions. They must consider updated information provided by the contractor regarding relevant PPI.

Some aspects of relevance include the type of effort (e.g., development, production, repair), and the business sector. The objective of the screening is to remove from consideration those contract references that are clearly *unrelated* to the type of effort sought. Other members of the source selection team may be consulted as necessary for assistance in determining relevancy.

In some cases, previous contracts as a whole may be similar to the current contract while in others only portions of previous contracts may be relevant. One example would be the evaluation of the contractor's management, planning, and scheduling of subcontractors on a past service contract for a current production requirement calling for integration skills.

The evaluation group should consider the most recent data available. The best practice is to select similar efforts that are either still in progress or just completed, and that has at least one year of performance history. While the actual cut-off time should be determined by the contracting officer on a case-by-case basis, the currency of the information requested should be determined by the commodity and the specific circumstances of the acquisition.

The Comptroller General recommends use of solicitation language that evokes the term of "for the same or similar items" that may ensure that the government does not overly restrict its ability to consider an array of information. PPI relating to the recent or ongoing production of a transport aircraft, for example, would be relevant for the source selection for production of a new transport aircraft of similar range or payload. When considering the relevance of PPI to be used in making a source selection decision, the following should be considered:

- the nature of the business area(s) involved

- the required levels of technology

- the contract types

15

- the similarity of materials and production processes

- the location of work to be performed

- the product/service similarity

- the similar scope

One specific relevancy issue that should always be clearly articulated in the solicitation is relevancy of the proposed performance **location**. When procuring commodities, the PPI for work performed at the proposed performance location will be considered relevant for assessing performance risk for the work to be performed. Mergers and acquisitions should be considered when determining what information may be considered relevant. Past performance evaluations are typically conducted only for the specific site where work is proposed for future performance. Performance within companies may vary widely from site to site or specific address. When evaluating performance of services or commercial items, however, corporate past performance may be a consideration. Tailor the PPI criteria in the solicitation to clarify whether assessing global corporate capability really assesses company experience not past performance. If more than one site is proposed for performance then each site should be evaluated for the type of effort proposed for performance at that site.

All PPI older than three years beyond the completion of contract performance should be purged from DoD records. Do not use any PPI in source selection evaluations that should have been purged from the files.

How Much Weight to Give Past Performance

Past performance should be given sufficient evaluation weight to ensure that it is meaningfully considered throughout the source selection process and will be a valid discriminator among the proposals received.

What are the Rating Categories?

In planning the acquisition, the evaluation group develops a rating scheme for evaluating past performance. The group may use the following definitions of performance risk to describe the results of its evaluation:

- **Unsatisfactory/Very High Performance Risk.** Based on the offeror's performance record, extreme doubt exists that the offeror will successfully perform the required effort.

Appendix B **273**

- **Marginal/High Performance Risk.** Based on the offeror's performance record, substantial doubt exists that the offeror will successfully perform the required effort.

- **Satisfactory/Moderate Performance Risk.** Based on the offeror's performance record, some doubt exists that the offeror will successfully perform the required effort. Normal contractor emphasis should preclude any problems.

- **Very Good/Low Performance Risk.** Based on the offeror's performance record, little doubt exists that the offeror will successfully perform the required effort.

- **Exceptional/Very Low Performance Risk.** Based on the offeror's performance record, no doubt exists that the offeror will successfully perform the required effort.

- **Unknown Performance Risk.** No performance record identifiable. See "How to Evaluate Contractors with No Relevant Past Performance."

How to Evaluate Contractors with No Relevant Past Performance

In most cases the evaluation group will find some related government or other public or private past performance information for each contractor and subcontractor. Such information will usually surface if the evaluation approach allows a broad interpretation of relevancy or takes into account information regarding the past performance of predecessor companies, key personnel who have relevant experience, or subcontractors that will perform key aspects of the requirement. This flexibility will take on increasing importance as the department modernizes through the use of commercial items.

Occasionally, however, an evaluation group may not find any relevant information. In those cases, you must treat an offeror's lack of past performance as an unknown performance risk, having no positive or negative evaluative significance. This allows the government to evaluate past performance in a manner that is fair to newcomers. The method and criteria for evaluating offerors with no relevant past performance information should be constructed for each specific acquisition to *ensure that such offerors are not evaluated favorably or unfavorably on past performance.*

You may use a variety of rating methods to evaluate offerors with no past performance history. Regardless of the method selected, the solicitation must clearly describe the approach that will be used for evaluating offerors with no

274 PAST PERFORMANCE HANDBOOK

relevant performance history. Solicitations should encourage offerors to identify PPI that may be judged related or relevant to the specific acquisition.

Rating schemes articulated in the solicitation, may allow agencies to drop the past performance evaluation factor when making its award decision, after discovering that one of the competitors has no past performance history.

Public versus Private Competitions

When public/private competitions are conducted, the USD (A&T) has determined that the same mandatory DoD PPI evaluation elements and ratings by business sector shall be used to evaluate past performance for both public and private firms. This applies to any depot competition conducted.

What to Include in the Solicitation

The solicitation, at a minimum, must clearly describe the approach you will use to evaluate past performance. This includes what past performance information you will evaluate (including the anticipated method of PPI collection), how it will be evaluated, its weight or relative importance to the other evaluation factors and subfactors, the PPI you anticipate will be relevant for the proposed performance location, and how you will evaluate offerors with no past performance history. The amount of information you request should be tailored to the circumstances of the acquisition, and reasonable so as not to impose excessive burdens on offerors or evaluators. The proposal evaluation information, at a minimum, should clearly state that:

- The government will conduct a performance risk evaluation based upon the past performance of the offerors and their proposed major subcontractors as it relates to the probability of successfully performing the solicitation requirements;

- In conducting the performance risk evaluation, the government may use data provided by the offeror and data obtained from other sources; and

- The government may elect to consider data obtained from other sources that it considers current and accurate, but should ensure the solicitation contains a request for the most recent information available.

The proposal submission instructions must, at a minimum, instruct offerors to submit recent and relevant information concerning contracts and subcontracts (including Federal, State, and local government, and private) that demonstrate their ability to perform the proposed effort.

Appendix B **275**

Source selection teams may want to limit the information requested to a summary of the offeror's performance for each contract or subcontract. The summary should include contract numbers, contract type, description and relevancy of the work, dollar value, contract award and completion dates, and names, phone numbers, and e-mail addresses for references in contracting and technical areas.

In addition, offerors should be given the opportunity to explain why they consider the contracts they have referenced as being relevant to the proposed acquisition. The instructions should also permit offerors to provide information on problems encountered on such contracts and the actions taken to correct such problems. Also, it is important that the offeror specifically describe the work that major subcontractors will perform so that the evaluation group can conduct a meaningful performance risk evaluation on each major subcontractor.

One best practice is to use presolicitation exchanges of information with industry (e.g., draft solicitations or presolicitation/prepoposal conferences) to explain the approach you will use to evaluate performance risk. Although the solicitation must contain all evaluation factors and sub-factors and describe the approach to the evaluation, presolicitation exchanges can help to ensure that potential offerors have a clear understanding of how their past performance will be evaluated.

THE PAST PERFORMANCE EVALUATION PROCESS

If the solicitation states that past performance will be an evaluation factor, the government has broad discretion regarding the type of data to be considered. This means that the government may consider a wide array of information but is not compelled to rely on all the information available. Solicitations must clearly describe the past performance, type, age and location, that will be considered relevant in evaluating an offeror's proposal. The Government should reserve the option in the solicitation to consider other information that may be evaluated. While you may want to consider information over a specified time period, you may want to evaluate only the most recent information, e.g., data within the last six months.

Past performance information may be considered under other non-cost factors, in addition to being considered as part of a performance risk assessment, however be careful not to evaluate the same information twice.

A best practice is to limit the past performance evaluation to a few most recent and relevant contracts.

276 PAST PERFORMANCE HANDBOOK

Evaluation of PPI

PPI is one indicator of an offeror's ability to perform the contract success-fully. The currency and relevance of the information, source of the information, context of the data, and general trends in contractor's performance shall be considered.

> Personnel collecting PPI for use in a particular source selection should consider whether the data received comes from reputable and reliable sources.

Government evaluators are cautioned to ensure that the information submit-ted by the contractor is verified with some other source and that information known to the evaluators or other sources, that conflicts with the offeror's infor-mation is considered. Apparent discrepancies should be resolved prior to a fi-nal evaluation rating being assigned.

The assessment group must ensure an offeror has had the opportunity to comment on all adverse past performance information before presenting the adverse information to source selection officials.

Past performance is *now* one of the defined areas of clarification that a con-tracting officer should explore with contractors even when planning to award without discussions. Include any concern about an offeror's past performance, including relevancy and any adverse past performance information on which the offeror has not previously had an opportunity to comment.

> The Government should share all relevant PPI with contractors as part of the past performance evaluation during the source selection pro-cess, and must share adverse PPI on which contractors have not had the opportunity to comment.

Currency of PPI

If the contractor submits information during the source selection process, either as part of the proposal or during exchanges, it should be considered by the government, particularly if it is more current than the available govern-ment information.

On the other hand, agencies are under no duty to seek out more current in-formation that may exist outside the proposal, unless it is known by the evalu-ators at the specific buying command.

20

Appendix B **277**

Additionally, it is appropriate for the evaluation team to use information that was gathered under an earlier solicitation to evaluate a contractor's past performance.

Ordinarily, PPI, which relates to less current performance should be given less weight than current PPI, however guidance should be tailored to the nature of item or service being acquired. On the other hand, trends may be developed from PPI data that are strong indicators of risk associated with future performance of contracts. Buying activities and source selection officials should consider the need to appropriately weigh "older" PPI, but also properly accept its value when used in trend analyses that extend through recent periods of performance.

Teaming Arrangements

When two contractors decide to team together to perform a proposed effort they usually enter into a joint venture business arrangement. To evaluate past performance in this situation, each contractor's proposed efforts should be evaluated for the portion or type of effort that firm will perform. If it is not possible to distinguish responsibility, a performance assessment shall be performed for the entire effort and filed in each contractor's file.

Mergers and Acquisitions

The Comptroller General has upheld decisions that acquiring firms should share responsibility for a previous company's troubled reputation, if the acquiring firm wants to capitalize on the firm's technical skills. Common sense should rule the relevancy determinations when mergers and acquisitions are involved. If few changes have occurred at the performance location, then the previous firm's past performance record should be used to assess performance risk.

Subcontractor Past Performance

Common sense should govern when source selection officials choose to consider subcontractor past performance. A special problem arises with respect to subcontractors. Past performance information pertaining to a subcontractor cannot be disclosed to a private party without the subcontractor's consent. Because a prime contractor is a private party, the government needs to obtain the subcontractor's consent before disclosing its past performance information to the prime during negotiations. There are a variety of ways to obtain subcontractor consent. For example, the solicitation could require the prime to submit

278 PAST PERFORMANCE HANDBOOK

the consent of its principal subcontractors along with the prime's proposal to the government.

It is risky to rely solely on the past performance of a subcontractor to downgrade the predicted performance of a prime contractor. Before downgrading the predicted performance of a prime contractor based on the poor past performance of a subcontractor, consider the proposed subcontractor's contribution to the overall proposed effort and the likely impact of the predicted risky or poor performance. On the other hand, experience of a subcontractor that contributes to the overall expertise of a prime contractor should be considered.

What Sources of Data are Available?

PPI is obtained from a variety of sources, including references cited by offerors in their proposals, telephone interviews, surveys, or electronic databases. Upon receipt of proposals and any information on past contracts from government or commercial sources, the evaluation group will assess which of the offeror's past contract efforts relate to the solicitation requirements. These assessments of relevancy are judgment calls.

When a solicitation requires submission of references as an evaluation criterion, then government information obtained from those references and provided by the offeror may be considered in evaluating past performance.

Can the Evaluation Group Use Commercial References?

It is permissible to use other public and private references such as Dun and Bradstreet, information received from commercial and foreign government sources, awards of excellence or vendor quality certifications that reflect on companies performing the work, when appropriate. These references should be relevant to the effort set out in the solicitation.

The evaluation group should verify information received from all sources, whether contained in government evaluation reports on completed work, a database, or other public or private sources, to ensure accuracy. The verification must seek to identify supporting rationale for any evaluation report so that performance evaluations always rely on supportable data.

How to Assign Performance Risk Ratings

Once the data gathering efforts are completed, the entire evaluation group needs to assess all offerors and assign performance risk ratings. The evaluation

Appendix B   **279**

group should note instances of good or poor performance and relate them to the solicitation requirements and evaluation factors. Again, it is helpful for the evaluation group to review the statement of work, specifications, and the evaluation approach described in the solicitation. If the evaluation group identifies past performance problems, it should consider the context of the problems and any mitigating circumstances.

The evaluation group should not limit its inquiry solely to the proposing entity if other corporate divisions, contractors or subcontractors will perform a critical element of the proposed effort. The performance record of those organizations should be assessed in accordance with the solicitation. Performance risk assessments should consider the number and severity of problems, the ***demonstrated*** effectiveness of corrective actions taken (not just planned or promised), and the overall work record.

The evaluation group's assessment is usually based upon subjective judgment of supportable data. It is not intended to be a mechanical process or a simple arithmetic function of an offeror's performance on a list of contracts. Rather the information deemed most relevant and significant by the group should receive the greatest consideration. The assessment should include a description of the underlying rationale for the conclusions reached. The rationale should be reasonable, and adequately documented to support the conclusion.

A word of caution is appropriate concerning offeror promises to correct past performance failures, as opposed to actions already taken to correct such failures. A promise to improve does not change past performance and should be considered under proposal risk rather than performance risk. However, ***demonstrated*** corrective actions reflect a commitment to rectify past performance problems, and therefore, can lower the risk of similar performance failures.

Exchanging Past Performance Information with Offerors

The contracting officer must provide offerors with the opportunity to comment on adverse past performance information on which offerors have not had a previous opportunity to comment. This practice ensures fairness for the competing offerors. The validation process is particularly important when the adverse information is provided by only one reference, or when there is any doubt concerning the accuracy of the information. Usually, adverse information reflects performance that was less than satisfactory, although this is a judgment call that will depend upon the circumstances of the acquisition. Note that while the government must disclose past performance problems to offerors, including the identity of the contract on which the information is based, it shall not disclose the names of individuals who provided information about an offeror's past performance.

280 PAST PERFORMANCE HANDBOOK

When discussing adverse past performance information with industry during a source selection, agencies have often been concerned regarding the level of detail necessary for this exchange of information. Experience has indicated that *summarizing past performance information into problem categories is acceptable as long as the government agency revealed sufficient information to give the offeror a fair and reasonable opportunity to respond to the problems identified.* Verbal, informal PPI requests should be followed by a written request. If PPI will be relied upon in making a competitive range determination or source selection award, this information should be shared with the contractor.

What to Include in the Evaluation Assessment Report

While not wanting to say too much or too little in the evaluation report, the goal is to provide clear, reasonable, and rational analysis of the past performance of the offerors. The evaluation group must provide the source selection authority with sufficient information to make informed judgments. Again, the evaluation group should provide a recommendation and a well-reasoned, well-supported rationale for the recommendation.

Conclusionary statements must be supported by the underlying factual basis. The best practice is to state the conclusion and provide specific strengths and weaknesses that support the conclusion. To ensure that the risk assessments provide the necessary background information and are structured consistently, the entire evaluation group should review and evaluate the report on each offeror. During this review, the evaluation group should correct statements that appear unsupported, inconsistent, or unnecessary. The conclusion may be a single overall rating/assessment supported by specific description of the offerors past performance as it relates to the specific acquisition.

Occasionally the evaluation group will be unable to arrive at a unanimous agreement on a particular risk assessment. If this occurs, the evaluation group may include the dissenting opinion as part of the assessment report.

Reporting the Past Performance Evaluation Results

The evaluation group's submission of the past performance evaluation report usually completes the major portion of its work. The evaluation group leader should remind the source selection official of the purpose of the group and the past performance evaluation approach described in the solicitation. This report should address offerors with no past performance history. This is to ensure that everyone fully comprehends the significance of the results being reported. Experience reveals that source selection officials are more apt to rely upon evaluation group results if they thoroughly understand the process.

Appendix B **281**

How to Handle Past Performance Information

Information concerning the past performance of an offeror or of its proposed subcontractors should be treated as deliberative information, marked "For official use only." The evaluation of past performance of a contractor for a specific source selection is actually source selection information. This information frequently includes information that is proprietary, such as trade secrets and confidential commercial or financial data that would not be released under the Freedom of Information Act. Current laws, regulations, and policies governing storage, access, disclosure, and marking of source selection and proprietary information must be observed at all times. Questions concerning the procedures for the handling of past performance information should be referred to the contracting officer or legal counsel for resolution.

The evaluation group must retain the records of its evaluation activity throughout the source selection process. Upon contract award or cancellation of the solicitation, all evaluation group records are provided to the contracting officer for retention along with the other source selection documents.

Using Past Performance When Not Required In The Request For Proposal

There are circumstances when the contractor will submit past performance information even when it is not a stated criterion of the solicitation. You are not obliged to consider past performance information submitted by the contractor, when it is not a stated evaluation criteria. However, it may be considered as experience under other evaluation criteria.

Use of Passive PPI

For the Operations Support sector, the collection threshold for report card information is $5,000,000. Under the $5,000,000 threshold, buying activities should continue to accumulate and use contractor performance data from existing management information systems that already capture data on timeliness of delivery and quality of product or service. (Examples of such performance information collection systems include "Red/Yellow/Green" and "Automated Best Value Method.") While passive systems may continue to be used, DoD wide implementation of collection and use of PPI through passive performance information collection systems is not mandatory until the collection system is fully automated across DoD. Use of passive PPI depends on the existence of databases that collect data on an ongoing basis.

282 PAST PERFORMANCE HANDBOOK

APPENDIX A
DEFINITIONS, REFERENCES, AND GAO CASES

Adverse PPI. PPI that supports a less than satisfactory rating on any evaluation element or any unfavorable comments received from sources without a formal rating system.

Best Value. The expected outcome of an acquisition that, in the Government's estimation, provides the greatest overall benefit in response to the requirement.

Business Sectors. Groups of goods or services with similar characteristics, or similar requirements for engineering development, manufacturing, or technology. The DoD PPI business sectors are: Systems, Operations Support, Services, Information Technology, Construction and Architect-Engineering Services, and Science and Technology.

Contractor Experience. The Contractor's experience, in a particular area of expertise, that does not use performance data as a qualifier of that experience (e.g. 20 years of experience as a software firm).

Contractor Past Performance Assessments. The written or oral result of taking performance data and considering it in the context of a particular contract's scope and requirements.

Key Business Sectors. Four global business sectors that represent the areas that comprise the greatest workload for DoD: Systems, Operations Support, Services, and Information Technology.

Passive PPI. Any method of past performance assessment that relies on information obtained from a number of external pre-existing information sources managed by the Department of Defense. These sources may include contract administration, quality, reliability, and payment information.

Past Performance Evaluations. Past performance evaluations occur when the PPI assessments are considered in the context of a source selection.

Past Performance Information (PPI). Information submitted with the offeror's proposal, contractors' references, contractor reports cards, survey data, or other data available to the source selection authority.

Performance Assessment Elements. The mandatory assessment elements for the DoD business sectors.

Appendix B **283**

Performance Assessment Reports. Contractor performance assessments are one source of PPI. They are in essence, "report cards" on how well a contractor is performing or has performed on an individual contract.

Performance Risk. Evaluation of the risk of performance as it relates to the probability of the offeror successfully completing the solicitation's requirements based on previous demonstrated relevant performance.

Proposal Risk. The evaluated risk associated with the offeror's proposed approach to meeting the requirements of the solicitation, for each of the non-cost evaluation factors, other than past performance.

Relevancy. Information that has a logical connection with the matter under consideration and applicable time span.

Unique Business Sectors. Two unique business sectors which are separate from the four key business sectors are: Science & Technology and Construction and Architect-Engineering.

REFERENCES

References that are noted here prescribe policies/requirements for collecting and using past performance information:

Federal Acquisition Regulation (FAR) Parts 9, 15, 19, 36, and 42

DoD

Under Secretary of Defense (Acquisition and Technology) policy memo titled, "Automation of Past Performance Information," dated 20 February 1998.

Under Secretary of Defense (Acquisition and Technology) policy memo titled "Competition between Public Sector (Organic) Maintenance Depots and Private Sector Commercial Firms", dated May 2, 1997, Paul Kaminski

Defense Acquisition Council Class Deviation 99-00002

Navy

Assistant Secretary of the Navy (RD&A) memo of March 13, 1998, "Use of Contractor Past Performance Information in Source Selection."

Assistant Secretary of the Navy (RD&A) memo of February 2, 1998, "Implementation of Contractor Performance Assessment Reporting System (CPARS)"

284 PAST PERFORMANCE HANDBOOK

Army

Army Material Command Source Selection Guide (Pamphlet No. 715-3, Contracting for Best Value, 1 January 1998)

Air Force

AFFARS Part 5315
AFMC Pamphlet 64-113, Volume 1, PRAG Guide
AFMCI 64-107 CPARS Instruction
Contracting Policy Memo 98-C-05, 10 April 1998, "Past Performance Information (PPI) Collection Requirements"

GAO CASES

p. 7, Proposal Risk versus Performance Risk
Questech, Inc. B-236028, Nov. 1, 1989, 89-2 CPD ¶ 407
p. 8, Past Performance versus Responsibility Determinations
Smith of Galeton Gloves, Inc., B-271686, July 24, 1996; Corvac, Inc., supra note 127; Tiernay Turbins, Inc., B-226185, June 2, 1987, 87-1 CPD ¶ 563; Johnston Communications, B-221346, February 28, 1986, 86-1 CPD ¶ 211.
p. 10, PPI Relevancy
Ashland Sales and Service Co., B-259625-2, April 14, 1995, 95-1 CPD ¶ 198.
p. 14, The Past Performance Evaluation Process
Young Enterprises, Inc., B-256851.2, August 11, 1994, 94-2 CPD ¶ 159.
p. 15, Currency of PPI
American Video Channels Inc., B-236943, January 18, 1990, 4 CGEN ¶ 103,982
p. 15, Mergers and Acquisitions
Heritage Reporting Corporation, B-228008, October 15, 1987, 87-2, CPD ¶ 363
p. 17, Exchanging Past Performance Information with Offerors
Pacific Architects & Engineers, Inc., Comp. Gen. Dec. B-274405.2, 97-1 CPD ¶ 42
p. 18, Using Past Performance when not required in the Request for Proposal
NDI Engineering Co., B-245796, January 27, 1992, 92-1 CPD 5

Appendix B **285**

APPENDIX B
BUSINESS SECTORS

KEY BUSINESS SECTORS

Systems—Generally, this sector includes products that require a significant amount of new engineering development work. Includes major modification/upgrade efforts for existing systems, as well as acquisition of new systems, such as aircraft, ships, etc. Also includes program budget account code 6.4-funded projects. More specifically—

Aircraft: Includes fixed and rotary wing aircraft, and their subsystems (propulsion, electronics, communications, ordnance, etc.)

Shipbuilding: Includes ship design and construction, ship conversion, small craft (e.g., rigid inflatable boats) and associated contractor-furnished equipment, as well as ship overhaul and repair.

Space: Includes all satellites (communications, early warning, etc.), all launch vehicles, strategic ballistic missiles, and all associated subsystems, including guidance and control.

Ordnance: Includes all artillery systems (except non-Precision Guided Munitions (PGM) projectiles), tactical missiles (air-to- air, air-to-ground, surface-to-air, and surface-to-surface) and their associated launchers, and all PGM weapons and submunitions, such as the Joint Direct Attack Missile, the Sensor-Fused Weapon and the "Brilliant Antitank" weapon.

Ground Vehicles: Includes all tracked combat vehicles (e.g., tanks and armored personnel carriers), wheeled vehicles (e.g., trucks, trailers, specialty vehicles), and construction and material handling equipment requiring significant new engineering development. Does not include commercial equipment typically acquired from existing multiple award "schedule" contracts (e.g., staff cars, base fire trucks, etc.)

Training Systems: Generally, includes computer-based (or embedded) virtual and synthetic environments and systems of moderate to high complexity capable of providing training for air, sea, and land based weapons, platforms, and support systems readiness. Does not include operation and maintenance support services beyond the scope of the initial training system acquisition, or basic and applied research in these areas.

286 PAST PERFORMANCE HANDBOOK

Other Systems: Includes technologies and products that, when incorporated into other systems such as aircraft and ships, are often categorized as subsystems. However, many of these products are often acquired as systems in their own right, either as "stand-alone" acquisitions or as the object major modification/ upgrade efforts for ships, aircraft, etc. Examples of other systems include Command, Control, Communication, Computer and Intelligence (C4I) systems, airborne and shipborne tactical computer systems, electrical power and hydraulic systems, radar and sonar systems, fire control systems, electronic warfare systems, and propulsion systems (turbine engines—aviation and maritime, diesel engine power installations—maritime and combat vehicle). Does not include tactical voice radios with commercial equivalents, personal Global Positioning System (GPS) receivers, non-voice communication systems with commercial equivalents (See Operations Support and Information Technology sectors).

Services—Generally, this sector includes all contracted services except those which are an integral part of a systems contract or related to "Science & Technology," "Construction & Architect—Engineering Services," "Information Technology", and "Health Care." Services are further defined below:

Professional/Technical & Management Support Services: Includes all consultant services—those related to scientific, health care services, and technical matters (e.g., engineering, computer software engineering and development), as well as those related to organizational structure, human relations, etc. Includes office administrative support services (e.g., operation of duplication centers, temporary secretarial support, etc.). Does not include any basic or applied research that will result in new or original works, concepts or applications, but does include contract advice on the feasibility of such research, as well as evaluation of research results.

Repair & Overhaul: Services related to the physical repair and overhaul of aircraft, ground vehicles, etc., and any associated subsystems or components. Includes condition evaluations of individual items received for repair or overhaul, but does not include evaluations of the feasibility or the benefits of the overall project. Does not include Ship Repair and Overhaul that is included in the Shipbuilding sector.

Installation Services: Includes services for grounds maintenance (grass cutting, shrubbery maintenance or replacement, etc.). Includes services related to cleaning, painting, and making minor repairs to buildings and utilities services, etc. Includes contracted security and guard services. Includes installation and maintenance of fencing. It also includes minor electrical repairs (e.g., replacing outlets, changing light bulbs, etc.), minor road surface repairs (patching cracks, filling in potholes, etc.), relocation of individual telephone lines and connections, snow removal. (See "Construction for the installation services covered by that sector.)

30

Appendix B   **287**

Transportation and Transportation-Related Services: Includes services related to transportation by all the land, water, and air routes, and transportation efforts which support movement of U.S. forces and their supplies during peacetime training, conflict, or war. Consists of those military and commercial efforts, services and systems organic to, contracted for, or controlled by the DoD.

Information Technology—This sector includes any equipment or interconnected system or subsystem of equipment, that is used in the automatic acquisition, storage, manipulation, management, movement, control, display, switching, interchange, transmission or reception of data or information. Generally, includes all computers, ancillary equipment, software, firmware and similar procedures, services (including support services), and related resources. Does not include any military-unique C4I systems and components included under Systems, such as JTIDS, Aegis, etc. More specifically—

Software: A set of computer programs, procedures, and associated documentation concerned with the operations of a data processing system; e.g., compilers, library routines, manuals and circuit diagrams. Information that may provide instructions for computers; data for documentation; and voice, video, and music for entertainment and education.

Hardware: Physical equipment as opposed to programs, procedures, rules and associated documentation. In automation, the physical equipment or devices forming a computer and peripheral components.

Telecommunications Equipment or Services: Circuits or equipment used to support the electromagnetic and/or optical dissemination, transmission, or reception of information via voice, data, video, integrated telecommunications transmission, wire, or radio. The equipment or service must be a complete component capable of standing alone. This includes the following type of items; telephones, multiplexers, a telephone switching system, circuit termination equipment, radio transmitter or receiver, a modem, card cage with the number and type of modem cards installed, etc. This does not include the following type of items: a chip, circuit card, equipment rack, power cord, a microphone, headset, etc.

Operations Support—Generally, this sector includes spares and repair parts for existing systems. Also includes products that require a lesser amount of engineering development work than "Systems," or that can be acquired "build-to-print," "non-developmental," or commercial off the shelf. More specifically—

Mechanical: Includes transmissions (automotive and aviation), landing gear, bearings, and parts/components related to various engines (turbine wheels, impellers, fuel management and injection systems, etc.)

288 PAST PERFORMANCE HANDBOOK

Structural: Includes forgings; castings; armor (depleted uranium, ceramic, and steel alloys); and steel, aluminum, and composite structural components. Does not include "bare" airframes, ships, or combat vehicles (i.e., without engines and electronics).

Electronics: Includes parts and components related to digitization, guidance and control, communications, and electro-optical and optical systems. Includes individual resistors, capacitors, circuit cards, etc., as well as "modules" such as radio-frequency receivers and transmitters. Includes tactical voice radios, personal Global Positioning System receivers, etc.

Electrical: Includes electric motors, thermal batteries, auxiliary power units, and associated spares and component parts.

Ammunition: Includes all small arms ammunition and non-Precision Guided Munitions artillery rounds.

Troop Support: Includes all food and subsistence items. Includes all clothing and textile-related items, including uniforms, tentage, personal ballistic protective gear, life preservation devices, etc. Includes all medical supplies and equipment, including medicines and diagnostic equipment (X-ray machines, etc.). Does not include any recreational or morale/welfare items.

Base Supplies: Includes all consumables and personal property items needed to maintain installations, bases, ports, etc. Includes small tools and cleaning and preservation equipment and supplies (paints, brushes, cleaning solvents, etc.). Does not include any grounds maintenance, construction, security, or other types of services.

Fuels: Includes all bulk fuels, lubricants, and natural gas, coal, storage, and other commodities and related support services.

UNIQUE BUSINESS SECTORS

Architect—Engineering Services: Professional services of an architectural or engineering nature, as defined by State law, if applicable, which are required to be performed or approved by a person licensed, registered, or certified to provide such services. These services include, research, planning, development, design, construction, alteration, or repair of real property. Incidental services include studies, investigations, surveying and mapping, tests, evaluations, consultations, comprehensive planning, program management, conceptual designs, plans and specifications (drawings, specifications and other data for and preliminary to the construction), value engineering, construction phase services,

Appendix B **289**

soils engineering, drawing reviews, preparation of operating and maintenance manual, and other related services.

Construction: Construction, alteration, or repair (including dredging, excavating, and painting) of buildings, structures, or other real property. The terms "buildings, structures, or other real property" includes but are not limited to improvements of all types, such as bridges, dams, plants, highways, parkways, streets, subways, tunnels, sewers, mains, power lines, cemeteries, pumping stations, railways, airport facilities, terminals, docks, piers, wharves, ways, lighthouses, buoys, jetties, breakwaters, levees, canals, and channels. Construction does not include the manufacture, production, furnishing, construction, alteration, repair, processing, or assembling of vessels, aircraft, or other kinds of personal property. Design-Build: Combining design and construction in a single contract with one contractor.

Science and Technology—Includes all contracted basic research and some applied research. Includes construction of "proof-of-principle" working prototypes. Includes projects funded by program budget accounts 6.1 (Basic Research), 6.2 (Exploratory Development), and 6.3 (Advanced Technology Development), but does not include projects funded by 6.4 accounts or similarly oriented appropriations. (Those projects are covered by the Systems sector).

290 PAST PERFORMANCE HANDBOOK

APPENDIX C
PPI EVALUATION AND REPORT THRESHOLDS

BUSINESS SECTOR	DOLLAR THRESHOLD[1]	REVIEWING OFFICIAL[2]
Systems (includes new development and major modifications)	≥$5,000,000	One level above the program manager.[3]
Services	≥$1,000,000	One level above the assessing official.
Operations Support	≥$5,000,000[4]	One level above the assessing official.
Information Technology	≥$1,000,000	One level above the assessing official.
Construction	≥$500,000	One level above the assessing official.
Architect-Engineering	≥$25,000	One level above the assessing official.
Science & Technology	As required	One level above the assessing official.

[1]The contract thresholds for PPI collection apply to the "as-modified" face value of contracts; that is, if a contract's original face value was less th an the applicable threshold, but subsequently the contract was modified and the "new" face value is greater than the threshold, then a performance assessment (or assessments) should be made, starting with the first anniversary that the contract's face value exceeded the threshold. If the contract threshold is expected to exceed the collection threshold by exercise of option, modification or order, it may be advisable to initiate the PPI collection process prior to the value of the contract proceeding the threshold.

[2]Only required if there is a disagreement between the assessing official and the contractor.

[3]Or equivalent individual responsible for program, project, or task/job order.

[4]For contracts under the $5,000,000 threshold, buying activities should continue to accumulate contractor performance data until the DoD automated database is established. (An example of such performance information collection system is "Red/Yellow/Green".)

34

Appendix B **291**

APPENDIX D
PERFORMANCE ASSESSMENT ELEMENTS

KEY BUSINESS SECTOR ASSESSMENT ELEMENTS

Assessment Elements for the Systems Sector—DoD shall collect PPI on all contracts within the seven sub-sectors of the Systems Sector using the following Performance Assessment Review elements:

TECHNICAL (QUALITY OF PRODUCT). This element is comprised of an overall rating and six sub-elements. Activity critical to successfully complying with contract requirements must be assessed within one or more of these sub-elements. The overall rating at the element level is the Program Manager's integrated assessment as to what most accurately depicts the contractor's technical performance or progress toward meeting requirements. It is not a predetermined roll-up of the sub-element assessments.

Product Performance—Assess the achieved product performance relative to performance parameters required by the contract. Systems Engineering—Assess the contractor's effort to transform operational needs and requirements into an integrated system design solution.

Software Engineering—Assess the contractor's success in meeting contract requirements for software development, modification, or maintenance. Results from Software Capability Evaluations (SCEs) (using the Software Engineering Institute (SEI's) Capability Maturity Model (CMM) as a means of measurement), Software Development Capability Evaluations (SDCEs), or similar software assessments may be used as a source of information to support this evaluation.

Logistic Support/Sustainment—Assess the success of the contractor's performance in accomplishing logistics planning.

Product Assurance—Assess how successfully the contractor meets program quality objectives, e.g., producibility, reliability, maintainability, inspectability, testability, and system safety, and controls the overall manufacturing process.

Other Technical Performance—Assess all the other technical activity critical to successful contract performance. Identify any additional assessment aspects that are unique to the contract or that cannot be captured in another sub-element.

292 Past Performance Handbook

SCHEDULE—Assess the timeliness of the contractor against the completion of the contract, task orders, milestones, delivery schedules, administrative requirements, etc.

COST CONTROL—(Not required for Firm Fixed Price or Firm Fixed Price with Economic Price Adjustment)—Assess the contractor's effectiveness in forecasting, managing, and controlling contract cost.

MANAGEMENT—This element is comprised of an overall rating and three sub-elements. Activity critical to successfully executing the contract must be assessed within one or more of these sub-elements. This overall rating at the element level is the Program Manager's integrated assessment as to what most accurately depicts the contractor's performance in managing the contracted effort. It is not a predetermined roll-up of the sub-element assessments.

Management Responsiveness—Assess the timeliness, completeness and quality of problem identification, corrective action plans, proposal submittals (especially responses to change orders, engineering change proposals, or other undefinitized contract actions), the contractor's history of reasonable and cooperative behavior, effective business relations, and customer satisfaction.

Subcontract Management—Assess the contractor's success with timely award and management of subcontracts, including whether the contractor met small/small disadvantaged and women-owned business participation goals.

Program Management and Other Management—Assess the extent to which the contractor discharges its responsibility for integration and coordination of all activity needed to execute the contract; identifies and applies resources required to meet schedule requirements; assigns responsibility for tasks/actions required by contract; communicates appropriate information to affected program elements in a timely manner. Assess the contractor's risk management practices, especially the ability to identify risks and formulate and implement risk mitigation plans. If applicable, identify and assess any other areas that are unique to the contract, or that cannot be captured elsewhere under the Management element.

Assessment Elements for the Services, Information Technology and Operations Support Sectors—DoD shall collect PPI using the following assessment elements within the Services, Information Technology and Operations Support sectors.

QUALITY OF PRODUCT OR SERVICE—Assess the contractor's conformance to contract requirements, specifications and standards of good work-

Appendix B **293**

manship (e.g., commonly accepted technical, professional, environmental, or safety and health standards).

SCHEDULE—Assess the timeliness of the contractor against the completion of the contract, task orders, milestones, delivery schedules, administrative requirements (e.g. efforts that contribute to or effect the schedule variance).

COST CONTROL—(Not required for Firm Fixed Price or Firm Fixed Price with Economic Price Adjustment)—Assess the contractor's effectiveness in forecasting, managing, and controlling contract cost.

BUSINESS RELATIONS—Assess the integration and coordination of all activity needed to execute the contract, specifically the timeliness, completeness and quality of problem identification, corrective action plans, proposal submittals, the contractor's history of reasonable and cooperative behavior, customer satisfaction, timely award and management of subcontracts, and whether the contractor met small/small disadvantaged and women-owned business participation goals.

MANAGEMENT OF KEY PERSONNEL (For Services and Information Technology Business Sectors Only)—Assess the contractor's performance in selecting, retaining, supporting, and replacing, when necessary, key personnel.

294 PAST PERFORMANCE HANDBOOK

APPENDIX E
CONSTRUCTION & ARCHITECT-ENGINEERING

The Construction & Architect and Engineering past performance information is collected in two systems: Architect-Engineer Contract Administration Support System (ACASS) and Construction Contractor Appraisal Support System (CCASS). **ACASS** is an automated centralized database of information required for contracting with architect-engineer (A-E) firms. The database contains A-E qualification data (Standard Form 254), A-E performance evaluations (DD 2631) and DoD A-E contract award data. The ACASS Center is operated and maintained by the U.S. Army Corps of Engineers, Northwestern District, Portland, Oregon. Applicable acquisition regulations and the general functions of the system are summarized below.

The data in ACASS are required to be available to contracting offices, and used in procuring A-E services, by the following acquisition regulations: FAR Subpart 36.6 and Defense Acquisition Regulation Supplement (DFARS) Subpart 236.6. By providing a central database, easily accessible by interactive procedures, ACASS makes it unnecessary for contracting offices to maintain these files.

The ACASS Center notifies A-Es when a SF 254 update is due and deletes SF 254s of firms that do not respond. This fulfills the requirements of FAR 36.603(d) that SF 254 files be reviewed and updated at least once each year.

ACASS maintains A-E performance evaluations (DD2631) for six years and makes this data available to all users, making it unnecessary for the contracting offices to distribute them, as required by FAR 36.604(c).

ACASS provides interactive procedures that allow sorting of A-Es by user-selected parameters. This fulfills the requirement in FAR 36.603(c) that contracting offices classify A-Es with respect to location, experience, and capabilities. ACASS interactive procedures are used when an evaluation board needs classification of the firms on file.

DFARS 236.604 (c) requires that performance evaluations of A-E contractors be sent to the central database (the ACASS Center). DFARS 236.602-1 requires that DoD evaluation boards use performance evaluation data from the central database in procurement actions for A-E services.

Performance Ratings are described by one of the following five adjectives: excellent; above average; average; below average; and poor. These terms are

38

subjective and are not derived through use of any mathematical computations or formulas.

CCASS is an automated centralized database containing a six-year history of construction contractor performance evaluations (DD 2626). The CCASS Center is operated and maintained by the U.S. Army Corps of Engineers, Portland District, Portland, Oregon.

By providing a central database CCASS makes it unnecessary for contracting offices to distribute these files within the contracting community.

The data in CCASS are required to be available to contracting offices, and used in procuring construction contractor services, by the following acquisition regulations: FAR Subpart 36.2 and Defense Acquisition Regulation Supplement (DFARS) Subpart 236.2.

CCASS is used by the contracting officer in making pre-award responsibility determinations as well as for use in selection of construction contractor awards for excellence (DFARS 236.201).

Performance Ratings are described by one of the following five adjectives: Outstanding; Above Average; Satisfactory; Marginal and Unsatisfactory. These terms are subjective and are not derived through use of any mathematical computations or formulas.

296 PAST PERFORMANCE HANDBOOK

APPENDIX F
COMMON DOD ASSESSMENT RATING SYSTEM

The critical sentence in DoD's assessment rating system is the second sentence that recognizes the contractor's resourcefulness in overcoming challenges that arise in the context of contract performance.

Exceptional. Performance meets contractual requirements and exceeds many to the Government's benefit. The contractual performance of the element or sub-element being assessed was accomplished with few minor problems for which corrective actions taken by the contractor were highly effective.

Very Good. Performance meets contractual requirements and exceeds some to the Government's benefit. The contractual performance of the element or sub-element being assessed was accomplished with some minor problems for which corrective actions taken by the contractor were effective.

Satisfactory. Performance meets contractual requirements. The contractual performance of the element or sub-element contains some minor problems for which corrective actions taken by the contractor appear or were satisfactory.

Marginal. Performance does not meet some contractual requirements. The contractual performance of the element or sub-element being assessed reflects a serious problem for which the contractor has not yet identified corrective actions. The contractor's proposed actions appear only marginally effective or were not fully implemented.

Unsatisfactory. Performance does not meet most contractual requirements and recovery is not likely in a timely manner. The contractual performance of the element or sub-element contains serious problem(s) for which the contractor's corrective actions appear or were ineffective.

Note: At the heart of America's greatness is that we value competition, fair play and we love to win. We value outstanding performers. Outstanding performance is not measured by merely getting the job done. Outstanding performance is measured by resourcefulness. At the heart of DoD's past performance system is that we value, and want to reward, outstanding performance. To help us to be as objective and fair as possible in determining who is a winner we use evaluations. These evaluations do incentivize and reward performers for being resourceful. In fact, this promotes competition even in sole source environments and is valued by our society as being fair.

40

APPENDIX G
COLLECTION OF PPI DURING SOURCE SELECTION

The evaluation group may gather information using various databases, questionnaires, surveys, and telephonic inquiries. Experience indicates that questionnaires provide useful but incomplete information. One approach is to start by sending a questionnaire tailored to the source selection to each reference and to conclude by calling those who respond with pertinent information. Whether you send questionnaires or not, you will most likely conclude by calling the reference to obtain more detail or clarification. While telephone interviews are an excellent means to obtain information, innovations in the field of technology have afforded us with additional means of verification such as e-mail.

Questionnaires should be short, concise and consist of no more than a page to a page and a half of questions.

If a report card format is used as part of a survey request it should use the uniform assessment elements established for the DoD business sectors.

WHERE TO CONDUCT TELEPHONE INTERVIEWS

Following the screening of previous contracts for further in-depth review, the evaluation group should send questionnaires and/or initiate telephone calls to the identified references for those efforts. The interviewing and reporting of results are usually individual efforts conducted by each evaluation group member. However, it is sometimes helpful to collect information as a group through the use of conference calls.

HOW TO CONDUCT TELEPHONE INTERVIEWS

At least two references should be contacted on each previous contract effort selected for in-depth review. The current or previous contracting officer, program manager, and contracting officer's representative, whoever has the most relevant experience on the contract, often prove to be excellent sources of information. Additional references are often identified during the interviews. Maximum effectiveness occurs when the expertise of the evaluation group interviewer matches that of the reference.

Prior to initiating a telephone interview, a group member should gather all available information on a specific effort and draft a list of questions. There may be a common group of questions for all offerors and/or tailored questions

298 PAST PERFORMANCE HANDBOOK

for each offeror, depending upon the circumstances. These questions can either be sent as questionnaires to each reference or be used by the group member during the telephone interview.

At the start of each telephone interview, the group member should explain the purpose of the call and request voluntary assistance from the reference. The interviewer should explain that he or she will document the results of the conversation and send a copy of the memorandum to the reference for verification. There is usually no need to divulge the solicitation number, program description, or other identifying information to the reference. If you do so, you need to obtain a nondisclosure statement.

In most instances the reference will willingly provide the information requested. In those rare cases when the reference is reluctant to participate, the interviewer should assure the reference of anonymity. At the least, the reference should be requested to provide additional references.

It is important to pursue and document the underlying facts supporting any concluding statements received on a contractor. The evaluation group member can determine neither the magnitude of a reported problem nor its possible impact on the current risk assessment without first understanding the details surrounding the problem.

HOW TO DOCUMENT TELEPHONE INTERVIEWS

Immediately following a telephone interview, the group member must prepare a narrative summary of the conversation and send it to the reference for verification. E-mail and datafax transmissions are encouraged. The following step is extremely important.

Extra care must be taken to ensure accuracy, clarity, and legibility because these summaries often represent the only written back-up supporting the opinions and conclusions of the final assessment report.

In order to maintain accurate records and facilitate verification, the telephone record form should include the reference's name, full mailing and electronic addresses and telephone number, the date and time of the call, and the description of the contract effort discussed.

The evaluation group member should send the telephone memorandum to the reference, stating explicitly that if the reference does not object to its content within the time specified, it will be accepted as correct. The amount of time allowed for a response depends on the circumstances of each acquisition. Note

Appendix B **299**

that the reference need not sign a nondisclosure form if the group member withholds the identity of the program and solicitation number.

If a reference indicates that the narrative is incorrect, then a corrected narrative must be sent for verification. Experience indicates that in most instances, changes are minor. If, however, a reference expresses opposition to a record and satisfactory corrections cannot be agreed upon, the evaluation group should not rely on the record.

300 PAST PERFORMANCE HANDBOOK

Include this form with the solicitation's instructions to offerors to simplify the submission and evaluation of past performance information

(To be completed by the offeror)

1. Contract Number:

   _____

2. Contractor (Name, Address and Zip Code):

   _____

   _____

   _____

3. Type of Contract: Negotiated _____ Sealed Bid _____

   Fixed Price _____ Cost Reimbursement _____ Hybrid (explain) _____

   _____

4. Complexity of Work: Difficult _____ Routine _____

5. Description, location & relevancy of work: _____

   _____

   _____

   _____

   _____

6. Contract Dollar Value: _____

   Status: Active _____ Complete _____

7. Date of Award: _____

   Contract Completion Date (including extensions): _____

8. Type and Extent of Subcontracting: _____

   _____

9. Name, Address, Tel. No. & e-mail of the Procuring Contracting Officer and/or the Contracting Officer's Representative (COR) (and other references, e.g. Administrative Contracting Officer, if applicable):

   _____

   _____

   _____

   _____

Appendix B **301**

TYPICAL QUESTIONS AND IDEAS FOR TELEPHONE INTERVIEWS AND QUESTIONNAIRES

- Confirm the following data from the offeror's proposal:
  —Contract number
  —Contractor's name and address
  —Type of contract
  —Complexity of work
  —Description and location of work (e.g., types of tasks, product, service)
  —Contract dollar value
  —Date of award
  —Contract completion date (including extensions)
  —Type and Extent of Subcontracting
- Verify any past performance data to which you may have access
- If the award amount or delivery schedule changed, find out why.
- Ask what role the reference played (e.g., COR, contract specialist, ACO, etc.) and for how long.
- If a problem surfaced, ask what the Government and contractor did to fix it.
- Ask for a description of the types of personnel (skill and expertise) the contractor used and the overall quality of the contractor's team. Did the company appear to use personnel with the appropriate skills and expertise?
- Ask how the contractor performed considering technical performance or quality of the product or service; schedule; cost control (if applicable); business relations; and management.
- Ask whether the contractor was cooperative in resolving issues.
- Inquire whether there were any particularly significant risks involved in performance of the effort.
- Ask if the company appeared to apply sufficient resources (personnel and facilities) to the effort.
- If the company used subcontractors, ask: What was the relationship between the prime and subcontractors? How well did the prime manage the subcontractors? Did the subcontractors perform the bulk of the effort or just add depth on particular technical areas? Why were the subcontractors chosen to work on specific technical areas, what were those areas and why were they accomplished by the subcontractors rather than the prime?
- If a problem is uncovered that the reference is unfamiliar with, ask for another individual who might have the information.
- Ask if this firm has performed other past efforts with the reference's agency.
- Ask about the company's strong points or what the reference liked best.
- Ask about the company's weak points or what the reference liked least.
- Inquire whether the reference has any reservations about recommending a future contract award to this company.
- Inquire whether the reference knows of anyone else who might have past performance information on the offeror.

302 PAST PERFORMANCE HANDBOOK

TYPICAL TELEPHONE INTERVIEW RECORD

Solicitation Number: (for reference—do not disclose to person contacted)
Contractor: (Name and Address)
Person Contacted: (Name, Address, Phone #, e-mail address)
Date & Time of Contact:
Summary of Discussion:

Interviewer's Signature
Past Performance Group Member

Note: When interviewing, you may want to use an introduction similar to the following: This is (name). I'm calling in reference to contractor (name). I'll be asking you some questions that pertain to that contractor's record of past and current performance. The information you provide will be used to evaluate the award of federal contracts. Therefore it is important that your information be as factual and accurate as possible. A summary of this discussion will be sent to you for your records. If that summary is inaccurate or incomplete in any way, please contact me immediately. My telephone number/e-mail address is (#/e-mail).

****

TYPICAL TELEPHONE INTERVIEW CONFIRMATION (ELECTRONIC)

Attached is a summary of our telephone conversation on (date) concerning the past and current performance of (*name of contractor*). If I do not hear from you by (date), I will assume that the summary of our discussion is correct. Please contact me if you have any questions or comments. You may reach me at telephone (number) or e-mail (address). Thank you for taking the time to assist in this effort.

Reminders for Past Performance Evaluation Group Member:

- Discuss currency and relevance of information.
- Read summary to person contacted.
- Send confirmation to person contacted.
- Withhold the identity of your program and solicitation number, if practicable, to avoid having to obtain a non-disclosure statement from the person contacted.

46

Appendix B **303**

APPENDIX H
AUTOMATED PAST PERFORMANCE
INFORMATION SYSTEMS

Army

1. **System Nomenclature**
   Past Performance Information Management System (PPIMS)

   System Description:
   Web-based automated information management system for supplies, services and systems

   Dollar Threshold
   Mandatory thresholds according to DoD policy; HCAs may establish lower thresholds

   Operational Date:
   10/1/97

   Type System:
   Web-based using NT/SQL Server/DBMS

   Current Users
   Army

   Applicable Regulations
   AFARS

   Point of Contact:
   Functional—Susan Erwin: 703-681-9292
   Technical—Terry Thacker: 540-731-3459

2. **System Nomenclature:**
   Architect-Engineer Contract Administration Support System (ACASS)

   System Description:
   ACASS is an automated database of information on architect-engineers (A-E) firms maintained by the Portland (Oregon) District of the U.S. Army Corps of Engineers.

   The purpose of the ACASS is threefold: 1) measure Past Performance, 2) has Standard Form 254, except for block 11, and 3) gives summaries of DD 250 for actions over $25,000.

   Dollar Threshold:
   All contract actions above $25,000

304 PAST PERFORMANCE HANDBOOK

Operational Date:
ACASS was developed in 1976.

Type System:
Oracle-based system (mainframe) but there is also read-only access on the Internet.

Current Users: *DoD and the Federal Sector*

Applicable Regulations:
FAR Part 36; DFAR Part 236

Point of Contact:
Functional: Donna Smigel (202) 761-0336
Technical: Kim Morrow (503) 808-4590
Mail requests for access to ACASS, on agency letterhead, along with your funding (MIPR or LOI) to: U.S. Army Corps of Engineers, Portland District, CENWP-CT-I, ACASS Center, P.O. Box 2946, Portland, OR 97208-2946

3. **System Nomenclature:**
Construction Contractor Appraisal Support System (CCASS)

System Description:
CCASS is an automated database of information on construction contractors maintained by the Portland (Oregon) District of the U.S. Army Corps of Engineers.

Dollar Threshold:
Above $100,000 (they got a waiver to the $500,000 rule)

Operational Date:
1985

Type System:
Oracle-based system (mainframe) but there is also read-only access on the internet.

Current Users:
Army, Navy

Applicable Regulations:
FAR Part 36; DFAR Part 236

Point of Contact:
Kim Morrow (503) 808-4590

Navy

4. **System Nomenclature:**
Product Data Reporting and Evaluation Program (PDREP)

Appendix B **305**

System Description:
PDREP is an automated system containing quality, delivery, and other performance data on products/services supplied to the Navy. Database is used by Red Yellow Green (RYG) program (a subset of PDREP), technical, quality, contracting groups and other DoD Service programs.

Dollar Threshold:
none

Operational Date:
1983

Type System:
Oracle-based client server system. Internet accessible. A World Wide Web site is available at www.nslctsmh.navsea.navy.mil.

Current Users:
Navy, Army, Marine Corps, Coast Guard, DLA

Applicable Regulations:
FAR Part 42, 15, 12 and 13, SECNAVINST 4855.3

Point of Contact:
John Deforge 603-431-9460 x450
Paul Couture 603-431-9460 x480

5. **System Nomenclature:**
Department of the Navy Contractor Performance Assessment Reporting System (CPARS)

System Description:
CPARS is an automated database for collection of contract performance information in Systems, Operations Support, Information Technology, and Services sectors. The Systems sector contains a subset for ship repair and overhaul.

Dollar Threshold:
From $500K to over $5M, depending on business sector.

Operational Date:
April 1998

Type System:
Oracle-based system with World Wide Web accessibility (www.nslcptsmh.navsea.navy.mil)

Current Users
Navy and Marine Corps

Applicable Regulations:
FAR Part 42, 15, DON CPARS Guide, February 2, 1998.

306 PAST PERFORMANCE HANDBOOK

Point of Contact:
Wendell Smith 603-431-9460 x451
Paul Couture 603-431-9460 x480

Air Force

6. System Nomenclature:
Contractor Performance Assessment Reporting System (CPARS)

System Description:
Data on contractor past performance for all qualifying contracts.

Dollar Threshold:
$5,000,000 and above.

Operational Date:
1986

Type System:
System data is available on the Internet at http://www.afmc.wpafb.af.mil/
HQ-AFMC/PK/pkpa/cpars.htm

Current Users:
Air Force

Applicable Regulations:
AFMCI 64-107

Points of Contact:
Ms. Lois Todd (937) 257-4657 or DSN 787-4657
Roger Hanson (937) 257-6057 or DSN 787-6057

Defense Logistics Agency

7. System Nomenclature:
Automated Best Value System (ABVS)

System Description:
ABVS is a DLA Automated application system which collects and analyzes
existing past performance data and translates it into a numeric score which
can be used as a tool in making a comparative assessment of performance
risk and price among offerors for best value award decisions.

Dollar Threshold:
Information is collected at all dollar thresholds

Operational Date:
1994

Appendix B **307**

Type System:
HP/Oracle-Based Client Server system.

Current Users:
Inventory control Points in DLA

Applicable Regulations:
FAR Part 15, Defense Logistics Acquisition Regulation Part 15.

Point of Contact:
Melody Reardon 703-767-1362

DEFENSE INFORMATION SYSTEMS AGENCY (DISA)

8. System Nomenclature:
Contractor Past Performance Evaluation Toolkit

System Description:
CPARS is an automated database for collection, storage and retrieval of contract performance information in Systems, Operations Support, Information Technology, and Services sectors. The Systems sector contains a subset for ship repair and overhaul. CPARS is an EA-21 (Electronic Acquisition for the 21st Century) initiative under PEO-ARBS (The Program Executive Officer for Acquisition Related Business Systems).

Dollar Threshold:
Mandatory for $1M and above

Operational Date:
October 96

Type System:
Web-based. Client hardware—any x86 PC, MAC, Unix workstation capable of client software. Client software—Netscape Navigator 2.02 or higher; Microsoft Internet Explorer 3.0 or higher

Current Users:
DISA contracts

Applicable Regulations:
FAR Parts 15 and 42; USD (A&T) Nov 20, 1997 policy memo

Point of Contact:
Mary Jenkins (BJ) (703) 681-1681/DSN 761
Nathan Maenle (703) 681-1673/DSN 761

INDEX

A

A. G. Cullen Construction, Inc., 69, 190
ABVM. *See* Automated Best Value Model
access control list (ACL), 176
Acepex Management Corp., 198
acquisition team, contract performance evaluations, 2
administrative contracting officer (ACO), 40
Advanced Data Concepts, Inc. (ADC), 87–88
adverse information, correct *versus* incorrect, 98–99
agency contract databases, 39
agency reviews, disagreements regarding, 166–167
Airwork Limited-Vinnell Corp. (AWV), 114–115
Alliant Techsystems, Inc., 200
Architect-Engineer Contract Administration Support System (ACASS), 173–175
architect-engineer contracts, 127
Armed Services Board of Contract Appeals, 188
Audit and Records—Negotiation (Far clause 52.215-2), 59
audit personnel, acquisition team members, 2
authority, establishing well-defined lines of, 9
Automated Best Value Model (ABVM), 76, 195

automation, contractor performance evaluation system, 144–145
award decision, role of source selection official, 111
award evaluations, obtaining past performance information, 40
AWV. *See* Airwork Limited-Vinnell Corp.

B

background information, contractor performance evaluation system, 140
basis of evaluation, post-award contractor review, 160
Best Practices for Collecting and Using Current and Past Performance Information, 17, 33
best value, determining, 113–115
billing, 23
Black and Veatch Special Projects Corp., 186
blind employees, nonprofit agencies, 127
BMAR, 72–74
Boland Well Systems, Inc., 52–53
business relations
contractor, providing past performance information, 48
contractor performance evaluation system, post-award, 136
Office of Federal Procurement Policy evaluation criteria, 2
subfactors, pre-award past performance, 23, 26–27

310 PAST PERFORMANCE HANDBOOK

C

CCASS. *See* Construction Contractor Appraisal Support System, U. S. Army Corps of Engineers
Centrex, 95
Certificate of Competency (COC), 22
Cessna Aircraft Co., 188
challenging accuracy of past performance information, 188–190
challenging agency past performance evaluations, 185–188
Charleston Marine Containers, Inc., 192
checking references
  problems related to, 86
  requirement to check all, 86–87
  when questionnaires are not returned, 87–89
Chemical Demilitarization Associates, 188
citing other firms, past performance information, 55
COC. *See* Certificate of Competency
color coding systems, 33–34, 103–104
comments, submitting on performance evaluations, 182–183
commercial items
  evaluating management issues, 9
  evaluation basis, contractor performance evaluations, 4
Communities Group (TCG), 67–68
The Community Partnership LLC, 190
comparative assessment, 21
competency, personnel qualification, 10
competitive range
  past performance problems, 107
  using past performance to determine, 1
compliance with solicitation requirements, pre-award evaluation factor, 11–12
compliance with subcontracting plan goals, 136
Comptroller General. *See also* legal issues
  attributing past performance to another firm, 78–79
  best value, determining, 114–115

  clarifying adverse past performance for awards made without discussions, 69
  combining past performance with prior experience, 18–19
  documenting tradeoff determinations, 118–121
  electronic databases, 56–59
  failure to comply with RFP requirements, 49–53
  failure to respond to questions, 70–71
  government inability to contact all references, 87–88
  key personnel, past performance, 80–82
  no past performance history, 75–77
  past performance/price tradeoffs, 115–118
  prospective performance, impact of past performance upon, 67–68
  questionnaires not returned, 87–89
  rating systems, evaluating circumstances and scores, 100
  rebuttal opportunities, offering, 94–97
  relevance, past performance information, 19–20, 72–74
  subcontractor past performance, 82–83
  successful rebuttals, 97–98
  sufficient evidence regarding poor past performance, 92–93
  using information close at hand, 89–91
  using personal knowledge, 92
Construction Contractor Appraisal Support System (CCASS), U. S. Army Corps of Engineers, 56–59, 173–175
construction contracts, 127
contacting contractor, post-award contractor review, 161
content requirements, contractor performance evaluation system, 135
context, past performance information, 64–65
continuing services, procurement of, 17
contract administration, 127
Contract Clauses, Section I, 4
contract planning, providing past performance information, 59–61

contract references, provided by offeror, 2
contracting officer's representative
   (COR), 68
contracting officer's technical
   representative (COTR), 40
contractor, providing past performance
   information
     business relations, 48
     citing other firms, 55
     contract planning, 59–61
     cost performance, 48
     describing in proposals, 49
     disassociated contracts, 54
     discussions, 55–56
     electronic databases, 56–59
     failure to provide, 49–53
     importance of, 46
     performance quality, 47
     schedule performance, 47–48
contractor input, post-award contractor
   review
     basis of evaluation, 160
     contacting contractor, 161
     contractor review process, 161–162
     correcting factual errors, 162
     fairness, 161
     final rating, 161
     government review process, 160
     inconsistent evaluations, 164
     inflated ratings, 163
     low ratings, 164
     negative ratings, 164
     notifying contractor, 159–160
     providing additional information, 162
     rating procedures, 160
     rebutting government assessment, 163
     resolution of disagreements, 160–161
     satisfactory ratings, 163
contractor performance assessment
   report (CPAR), 188
contractor performance evaluation
   system, post-award
     automation, 144–145
     business relations, 136
     compliance with subcontracting plan
       goals, 136
     content requirements, 135

     cost control, 136
     designing a form, 141
     end users, 137–138
     format, 139–141
     key personnel, 138
     management of key personnel, 137
     narrative summaries, 138–139
     OFPP guide, 142–143
     quality of product or service, 136
     rating systems, 138–139
     sample form, 143–144
     signatures, 145
     standard forms, 141–142
     timeliness, 136
contractor performance evaluations
   award fee payments, 130
   business relations criteria, 131
   compliance, rating, 132
   compliance problems, 125–126
   contractor review, 131–132
   cost control criteria, 131
   criteria, 2
   evaluating *versus* accepting/rejecting,
     128
   exemptions, 127
   frequency, 129
   impact on future contracts, 126
   incentive payments, 130
   information sources, 2
   interim, 129
   performance requirements, 2
   purpose, 2, 126–127
   quality criteria, 130
   rating performance, 131
   responsibility for, 129
   retention requirements, 1
   timeliness criteria, 130
   timing, 2, 129, 131
contractor performance reports
   contents, 127
   evaluating *versus* accepting/rejecting
     performance, 128
   government, obtaining past
     performance information, 39–40,
     45–46
   lack of government-wide reporting
     form, 96

312 Past Performance Handbook

Contractor Performance System,
  National Institutes of Health, 176
contractor review process, 140, 161–162
COR. *See* contracting officer's
  representative
corporate experience. *See* prior
  experience
correcting factual errors, post-award
  contractor review, 162
cost
  contractor performance evaluation
    system, 140
  pre-award evaluation factor, 8
cost control
  assessments, 137
  contractor performance evaluation
    system, post-award, 136
  Office of Federal Procurement Policy
    evaluation criteria, 2
  subfactors, pre-award past
    performance, 23, 25–26
cost performance, 48
COTR. *See* contracting officer's technical
  representative
Court of Federal Claims, 181
CPAR. *See* contractor performance
  assessment report
CRAssociates, Inc., 191
criteria, contractor performance
  evaluations, 2
cross-utilization, staffing, 9
Crown Clothing Corporation, 199
currency, past performance information,
  63–64, 185–188

D

D&B. *See* Dun and Bradstreet
Deliveries or Performance, Section F, 4
*Description/Specifications/Statements of
  Work,* Section C, 4
designing a form, contractor
  performance evaluation system, 141
Digital Systems Group, Inc., 191
diluting importance of past performance,
  18–19

disagreements
  agency reviews, 166–167
  definition, 165–166
  final decision, 169
  level above the contracting officer, 165
  parties, 165–166
  requesting reviews, 167–168
  reviewer responsibilities, 168
disassociated contracts, 54
discussions
  contractor, providing past
    performance information, 55–56
  enhancing contractor position with,
    184
  past performance problems, 107–108
documentation
  past performance, pre-award
    evaluation factor, 31
  tradeoff determinations, 118–121
documenting evaluation findings, 106
DOD. *See* United States Department of
  Defense
DOE. *See* United States Department of
  Energy
Dragon Services, Inc., 97–98
Dun and Bradstreet (D&B), 189
DynCorp, 114–115

E

Eagle, 120–121
electronic databases, past performance
  information, 56–59
end user surveys, obtaining past
  performance information, 39
end users, 137–138
Engineered Air Systems Inc., 189, 192
Engineering & Computation, Inc., 195
evaluating past performance
  applying rating systems, 99–101
  avoiding problems, 107–108
  challenges, 121–123
  checking references, 86–89
  color coding system, 103–104
  criteria, 85
  documenting findings, 106–107

Index **313**

numerical scoring systems, 101–103
performance risk, 105–106
personal knowledge, 91–94
rebuttal opportunities, 94–99
using information close at hand, 89–91
evaluation basis, 4
evaluation factors, pre-award
compliance with solicitation
requirements, 11–12
cost or price, 8, 13–14
discriminating among offerors, 13
limiting number of, 13
management capability, 8–9
past performance, 11–12
personnel qualifications, 10–11
prior experience, 9–10
quality, 3–14
relative importance of, 16
tailoring to procurement, 12–13
technical excellence, 8
Evaluation Factors for Award, Section M, 4
evaluation report, contractor
performance evaluation system, 140

F

failure to provide past performance
information, 49–53
fairness, post-award contractor review, 161
FDC. *See* Federal Data Corporation
Federal Data Corporation (FDC), 68
Federal Environmental Services, 199
Federal Prison Industries, Inc., 127, 185
Federal Procurement Data Systems
(FPDS), 39
final decision, disagreements concerning,
169
final evaluation, contractor performance
evaluation system, 140
final rating, post-award contractor
review, 161
financial personnel, acquisition team
members, 2
fixed-price contracts
evaluation factors, 14
indefinite quantity, 19

format, contractor performance
evaluation system, 139–141
Fort Bragg, 97
FPDS. *See* Federal Procurement Data
Systems

G

G. Marine Diesel, 89
GAO. *See* Government Accounting Office
General Services Administration (GSA),
49–51, 78–79, 102–103
general trends, past performance
information, 65
GFP. *See* government furnished property
government, obtaining past performance
information
agency contract database, 39
award evaluations, 40
contractor performance reports, 39–40,
45–46
end user surveys, 39
incentive fee payment evaluations, 40
obtaining answers from other
agencies, 43–44
offerors providing references, 44–45
primary source, 37
private sector sources, 39
questions, developing for reference
checks, 41–43
reference checks, conducting, 40–41
references, requesting, 38–39
Government Accounting Office (GAO).
See also protests
affiliates, 198–201
challenging accuracy of past
performance information, 188–190
challenging agency evaluations, 185–
187
consistency, 192
consistent practices, 181
Court of Federal Claims, 181
exchanges regarding past
performance, 190–192
history of claims/disputes, 196
incumbent contractors, 197

314 PAST PERFORMANCE HANDBOOK

key personnel, 198–201
reasonableness of evaluation
methodology, 194–196
subcontractors, 198–201
government actions contributing to
offeror's deficient performance, 71–72
government furnished property (GFP),
71
government review process, post-award
contractor review, 160
Green Valley Transportation, Inc., 194
GSA. *See* General Services
Administration
GTS Duratek, Inc., 89, 187

H

Hago-Cantu Joint Venture, 198
highest technically rated proposal, 112
HLC Industries, Inc., 186
Housing and Urban Development
(HUD), 67–68
Hughes Georgia, Inc., 195

I

IBSI. *See* International Business Systems,
Inc.
IGIT, Inc., 86
incentive fee payment evaluations, 40
inconsistent evaluations, post-award
contractor review, 164
inflated ratings, post-award contractor
review, 163
information sources, past performance, 2
initial evaluation
business relations, 156
comments, 153–154
contracting officer's responsibility, 147
contractor performance evaluation
system, 140
cost control, 155–156
forms, 147–149
incomplete information, 153
initial performance assessment, 149–150
objectivity, 152
quality of product or service, 154–155
rating performance, 151–152
requirements, 150–151

time needed to prepare, 156–157
timeliness, 155
Inspection and Acceptance, Section E, 4
*Instructions, Conditions, and Notices to
Offerors or Respondents,* Section L, 4
International Business Systems, Inc.
(IBSI), 90, 187, 195
ITT Federal Services International Corp.,
198

K

key personnel
contractor performance evaluation
system, post-award, 138
performance of, 79–82

L

lack of past performance history, 74–77
large systems acquisitions, 137
late delivery, 95–96
LDAP. *See* lightweight directory access
protocol
legal issues. *See also* protests
affiliates, 198–201
challenging accuracy of past
performance information, 188–190
challenging agency evaluations,
185–187
consistency, 192
Court of Federal Claims, 181
exchanges regarding past
performance, 190–192
Government Accounting Office, 181
history of claims/disputes, 196
incumbent contractors, 197
key personnel, 198–201
reasonableness of evaluation
methodology, 194–196
subcontractors, 198–201
legal personnel, acquisition team
members, 2
level above the contracting officer
disagreements, 165
obtaining reviews at, 183
lightweight directory access protocol
(LDAP), 176
Lockheed Aircraft Service Co., 189

logistic support/sustainment, DOD technical subelement, 137

low ratings, post-award contractor review, 164

lowest-priced proposal, 112

Lynwood Machine & Engineering, Inc., 186, 190, 192

M

maintaining past performance information
  NIH Contractor Performance System, 176
  Past Performance Automated Information System, 176
  problems with, 175
  system requirements, 172
  treating as source selection information, 171
  United States Army Corps of Engineers, 173–175

management assessments, DOD, 137

management capability, pre-award evaluation factor, 8–9

management of key personnel, contractor performance evaluation system, 137

management proposal, evaluation factors, 9

management responsiveness, DOD management subelement, 137

Management Solutions, 67–68

Management Technical Services, 197

Maytag Aircraft Corp., 191

measurable performance standards
  functions *versus* physical characteristics, 3
  objectivity, 3
  performance-based contracting methods, 3
  requirement for, 3

mechanization of contract administration system (MOCAS), 188

Menendez-Donnel & Assoc., 61

MOCAS. *See* mechanization of contract administration system

Modern Technologies Corp., 197

MTB Investments, Inc., 67–68

N

NAHB Research Center, Inc., 191

narrative summaries, contractor performance evaluation system, 138–139

National Aeronautics and Space Administration (NASA), 68

National Aerospace Group, Inc., 117, 195

National Institutes of Health (NIH), 176

NavCom Defense Electronics, 193

negative ratings, post-award contractor review, 164

Neil R. Gross & Co., 186

neutral ratings, past performance, 74–77

new firms, lack of past performance history, 74–77

NIH. *See* National Institutes of Health

nonprofit agencies, 127

Northeast MEP Services, Inc., 186

notifying contractor, post-award contractor review, 159–160

Nova Group, Inc., 196

numerical scoring systems
  GSA example, 102–103
  past performance, 32–33
  scoring example, 101
  subfactors, addressing, 102

O

obtaining answers from other agencies, past performance information, 43–44

Oceanometrics, Inc., 198–199

offerors providing references, past performance information, 44–45

Office of Federal Procurement Policy (OFPP)
  evaluation criteria, 2
  guidelines, 17, 142–143

Ogden Support Services, Inc., 194

Olympus Building Services, Inc., 186, 198

Omega World Travel, 92, 187

OneSource Energy Services, Inc., 190

OSI Collection Services, Inc., 192

Ostram, 72–74

overruns, 25

316 PAST PERFORMANCE HANDBOOK

P

parties, disagreements between, 165–166
past performance, pre-award evaluation factor
  color coding scoring system, 33–34
  defining in RFP, 29–30
  documentation, 31
  importance of, 17–18
  indicating how it will be evaluated, 30–31
  numerical scoring system, 32–33
  performance risk assessment, 34–35
  prior experience, combining with, 19–20
  prior experience, distinguishing from, 18–19
  requirement for, 11–12
  responsibility factor, distinguishing from, 20–22
  samples definitions, 27–29
  whether to use, 14–15
Past Performance Automated Information System (PPAIS), 176
past performance/price tradeoffs, 115–118
past performance problems, 42–43
past problems *versus* past successes, 22
PCO. *See* procuring contracting officer
peak workload conditions, staffing, 9
performance-based contracting methods, 3
performance-based service contracting, 17
performance history, lack of, 15
performance of key personnel, 79–82
performance of other companies, 78–79
performance/price tradeoff (PPT) technique, 52
performance quality
  contractor, providing past performance information, 47
  Office of Federal Procurement Policy evaluation criteria, 2
  subfactors, pre-award past performance, 23, 25
performance risk assessment, 15–16, 34–35, 105–105

personal knowledge
  sufficient evidence, 92–93
  validity, 94
  when to use, 91–92
personnel qualifications, pre-award evaluation factor, 10–11
personnel turnover, 9
pertinent education, personnel qualification, 10
Phillips Industries Inc., 76, 117
Phillyship, 89
physical characteristics, measurable performance standards, 3
post-award contractor performance evaluation system
  automation, 144–145
  business relations, 136
  compliance with subcontracting plan goals, 136
  content requirements, 135
  cost control, 136
  designing a form, 141
  end users, 137–138
  format, 139–141
  key personnel, 138
  management of key personnel, 137
  narrative summaries, 138–139
  OFPP guide, 142–143
  quality of product or service, 136
  rating systems, 138–139
  sample form, 143–144
  signatures, 145
  standard forms, 141–142
  timeliness, 136
post-award contractor performance evaluations
  award fee payments, 130
  business relations criteria, 131
  compliance, rating, 132
  compliance problems, 125–126
  contractor review, 131–132
  cost control criteria, 131
  evaluating *versus* accepting/rejecting, 128
  exemptions, 127
  frequency, 129
  impact on future contracts, 126
  incentive payments, 130

interim, 129
purpose, 126–127
quality criteria, 130
rating performance, 131
responsibility for, 129
timeliness criteria, 130
timing, 129, 131
post-award contractor review, contractor input
basis of evaluation, 160
contacting contractor, 161
contractor review process, 161–162
correcting factual errors, 162
fairness, 161
final rating, 161
government review process, 160
inconsistent evaluations, 164
inflated ratings, 163
low ratings, 164
negative ratings, 164
notifying contractor, 159–160
providing additional information, 162
rating procedures, 160
rebutting government assessment, 163
resolution of disagreements, 160–161
satisfactory ratings, 163
Power Connector, Inc., 185
PPAIS. *See* Past Performance Automated Information System
PPT. *See* performance/price tradeoff technique
price
contractor performance evaluation system, 140
pre-award evaluation factor, 8
tradeoff with past performance, 113
primary source, past performance information, 37
prior experience
combining with past performance, 19–20
distinguishing from past performance, 18–19, 78
pre-award evaluation factor, 9–10
private sector sources, past performance information, 39
problems, early identification of, 9

procurements in excess of $100,000
annual contractor performance evaluations, 127
past performance, 12, 20
procuring contracting officer (PCO), 40
product assurance, DOD technical subelement, 137
product performance, DOD technical subelement, 137
program management, DOD management subelement, 137
prospective performance, impact of past performance upon
award made without discussions, 69
contract claims, 70
determining, 66
failure to respond to questions, 70
Housing and Urban Development example, 67–68
NASA example, 68
protests. *See also* legal issues
attributing past performance to another firm, 75–77, 78–79
best value, determining, 114–115
clarifying adverse past performance for awards made without discussions, 69
combining past performance with prior experience, 18–19
documenting tradeoff determinations, 118–121
electronic databases, 56–59
failure to comply with RFP requirements, 49–53
failure to respond to questions, 70–71
government inability to contact all references, 87–88
key personnel, past performance, 80–82
no past performance history, 75–77
past performance/price tradeoffs, 115–118
prospective performance, impact of past performance upon, 67–68
questionnaires not returned, 87–89
rebuttal opportunities, offering, 94–97
relevance, past performance information, 19–20, 72–74

subcontractor past performance, 82–83
successful rebuttals, 97–98
sufficient evidence regarding poor past
performance, 92–93
using information close at hand, 89–91
using personal knowledge, 92
providing additional information, post-
award contractor review, 162

Q

QRI/Hampton Roads, 93
quality
contractor performance evaluation
system, 136
evaluation factor, 13–14
performance-based contracting
methods, 3
Quality Elevator Co., 186
quantity, performance-based contracting
methods, 3
questions, developing for reference
checks, 41–43

R

RAMCOR Services Group, Inc., 192
rating procedures, 160
rating systems
color coding systems, 103–104
contractor performance evaluation
system, post-award, 138–139
evaluation narratives, 99–100
numerical systems, 101–103
performance risk, 105–105
rebuttal opportunities, adverse past
performance
government actions, 94–98
offeror actions, 98–99, 163
reference checks, conducting, 40–41
references, requesting, 38–39
relevance, past performance information,
64, 72–74, 185–188
request for proposal (RFP)
defining past performance in, 29–30
evaluation criteria, 2
past performance problems, 107

Section C, 4
Section E, 4
Section F, 4
Section I, 4
Section L, 4, 29, 31
Section M, 4, 29–30, 85
requesting reviews, 167–168
requirement to evaluate past
performance, 1
resolving disagreements
agency reviews, 166–167
definition, 165–166
final decision, 169
level above the contracting officer, 165
parties, 165–166
requesting reviews, 167–168
reviewer responsibilities, 168
responsibility determination prior to
award, 1
responsibility factor, distinguishing from
past performance, 20–22
résumés, 11
retention plans, staffing, 9
reviewer responsibilities, disagreements,
168
RFP. *See* request for proposal
risk, past performance, 15–16

S

sample form, contractor performance
evaluation system, 143–144
satisfactory ratings, 163
Saudi Arabian National Guard, 114
SBA. *See* Small Business Administration
schedule assessments, DOD, 137
schedule performance
contractor, providing past
performance information, 47–48
Office of Federal Procurement Policy
evaluation criteria, 2
subfactors, pre-award past
performance, 23, 25
SDS International, 200
SEB. *See* source evaluation board
Section C, *Description/Specificatons/
Statements of Work*, 4

Section E, *Inspection and Acceptance*, 4
Section F, *Deliveries or Performance*, 4
Section I, *Contract Clauses*, 4
Section L, *Instructions, Conditions, and Notices to Offerors or Respondents*, 4, 29, 31
Section M, *Evaluation Factors for Award*, 4, 29–30, 85
Service Star USA, Inc., 79
services, description of, 140
severely disabled employees, nonprofit agencies, 127
SF. *See* Standard Form
sharing past performance information, 172–173, 176–178
Si-Nor, Inc., 120–121, 194
signatures, contractor performance evaluation system, 145
Small Business Administration (SBA), 21, 51, 91
software engineering, DOD technical subelement, 137
sole source evaluation, 1–2
solicitation factors, 192–194
solicitation provision, 4
source evaluation board (SEB), 68
source selection decision
    simple *versus* complicated, 111–112
    source selection official, 111
source selection official, 111
sources, past performance information, 64
SOW. *See* statement of work
staffing, appropriate level and labor mix, 9
Standard Form 279, 39
Standard Form 1420, 141–142, 173
Standard Form 1421, 141–142, 174
Standard Form 1449, 4
standard forms, contractor performance evaluation system, post-award, 141–142
statement of work (SOW), 12
subcontract management, 24
subcontractor management, DOD management subelement, 137
subcontractors, performance of, 82–83

subfactors
    business relations, 23, 26–27
    cost control, 23, 25–26
    past problems *versus* past successes, 22
    performance quality, 23, 25
    schedule performance, 23, 25
supplies, description of, 140
systems engineering, DOD technical subelement, 137

T

Tara, 117
TCG. *See* Communities Group
TEAM Support Services, Inc., 187, 196
technical assessments, DOD, 137
technical evaluation factor
    management capability as subfactor of, 9
    staffing as subfactor of, 9
technical excellence, pre-award evaluation factor, 8
Thomas Brand Siding case, 44
timeliness
    contractor performance evaluation system, post-award, 136
    performance-based contracting methods, 3
TLT Construction Corp., 56–59
tradeoff decisions, 1
Tri-Way, 93

U

uniform contract format, 4
United States Air Force, 80–82, 114–115, 120–121, 186
United States Army, 97–98
United States Army Corps of Engineers (USACE), 56–59, 173–175
United States Department of Defense (DOD), 137, 174
United States Department of Energy (DOE), 87
United States Navy, 75–76, 91, 93
Universal Building Maintenance, Inc., 201

upper-level review, 140
USACE. *See* United States Army Corps of Engineers
using information close at hand, 89–91
USS Defense Systems, Inc., 193

V

Veterans Administration, 90–91

W

Walsh Distribution, Inc., 186
weights
    assigning to evaluation factors, 17
    associated with past performance, 46
workload fluctuations, offer's ability to react to, 9